Essential Essays for the Study of the Military in First-Century Palestine

Essential Essays *for the* Study of the Military *in* First-Century Palestine

Soldiers and the New Testament Context

EDITED BY

Christopher B. Zeichman

PICKWICK *Publications* • Eugene, Oregon

ESSENTIAL ESSAYS FOR THE STUDY OF THE MILITARY IN FIRST-CENTURY PALESTINE
Soldiers and the New Testament Context

Pickwick Publications
An Imprint of Wipf and Stock Publishers
199 W. 8th Ave., Suite 3
Eugene, OR 97401

www.wipfandstock.com

PAPERBACK ISBN: 978-1-5326-5638-5
HARDCOVER ISBN: 978-1-5326-5639-2
EBOOK ISBN: 978-1-5326-5640-8

Cataloging-in-Publication data:

Names: Zeichmann, Christopher B., editor.

Title: Essential essays for the study of the military in first-century Palestine : soldiers and the New Testament context / edited by Christopher B. Zeichmann.

Description: Eugene, OR: Pickwick Publications, 2019. | Includes bibliographical references and index.

Identifiers: ISBN: 978-1-5326-5638-5 (paperback). | ISBN: 978-1-5326-5639-2 (hardcover). | ISBN: 978-1-5326-5640-8 (ebook).

Subjects: LCSH: Rome—Army. | Bible—New Testament—History of contemporary events. | Palestine—Social life and customs—To 70 A.D.

Classification: BS2361.3 Z451 2019 (print). | BS2361.3 (epub).

Manufactured in the U.S.A. NOVEMBER 1, 2019

Contents

Acknowledgments | *vii*
List of Contributors | *ix*
Introduction | *xi*
Abbreviations | *xxi*

1. The Roman Army (1933) | T. R. S. Broughton | 1
2. The Roman Army in Judaea under the Procurators: The Italian and the Augustan Cohort in the Acts of the Apostles (1982–83; 2019 addenda) | Michael P. Speidel | 26
3. The Beginning of the Roman Defensive System in Judaea (1983) | Israel Shatzman | 37
4. The Roman Army in the Galilee (1992) | Ze'ev Safrai | 67
5. Jewish Military Forces in the Roman Service (2004) | Jonathan P. Roth | 79
6. Sons of Israel in Caesar's Service: Jewish Soldiers in the Roman Military (2006) | Andrew J. Schoenfeld | 95
7. 'Romans Go Home'? Rome and Other 'Outsiders' as Viewed from the Syro-Arabian Desert (2014; 2019 addenda) | Michael C. A. Macdonald | 108

Further Reading: Annotated Bibliography | 133
Index of Ancient Sources | 143

Acknowledgments

THIS BOOK WOULD NOT be possible without others' extensive help. First, and most obviously, are the authors and publishers who granted permission to use their work; the specifics of these permissions can be found below. Their recognition of the importance of these articles—some of which have long been out of print—and the need to bring them to a wider audience is deeply appreciated. Particular appreciation is extended to Michael P. Speidel and Michael C. A. Macdonald who offered addenda for their reprints. Thanks also to Zeba Crook for helping procure one particularly obscure reference.

I would also like to extend my appreciation to the librarians at the University of Toronto for helping procure many of the chapters found here, especially Karen Wishart at the Emmanuel College Library who has supported this and related research in various ways. My aspiration is that the present book will be of aid to theological librarians—providing access to important publications at a modest price.

T. R. S. Broughton, "Note XXXIII: The Roman Army," originally appeared in *The Acts of the Apostles: Additional Notes and Commentary*, edited by Kirsopp Lake and Henry Cadbury (The Beginnings of Christianity 5; London: Macmillan, 1933), 427–45. Original publication is in the public domain.

Michael P. Speidel, "The Roman Army in Judaea under the Procurators: The Italian and the Augustan Cohort in the Acts of the Apostles," originally appeared in *Ancient Society* 13–14 (1982–83) 233–40. It appears here by permission of Peeters Publishers and with the approval of Michael P. Speidel. Addenda appear courtesy of Michael P. Speidel.

Israel Shatzman, "The Beginning of the Roman Defensive System in Judaea," originally appeared in *American Journal of Ancient History* 8 (1983) 130–60. It appears here by permission of Gorgias Press.

Ze'ev Safrai, "The Roman Army in Galilee," originally appeared in *The Galilee in Late Antiquity*, edited by Lee I. Levine (New York: Jewish Theological Seminary of America, 1992), 103–14. It appears here by permission of the Jewish Theological Seminary of America and with the approval of Ze'ev Safrai.

Jonathan P. Roth, "Jewish Military Forces in the Roman Service," was originally read at the Josephus section of the Society of Biblical Literature annual meeting, 23 November 2004 at San Antonio, Texas. It appears here courtesy of Jonathan P. Roth.

Andrew J. Schoenfeld, "Sons of Israel in Caesar's Service: Jewish Soldiers in the Roman Military," originally appeared in *Shofar* 24/3 (2006) 115–26. It appears here by permission of Purdue University Press.

Michael C. A. Macdonald, "'Romans Go Home'? Rome and Other 'Outsiders' as Viewed from the Syro-Arabian Desert," originally appeared in *Inside and Out: Interactions between Rome and the Peoples of the Arabian and Egyptian Frontiers in Late Antiquity*, edited by Jitse H. F. Dijkstra and Greg Fisher (Late Antique History and Religion 8; Leuven: Peeters, 2014), 145–63. It appears here by permission of Peeters Publishing and with the approval of Michael C. A. Macdonald. Addenda appear courtesy of Michael C. A. Macdonald.

Contributors

T. R. S. Broughton (1900–1993) was a Canadian scholar of Classics who studied at the University of Toronto and the University of Chicago before receiving his PhD at Johns Hopkins University in 1928. He taught at Victoria College (Toronto), Amherst College, Bryn Mawr College, and the University of North Carolina at Chapel Hill. His most famous work is *Magistrates of the Roman Republic* (3 vols., 1951–86).

Michael C. A. Macdonald is on the Faculty of Oriental Studies at the University of Oxford and an Honorary Fellow at Wolfson College. He is a specialist in early Arabic and its epigraphy and is the academic director of the Online Corpus of the Inscriptions of Ancient North Arabia (OCIANA). He is also academic director of the project Ancient Arabia: Languages and Cultures. His major works include *Literacy and Identity in Pre-Islamic Arabia* (2009); he also edited *The Development of Arabic as a Written Language* (2010).

Jonathan P. Roth is Professor of History at San Jose State University. He received his PhD in ancient history at Columbia University. He founded and serves as the Director of San Jose State's Burdick Military History Project. His major works include *The Logistics of the Roman Army at War (264 B.C.—A.D. 235)* (1999), and *Roman Warfare* (2009).

Ze'ev Safrai is Professor of Israel Studies at Bar-Ilan University in Ramat Gan, Israel. He received his PhD from Hebrew University. His major works include *The Macmillan Bible Atlas* (3rd ed., with Anson F. Rainey, 1993) and *The Economy of Roman Palestine* (1994).

Andrew J. Schoenfeld is a physician and orthopaedic surgeon. He is an Associate Professor of Orthopaedic Surgery at Harvard Medical School and Brigham and Women's Hospital.

Israel Shatzman (1934–2017) was an Israeli ancient historian. He received his PhD from Hebrew University. His major works include *Senatorial Wealth and Roman Politics* (1975), *History of the Roman Republic* (1989), and *The Armies of the Hasmonaeans and Herod: From Hellenistic to Roman Frameworks* (1991).

Michael P. Speidel received his PhD in ancient history at the University of Freiburg. He has taught most of his career at the University of Hawai'i at Mānoa. His major works include *Guards of the Roman Armies: An Essay on the Singulares of the Provinces* (1978), *The Religion of Iuppiter Dolichenus in the Roman Army* (1978), *Roman Army Studies* (2 vols., 1982–1992), *Riding for Caesar: The Roman Emperors' Horse Guards* (1994), *Ancient Germanic Warriors: Warrior Styles from Trajan's Column to Icelandic Sagas* (2004), and *Emperor Hadrian's Speeches to the African Army: A New Text* (2007).

Introduction

Christopher B. Zeichmann

THE PURPOSE OF THE PRESENT VOLUME

Though Christianity's place within the Roman Empire has been a major topic of scholarly interest for the past two decades, there is strikingly little engagement with the Roman military; biblical commentators have generally focused on Roman ideology, Roman religion, and the like at the expense of the military. Indeed, sources both ancient and modern note that one of the primary motors of Romanization in the provinces was the military: its encampments gave rise to markets, its soldiers spoke Latin, its pay was in imperial coinage, its large administrative apparatus imposed Roman law, etc. This is readily witnessed in Judaea as well, particularly with the introduction of *legio X Fretensis* as a permanent garrison in 70 CE: Latin is an obscure language mostly on *tituli picti* until the Jewish War; denarii are rare until the Jewish War; the Jerusalem garrison partially replaced the economic vacuum left by the temple's destruction; and so on.

While biblical commentators may sometimes refer to Josephus and other military historians of antiquity, there is rarely deep engagement with the role of the army within the social landscape of Judaea, with a handful of exceptions (e.g., the demon named "Legion" in Mark 5:1–20). Consequently, it is not uncommon for prestigious scholars to make rudimentary mistakes when discussing the military in early Roman Palestine: confusing client kings' armies, auxiliaries, and legions, misrepresenting the demographics of the military, as well as little sense for the duties soldiers served in the

Roman East.[1] It is important to note that there is no shortage of important writings on the topic of the military in early Roman Palestine by classicists and military historians. Indeed, there are abundant publications on these and related matters.

That said, a few factors might explain the reluctance of New Testament scholars to engage in serious study of the Roman military. Namely, that these works are often not particularly accessible for New Testament scholars, who might reasonably benefit from their study. This "inaccessibility" operates in two senses of the word: not easy to *understand* and not easy to *find*.

First, study of the Roman army tends to be an arcane and boring topic. For evidence, one need only read an article or two about the latest military diploma discovery, which at their most interesting are protracted prosopographies of the legates, tribunes, and other commanders, indicating which auxiliary cohort was where at what time. Even archaeological discoveries of military assemblages within Palestine are barely readable by those not already initiated into the study of militaria, since the ensuing discussion tends to revolve around comparison of, say, belt buckles found at Masada with those at sites in Britannia, Dacia Superior, and so on. The implications of such studies are often unclear: what knowledge this might contribute to our understanding of the military's organization, functions, trade patterns, economic relations, and many other topics may be opaque to novice students of the Roman army. The general dearth of military studies *within* New Testament scholarship further contributes to its absence, as commentators have little groundwork to build upon and few accessible points of entry.

Second, many important articles and book chapters are not easy to find due to its publication venue. Many important articles are in journals

1. For instance, New Testament scholars often emphasize the *Roman* character of the pre-War garrison to a point of caricature in service of one or another rhetorical or social historical point: Wendy Cotter, "Cornelius, the Roman Army and Religion," in *Religious Rivalries and the Struggle for Success in Caesarea Maritima* (ed. Terence L. Donaldson; Studies in Christianity and Judaism 8; Waterloo: Wilfrid Laurier University Press, 2000), 279–301; Daniel Cohen, "The Gerasene Demoniac: A Jewish Approach to Liberation before 70 CE," in *Judaism, Jewish Identities and the Gospel Tradition: Essays in Honour of Maurice Casey* (ed. James G. Crossley; BibleWorld; London: Equinox, 2010), 152–73; William J. Hamblin, "The Roman Army in the First Century," in *Masada and the World of the New Testament* (ed. John W. Welch, et al.; BYU Studies Monograph Series; Provo: Brigham Young University Press, 1997), 337–49. On the problems with this depiction, see Christopher B. Zeichmann, *The Roman Army and the New Testament* (Lanham, MD: Lexington/Fortress Academic, 2018), 1–21.

that are often not found in theological libraries or altogether absent from databases that are important within our field (e.g., ATLA, JSTOR). As such, there is little reason they would be on a New Testament scholar's "radar." Moreover, many important book chapters have been published in collected volumes that are otherwise irrelevant to the field and thus unlikely to be found in a theological library. Consider, for instance, the important work published by the *Limeskongress* and the Roman Frontier Studies book series. Such books often have a chapter or two relevant to the military in early Roman Judaea, though there is little reason most biblical scholars would encounter these works: their publication of relevant material is so inconsistent that it is hardly worth perusing the entire history of these books to find only a handful of useful nuggets. This is not to mention that these collected volumes often have very low print runs and sold at an exorbitant cost: a smaller theological library would be wise to avoid purchasing such collections.

The present volume aims to help with these myriad problems by living up to its title. First, this book provides important articles that are otherwise difficult to find or whose importance has been neglected by biblical scholars. That is to say, they are rendered "accessible" in both senses above: they are useful as starting points for the study of the military in Roman Palestine and can be purchased in a book entirely relevant to biblical studies at a modest cost.

This book should also give some sense of the issues that non-biblical scholars have identified as important to the study of military in New Testament Palestine. While biblical scholars have long had their own interpretive agenda regarding the military (e.g., Christian relationship with Roman ideology [e.g., Richard Horsley, Warren Carter], historical reliability of the Bible [e.g., Craig Keener, Ben Witherington III]), what do those who specialize in the field of the military in the Roman East make of the army's role in Judaea, Galilee, and Batanaea? Though there is often overlap between the areas of interest of New Testament scholars and military historians, points of divergence are also important: classics scholarship on the military can both reveal outdated assumptions among biblical commentators as well as open up new avenues for the study within the field of New Testament studies.

Finally, this book contains contributions spanning over eighty years. This scope of studies should facilitate a sense of how the fields have changed and continue to change. Readers might observe how some debates have more or less resolved, how methods of study have changed within the field of Roman military history, and what social-historical questions have fallen out of vogue. This is important, because it is not uncommon to find biblical academics citing as authoritative wildly out of date works on the Roman military as though that field of study has not undergone significant changes in the way the study of the New Testament has—and for similar reasons: explosion of papyrological and epigraphic finds, increased aware of knowledge production within a colonial context, important archaeological excavations, revised readings of primary sources, etc.

The present book also aims to make accessible the numerous military papyri and inscriptions relating to Roman Palestine by integrating the *Database of Military Inscriptions and Papyri of Early Roman Palestine* (*DMIPERP*) into the reprinted chapters. *DMIPERP* collects all published military inscriptions and papyri found *within* Palestine (broadly characterized as Judaea, Galilee, Batanaea, Decapolis, and Ascalon), found outside the region but mentioning people from Palestine or Palestinian military units. The database can be found online at www.ArmyOfRomanPalestine.com. The purpose of *DMIPERP* is to assist biblical scholars' engagement with this ample corpus of evidence without having to track down obscure archaeological reports or other publications: all entries include original language text, an English translation, discussion, and a bibliography. As far as the present volume is concerned, *DMIPERP* cross-references have been added whenever possible for the chapters included here, making it much easier to find the inscription/papyrus under discussion. One goal of this book is that scholars might see that there are valuable sources concerning the military in early Roman Palestine beyond the (often tendentious) text of Josephus.

Beyond the addition of cross-references to *DMIPERP*, these publications have been cleaned up in various ways to make the volume as reader-friendly as possible. Citations for both primary and secondary sources have been made clearer in a few chapters, such that in any chapter the first time there is a reference to a modern source, the citation is provided with full information (as opposed to unhelpful references like "*RE* s.vv." that are sometimes found in the original publication). A relatively consistent citation system has been imposed upon ancient sources, especially in the case of Josephus: all references are in the Niese/Loeb citation system, rather than the older and clunkier Whiston citation system. There were times when authors relied upon incredibly arcane citation systems; Broughton's important chapter, for instance, cites Roman military diplomas in a manner that is utterly incomprehensible. That said, it is fairly easy to ascertain what diploma he is discussing via context, so in the version of his chapter contained within this volume, the standard reference method for military diplomas has been adopted. In the case of Israel Shatzman's chapter, the citation system is so bizarre that its original publication contained an apology from the journal's editor, as it included competing citation methods (both author-date and full-footnote) within a single article: "The Editor regrets that unusual difficulties in checking the references in this article and in communications have delayed publication."[2] Needless to say, the present book presented an opportunity to reprint the article with a single, coherent citation system that did not require the reader to flip between three different pages to understand a given reference. Since some of these articles are older, "edition" number has been added wherever they might be helpful. This is not to mention the occasional typo found in original publications.

All of this should indicate that the text sometimes differs from the original publication, though this is mostly relegated to citations of primary and secondary sources. Should the exact citation system be important to the reader, they are advised to find the original publication. Editorial revisions and comments beyond citation clarifications and typo corrections are usually enclosed in [[double brackets]]. That is to say, these are *revised* texts, even if those revisions are as light and unintrusive as possible. Even so, it remains important to respect the structure of the original publication, which had its own logic; this means that chapters each have different heading systems, citation systems, spelling conventions, among many other peculiarities.

The act of reprinting also permitted the opportunity for author-initiated additions and changes. The articles by Michael Macdonald and Michael P. Speidel, for instance, contain addenda to the original article following their conclusion. These addenda provide valuable updates to the original article based on subsequent discoveries and academic discussion. In the case of Speidel, his addenda are a further update to the addenda published to his article in a 1992 reprint.[3]

2. Israel Shatzman, "The Beginning of the Roman Defensive System in Judaea," *American Journal of Ancient History* 8 (1983) 149.

3. The much briefer 1992 addenda can be found at Michael P. Speidel, *Roman Army Studies* (Mavors Army Researches 8; Stuttgart: Steiner, 1992), 2.232.

CONTENT

The following chapters are presented in chronological order rather than thematically. The focus of the present book is generally on articles published after Edward Luttwak's 1976 monograph *Grand Strategy of the Roman Empire*—a monograph of considerable importance, albeit one that has not fared well in criticism.[4] Luttwak argued that there were three successive "grand strategies" used by the Roman Empire; the most important for our purposes is that of the Julio-Claudians, which he terms a system of "client states and mobile frontiers." In short, Luttwak contends that the Julio-Claudians conceived of the Empire as a series of concentric circles that served to protect the innermost from harm; Rome and Italia were protected by the Senatorial provinces, which were in turn protected by the Imperial provinces, which were in turn protected by client states and tribes. Military garrisons were most prevalent in the outer-two rings, with non-Roman lives at stake in the outermost circle. By locating the Roman army proper in provinces and not allied kingdoms, it remained a mobile force that could quickly move to address nearby threats. Luttwak hesitates to call the outermost circle "buffer states," as these threats were not foreign powers (e.g., directed against Parthia), but against minor foreign threats and undermining unrest within these regions, especially unpacified populations: "client states absorbed the burden of providing peripheral security against border infiltration and other low-intensity threats."[5] This strategy served to expand the geographic extent of Roman power, pacifying one region before proceeding outward to maximize the empire's maintainable dominion.

The reception of Luttwak's work among Roman historians was not particularly kind. Luttwak is not a trained classicist, nor did he consult with any Roman historians while writing. His book thus has numerous errors of fact and while most of them are fairly minor (e.g., Agrippa I is incorrectly identified as Herod the Great's nephew), it does little to bolster one's confidence in his argument. Many other grievances might be articulated:

4. Edward N. Luttwak, *The Grand Strategy of the Roman Empire from the First Century A.D. to the Third*, 1st ed. (Baltimore: Johns Hopkins University Press, 1976). Luttwak published a second edition that has not fared well under academic criticism. Reviewers cite *inter alia* his extremely recalcitrant approach to forty years of critical engagement by other academics: Edward N. Luttwak, *The Grand Strategy of the Roman Empire from the First Century A.D. to the Third*, rev. ed. (Baltimore: Johns Hopkins University Press, 2016).

5. Luttwak, *Grand Strategy of the Roman Empire* (1st ed.), 24.

his lack of interaction with papyrology and epigraphy, lack of evidence that Romans actually thought in such abstract terms, supposition of continuity of strategy over imperial dynasties, rationalist assumptions about Roman planning, etc. Also concerning is Luttwak's employment as a defense specialist by numerous world powers. Consequently, one wonders about his effusive praise for the Julio-Claudian system, a system that in his description sounds eerily similar to the strategy of the U.S. in the Cold War—a system he personally helped develop and enact as a military advisor to the U.S. State Department, the U.S. Secretary of Defense, and the U.S. Navy, among many other branches of government.

The importance of Luttwak's work, however, is in the work that it inspired as response, leading to a massive shift in Roman military history from *Limesgeschichte* (i.e., study of forts along the *limites*) to frontier studies proper. The rise of postcolonial theory and related disciplines around this time entailed a short life-span for his book's authority—Luttwak shows no interest in "history from below," such that civilians are reduced to their friendliness or hostility to Roman rule (one is again reminded of the Cold War). One thus finds almost no interaction with papyrological scholarship, scholarship that would elucidate the actual function of the military in frontier regions. Luttwak instead relies heavily on the idealist and sometimes out-of-touch accounts of elite Roman historians, men who had little practical experience of life on the periphery of the Empire. Against the eminently rational and "realist" understanding of Roman power came suggestions of the opposite: an emphatically primitivist understanding of Roman rule, most fully articulated in the work of Benjamin Isaac—especially relevant in that he also uses Palestine as his primary example and limits his scope to the Roman East.[6]

While Luttwak depicts the Empire's growth and maintenance as the result of careful planning at high levels of administration, Isaac argues the opposite: Rome operated with little strategy beyond minimizing the chaos inherent to the Empire. Soldiers instead largely served to minimize the disorder of banditry and so on. Rome had little interest in expanding or securing its borders, instead primarily going to war for glory, gold, or to satisfy soldiers itching for a fight. This can be seen in Roman Judaea with the use of small fortifications; before the Jewish War, roads through the countryside of Judaea were peppered with fortlets that could only have served to

6. For more on Isaac's important contributions, see "Further Reading: Annotated Bibliography" at the close of this book.

address brigandage and other highly-localized, ad hoc, and quality-of-life concerns. Josephus and the rabbis attest Roman presence as reactive rather than proactive: within the province of Judaea and eventually Syria Palaestina, their presence largely responds to outbursts of violence and at their most proactive increased patrols around the time of Jewish holidays when there were crowds and pilgrims.

Response to Isaac's work was more favorable than that which Luttwak received. Criticism tended to stem from two specific concerns: the extent to which Judaea/Syria Palaestina was representative of the Roman East in general and Isaac's over-correction of Luttwak's modernism in favor of "arch-primitivism." The former criticism is well-taken: Palestine was subject to multiple large-scale revolts, its elites were unable to influence the population, and brigandage seems to have been a uniquely prevalent problem. For biblical scholars, however, this is hardly a reason to reject the importance of his work; rather, it would only require caution when generalizing about policies beyond the Southern Levant. Scholarly debate has largely concerned how to navigate the two ends of this pole, the modernist and primitivist understandings of Roman strategy; for further reading on the topic see the "Further Reading" chapter at the close of this book.

Despite the important criticism of Luttwak's work, it is a watershed in the study of the Roman army; a considerable portion of subsequent Roman military scholarship engages directly or indirectly with Luttwak's claims. Around this same time, the first volume of the revised English translation of Emil Schürer's *The History of the Jewish People in the Age of Jesus Christ (175 B.C.—A.D. 135)* was published, marking a watershed in the study of Hellenistic and early Roman Palestine, which itself included a vital discussion of the military in the region (1.360–368). Consequently, it makes little sense to have too much content published before these volumes, given the significant impact they have had on their respective fields.

Chapter 1 is the sole exception to the post-Luttwak, post-revised-Schürer scope of the book. Though T. R. S. Broughton's "The Roman Army" is quite old and often outdated, it is not only a widely cited and influential article, but one that acts as a viable, if flawed, introduction to the study of the military in early Roman Judaea. Broughton's contribution offers remarkable breadth that covers the most essential issues in a clear way, such that Michael P. Speidel regarded it as "The best general account of the Roman army in Palestine in the early period" fifty years after its initial publication.[7] One could make a strong argument that that remains the case today, though I hope my own 2018 monograph *The Roman Army and the New Testament* may usurp the title or at least offer more updated insights.

Chapter 2 is Michael Speidel's widely-cited article on the military under the Judaean procurators and the units depicted in Acts: namely the Italian (Acts 10) and Augustan (Acts 27) cohorts. Were these units present in pre-War Judaea as Acts depicts? Or should one be suspicious of Acts historicity in this regard? Speidel largely follows the contentions of Broughton on the matter, updating the argument and ultimately taking a stronger stance on the matter. Speidel's article, despite criticism, remains *the* essential article on these military units.

Chapter 3 is Israel Shatzman's engagement with the question of Roman grand strategy in the Negev desert of southern Judaea. While the beginning of the article is somewhat arcane, the body provides helpful information about how archaeologists ascertain military presence, as well as the significance of such a presence within Palestine. Shatzman's primary dialogue partner is Mordechai Gichon, who argued that Judaea had an extensive border defense system to protect Jewish civilians from desert bandits and other foreign threats. Much of Shatzman's discussion could be reiterated *mutatis mutandis* concerning Luttwak—a point which Shatzman makes explicit at one point.

Chapter 4 reprints Ze'ev Safrai's "The Roman Army in Galilee," the first chapter of the book to discuss Jesus' home country, where the vast majority of the Gospels takes place. The chapter provides a helpful overview of the changing military situation within the region, contending that it is helpful to distinguish between four different periods of Roman military presence, with soldiers playing distinct roles in each: the pre-War provincial period of 44–66 CE, the post-War period (70–120 CE), the middle-Roman period (120–300 CE), and the fourth century CE. This changing function of the military is important to consider, as it is common for New Testament scholars to anachronistically impose the characteristics of one period (often, the post-War period) on another (often, the life of Jesus).

Chapter 5 has never been published before and is presented in print for the first time here. Jonathan Roth's discussion of Jewish soldiers in Roman service was originally presented at the 2004 annual meeting of the Society

7. Michael P. Speidel, "The Roman Army in Judaea under the Procurators: The Italian and the Augustan Cohort in the Acts of the Apostles," *Ancient Society* 13–14 (1982–83) 233 n.1 = present volume, 27 n.1.

of Biblical Literature in the Josephus section (that year themed "The Jewish Revolt"). Here, Roth presents a compelling portrait of a complex role Jews played within the Roman army—a considerable issue rarely discussed by biblical scholars. In so doing, Roth offers anticipatory criticism of the widespread depiction of Rome as inherently hostile to the Jewish people, instead elaborating upon evidence of Jewish soldiers during the first century CE and why military service may have appealed to them.

Chapter 6 is Andrew Schoenfeld's article "Sons of Israel in Caesar's Service," which takes Roth's point farther, taking aim at the common assumption that Jews in the Roman army *must* have been apostates, despite a frequent lack of evidence to support such a strong claim. Schoenfeld instead argues that navigating ethnic identity in the military was often a complex issue, but hardly precluded soldiers from engaging in Jewish practices and continuing to identify with the religion.

Chapter 7 is written by Michael C. A. Macdonald on the relevance of Safaitic inscriptions for the study of the Roman military in the Levant. Safaitic—a language rarely discussed by biblical scholars, despite its extensive use in Palestine and neighboring regions—is an Arabic dialect that survives through a massive number of graffiti, mostly in the Syrian desert and north Arabia (i.e., Nabataean Arabia, not Saudi Arabia). Jewish wars, Herodian client kings, and other topics of interest to biblical scholars come up with surprising frequency in Safaitic graffiti. Moreover, these graffiti give acute insights to how those at the margins of the empire (and Roman society more broadly!) perceived and interacted with the Roman army. These graffiti can be found in the excellent searchable database *Online Corpus of the Inscriptions of Ancient North Arabia* (*OCIANA*): http://krcfm.orient.ox.ac.uk/fmi/webd/ociana.

This book concludes with an annotated bibliography for further reading on topics relevant to the study of the military and the New Testament. Should one wish to research any of the topics raised elsewhere in this book in further depth, several starting points are suggested.

Abbreviations

ANCIENT SOURCES

Appian	
B.C.	*Civil War*
Syr.	*Syrian Wars*
Aulus Hirtius	
bell. Alex.	*Alexandrian War*
Caesar	
bell. Civ.	*Civil War*
bell. Gall.	*Gallic War*
Pseudo-Caesar	
bell. Hisp.	*Spanish War*
Cicero	
Att.	*Letters to Atticus*
Fam.	*Letters to Friends*
Cod. Theod.	*Codex Theodosianus*
Pseudo-Hyginus	
Cast. mun.	*De Munitionibus Castrorum*
Jerome	
Ep.	*Epistles*
Josephus	
A.J.	*Antiquities of the Jews*
J.W.	*Jewish War*
Libanius	

Ep.	*Epistles*
Macrobius	
Sat.	*Saturnalia*
Not. Dig.	*Notitia Dignitatum*
Pliny	
Hist. Nat.	*Natural History*
Plutarch	
Ant.	*Antony*
Crass.	*Crassus*
Ptolemy	
Geog.	*Geography*
Rufinus	
HE	*Ecclesiastical History*
Socrates	
HE	*Ecclesiastical History*
Sozomenos	
HE	*Ecclesiastical History*
Suetonius	
Aug.	*Augustus*
Vesp.	*Vespasian*
Tacitus	
Ann.	*Annals*
Hist.	*History*
Theodoret	
HE	*Ecclesiastical History*

MODERN SOURCES

AAES	William Kelly Prentice, *Greek and Latin Inscriptions*. Publications of an American Archaeological Expedition to Syria in 1899–1900 pt. 3. New York: Century, 1908
ADAJ	*Annual of the Department of Antiquities of Jordan*
AE	*Année Epigraphique*
AJA	*American Journal of Archaeology*
ANRW	Hildegard Temporini and Wolfgang Haase, eds., *Aufstieg und Niedergang der römischen Welt: Geschichte und Kultur Roms im Spiegel der neueren Forschung*. Part II, Principat. Berlin: de Gruyter, 1972–
BARIS	British Archaeological Reports, International Series
BGU	*Aegyptische Urkunden aus den Königlichen Staatlichen Museen zu Berlin, Griechische Urkunden*. 15 vols. Berlin: Weidmann, 1895–1983
BJ	*Bonner Jahrbücher*
CIG	*Corpus Inscriptionum Graecarum*. 4 vols. Berlin: Academia Borussica, 1828–77
CIJ	Jean-Baptiste Frey, *Corpus Inscriptionum Judaicarum*. 2 vols. Paris: Pontifical Institute, 1936–52. Reprinted as *Corpus of Jewish Inscriptions: Jewish Inscriptions from the Third Century B.C. to the Seventh Century A.D.* Prolegomenon by Baruch Lifshitz. Library of Biblical Studies. New York: Ktav, 1975
CIL	*Corpus Inscriptionum Latinarum*. Berlin: Reimer, 1862–
CIS	*Corpus Insriptionum Semiticarum*. Paris: Imprimerie nationale, 1889–1954

CPJ	Victor A. Tcherikover, *Corpus Papyrorum Judicarum*. 3 vols. Cambridge: Harvard University Press, 1957–64
CSIR	*Corpus Signorum Imperii Romani*
DMIPERP	*Database of Military Inscriptions and Papyri of Early Roman Palestine* (http://www.armyofromanpalestine.com).
HSCP	*Harvard Studies in Classical Philology*
IEJ	*Israel Exploration Journal*
IGLS	[without volume number:] W. H. Waddington, *Inscriptions grecques et latines de la Syrie*. 4 vols. Paris: Didot, 1870
	[with volume number:] Louis Jalabert et René Mouterde, *Inscriptions grecques et latines de la Syrie*. Bibliothèque archéologique et historique. Paris: Geuthner, 1929–
IGRR	René Cagnat, Jules Toutain, Georges Lafaye, and Victor Henry, eds., *Inscriptiones Graecae ad Res Romanas Pertinentes*. 4 vols. Paris: Leroux, 1911–27
ILS	Hermann Dessau, ed., *Inscriptiones Latinae Selectae*. 3 vols. Berlin: Weidmann, 1892–1916
JRS	*Journal of Roman Studies*
KRS	*King Rescue Survey*. [Note: these inscriptions were formally published in *OCIANA*, see below]
LCL	Loeb Classical Library
LSJ	Henry George Liddell, Robert Scott, and Henry Stuart Jones, *A Greek-English Lexicon*. 9th ed. Oxford: Clarendon, 1940
OCIANA	*Online Corpus of the Inscriptions of Ancient North Arabia* (http://krc2.orient.ox.ac.uk/ociana/)
OGIS	Wilhelm Dittenberger, ed., *Orientis graeci inscriptiones selectae*. 2 vols. Leipzig: Hirzel, 1903–5

QDAP	*Quarterly of the Department of Antiquities in Palestine*
P.Ryl.	*Catalogue of the Greek and Latin Papyri in the John Rylands Library, Manchester*. 4 vols. Manchester: Manchester University Press, 1911–38
PUAES	Enno Littmann, David Magie, and Duane Reed Stuart, *Publications of the Princeton University Archaeological Expeditions to Syria 1904–5 and* 1909. Leiden: Brill, 1922–49
RBi	*Revue biblique*
RMD	Margaret Roxan and Paul Holder, eds., *Roman Military Diplomas*, 1954–
RMR	Robert O. Fink, ed., *Roman Military Records on Papyrus*. American Studies in Papyrology 26. Cleveland: Press of Case Western University, 1971
SBA	*Sammelbuch griechischer Urkunden aus Aegypten* (1915–)
SCI	*Scripta Classica Israelica*
SEG	*Supplementum Epigraphicum Graecum*
SIJ	F. V. Winnett, *Safaitic Inscriptions from Jordan*. Near and Middle East Series 2. Toronto: University of Toronto Press, 1957
TAPA	*Transactions of the American Philological Association*
WH	F. V. Winnett and G. L. Harding, *Inscriptions from Fifty Safaitic Cairns*. Near and Middle East Series 9. Toronto: University of Toronto Press, 1978
ZDMG	*Zeitschrift der deutschen morgenländischen Gesellschaft*
ZPalV	*Zeitschrift des deutschen Palästina-Vereins*
ZPE	*Zeitschrift für Papyrologie und Epigraphik*
ZWT	*Zeitschrift für wissenschaftliche Theologie*

1

The Roman Army[1]

T. R. S. Broughton

Acts has several references to the Roman army, and in the background of the story there is always a dimly perceived and changing mass of tribunes, centurions, and soldiers who sometimes limit the freedom and sometimes preserve the lives of the Christians who are in the foreground.

To describe the details which happen to be mentioned without explaining the system to which they belong seemed undesirable, if not impossible, nor is there any one book, at least in English, to which reference could conveniently be made. The following paragraphs therefore give (i.) a general description of the Roman military organization in the first century, (ii.) a discussion of the units of the Roman army in Syria and Palestine, (iii.) a note on the three most difficult references to military units in Acts.

1. [[The footnoting system of the original publication does not lend itself to new typesetting, so a different numbering system is deployed in this reprint—all footnotes from the original are retained with their full content. Moreover, all citations have been revised for clarity: secondary sources are given a full citation in their first occurrence and primary sources are provided in their standard and more accessible reference (e.g., *AE* or *CIL* instead of the *editio princeps*).]]

THE ORGANIZATION OF THE ROMAN ARMY IN THE FIRST CENTURY

(a) The Legion—The Regular army was divided into legions varying in number with the military needs of the Empire. The strength of a legion was about 6000 men divided into ten cohorts (σπεῖραι); these in turn were each divided into three maniples and six centuries. The tactical unit was the maniple, the administrative unit the cohort. There was also a body of legionary cavalry numbering in the first century 120 horse.[2] The commander of all forces in Syria was the imperial legate, but each legion also had as commander a legate of the senatorial order. With him were a group of subordinate officers, *beneficarii, stratores, cornricularii*, as an office staff. The legionary tribunes, six in number, whether senatorial, *laticlavi*, or equestrian, *angusticlavi*, combined military and administrative duties such as going the rounds, taking care of the list of soldiers in the corps, etc. They were usually young men doing military service at the beginning of their official career. In Greek they are regularly called χιλίαρχοι. The camp prefect, who also had a staff, was usually a veteran from the centurions *primipili*, thoroughly acquainted with the details of the service, and could in certain cases perform the duties of the legate of the legion in the latter's absence.

Of the subordinate officers the most important was the centurion, who was in command of a centuria, nominally of 100 men. There were 59 to a legion, and the first century had double the usual number of men. The centurions were ranked in a regular hierarchy from the *primus pilus*, who took part in the councils of war, to the *hastatus posterior* of the tenth cohort. This hierarchy represented the usual order of promotion. The centurions had closest contact with the soldiers of the line, and regulated duties, immunities, and punishments, so that the discipline of the legions depended chiefly on them. Officers subordinate to the centurions were the *optiones, imaginiferi, vexilarii*, etc. From these the centurions were promoted. Centurions were transferred from cohort to cohort and legion to legion as they were advanced in the service.[3] In general the centurion's

2. There has been doubt of the continuance of the legionary cavalry after the Augustan reorganization. The statement of Josephus, *J.W.* 3.120 εἵπετο δ' αὐτῷ τὸ ἴδιον τοῦ τάγματος ἱππικόν· ἴδιοι γὰρ ἑκάστου τάγματος εἴκοσι πρὸς τοῖς ἑκατόν ἱππεῖς, seems clear and definite.

3. See René Cagnat, "Legio," in Charles Darmenberg and Edmond Saglio, *Dictionnaire des antiquités grecques et romaines* (Paris: Hachette, 1911), 1047–93 (1056); Alfred von Domaszewski, *Die Rangordnung des römischen Heeres* (Bonn: Marcus & Weber,

opportunity for promotion ended with appointment to the post of *primus pilus* or of camp prefect.

The legionary soldier was *ipso facto* a Roman citizen, levied from a Roman town, or given Roman citizenship upon his entry into the service. The legal term of service was twenty years, but legionary soldiers were often kept in service for longer periods, particularly in the first century A.D. The centurions, whose position was more advantageous, often stayed still longer. The soldier's pay was probably a denarius a day, out of which he had to equip himself, secure any simple luxuries, or bribe the centurions for remissions of duties.[4] At the end of his service he received with his discharge a sum of money and a piece of land either in Italy or, as was more usual in the Empire, in soldier settlements in the provinces. Colonies were often set out in frontier lands with the double purpose of defence and development. In the east, however, the legions were resident in lands long since settled and developed; so soldier colonies were less numerous, and in general the veterans, of whom many were orientals by birth, soon merged into the people about them.[5]

After the Augustan reorganization the method of recruitment of the legions was in some measure local. At least the eastern and the western portions of the Empire became largely separate areas of recruitment, Africa, which in the time of Trajan had many soldiers from Asia Minor and Syria, being in the eastern area. In this policy two considerations were involved. The developed cities of the east, in the absence of Roman towns, had to be treated from the point of view of recruitment as analogous to the Roman cities of the west; and it was an advantage in each area to have soldiers already inured to the climate of their place of service. As a result, legions originally recruited in the west were early filled with Syrian soldiers. Antony had already recruited many Syrian soldiers into his legions. In the time of Vespasian the *legio III Gallica*, on the march to Italy in his interest, was composed of Syrians who, says Tacitus, saluted the rising sun, "as

1908), 90–97.

4. Tacitus, *Ann.* 1.17; cf. Pliny, *Hist. Nat.* 33.45.

5. For further information see W. Kubitschek and E. Ritterling, "Legio," in *Paulys Realencyclopädie der classischen Altertumswissenschaft* (ed. Georg Wissowa; Stuttgart: Metzler, 1924–26), 23.1186—24.1829 and literature there cited; H. M. D. Parker, *The Roman Legions* (Oxford: Clarendon, 1928).

the custom of the Syrians was."[6] Vespasian made Italy no longer liable to recruitment for the legions, and later on the levy became more purely local.[7]

(b) The Auxiliary Troops—Accompanying the legions in each province were auxiliary troops. These consisted of cavalry divisions or *alae* (ἴλαι), and of divisions either wholly or in large part consisting of infantry or *cohortes* (σπεῖραι). Special corps also were formed to meet special needs, such as slingers, archers, dromedary corps, etc. In the Augustan reorganization these troops were successors to the allied corps of the Republican army and supplied all the light-armed troops and almost all the cavalry used in the provincial armies. They were an integral part of the garrison forces, the cohorts being attached to the various legions, between five and seven to a legion, while the *alae* of cavalry were directly under the commander of the provincial army. In procuratorial provinces such as Judaea the garrison probably consisted almost wholly of auxiliary forces. They were recruited from the various dependent and allied peoples, of peregrine right, tribal names such as *Lucenses*, *Astures*, *Ituraei* being common in both eastern and western units. In the east, however, cohorts from cities also appear in the first century A.D., e.g. *Ascalonitani*, *Canatheni*, *Sebasteni*. Additional geographical titles such as *Dacica*, *Syriaca*, etc., probably refer to the service of cohorts in those regions before being moved, and are distinguishing epithets. Honorary cognomina, such as *Augusta*, *Claudia*, *Traiana*, are common, and in many cases refer to the organization of the unit under the emperor designated.[8]

A soldier in a cohort or an ala was normally not a Roman citizen, but regularly received citizenship at the end of his term of service. The *cohorts* and *alae civium Romanorum voluntariorum* were special formations. Free birth was a general condition of entrance into the legions, and this rule was broken only in cases of great national danger. Augustus only twice[9] used slaves and freedmen in the legions—during the Pannonian revolt and after the defeat of Varus. From Macrobius[10] we learn that in Germany and Illyricum he levied several cohorts of freedmen which he termed

6. Tacitus, *Hist.* 3.24.

7. W. Liebenam, "Dilectus," in *Paulys Realencyclopädie der classischen Altertumswissenschaft* (ed. Georg Wissowa; Stuttgart: Metzler 1905), 9.591–639.

8. Conrad Cichorius, "Cohors," in *Paulys Realencyclopädie der classischen Altertumswissenschaft* (ed. Georg Wissowa; Stuttgart: Metzler), 7.231–356; George L. Cheesman, *The Auxilia of the Roman Imperial Army* (Oxford: Clarendon, 1914).

9. Suetonius, *Aug.* 25; Dio Cassius 40.31–32

10. Macrobius, *Sat.* 1.11.33.

voluntariae. This is the probable origin of the *cohortes civium Romanorum voluntariorum*,[11] but the presence of *cohortes ingenuorum* among the volunteers suggests that the levy was not extended to freedmen until the freeborn had been exhausted. The *cohortes classicae* were probably cohorts originally formed from the fleet where freedmen could serve, and then turned to service on land.

An auxiliary *cohors peditata* was composed of infantry only, a *cohors equitata* of both infantry and cavalry. Most of the cohorts were of the latter type. A *cohors quingenaria* had a nominal strength of 500 men if *peditata*, if *equitata* of 380 infantry and 120 cavalry; a *cohors miliaria* had double the number in either case.[12] In practice there might be some modification. The *cohors I Augusta Lusitanorum* in A.D. 156 numbered, without its centurions and decurions, 363 foot, 114 horse, and 19 dromedarii.[13] Of 23 cohorts in Vespasian's army in A.D. 67, 10 had 1000 infantry each, and 13 had 600 infantry and 120 cavalry each.[14] In a *cohors miliaria peditata* there were 10 centuries, in a quingenaria 6. In a *cohors miliaria equitata* the infantry were divided into 10 centuries, in a *quingenaria* into 6; the cavalry were divided into *turmae*, but the number is uncertain. In the *cohors I Augusta Lusitanorum* above mentioned there were 6 centuries and 3 turmae. Each century was commanded by a centurion, each turma by a decurion, while other officers subordinate to them, the *optio*, *signifer*, etc., are found. Cohorts, if *quingenariae*, were commanded by *praefecti*, ἔπαρχοι, or if *miliariae*, by *tribuni*, χιλίαρχοι (cf. Acts 21:33). The post of tribune was equal in rank to the military tribuneship of a legion.

The majority of the alae were *quingenariae*, really of 480 men and 544 horses,[15] while the *miliariae* were composed of 1008 men and 1104 horses.[16] An *ala quingenaria* was divided into 16 turmae of 30 men and 34 horses each,[17] a *miliaria* into 24 turmae of 42 men and 46 horses each.[18]

11. Theodor Mommsen, *Res Gestae Divi Augusti ex Monumentis Ancyrano et Apolleniense* (2nd ed.; Berlin: Weidmann, 1883), 72.

12. Hyginus, *Cast. mun.* 27.

13. *BGU* 696.

14. Josephus, *J.W.* 3.66–67.

15. Alfred von Domaszewski, *Hygini Gromatici: Liber De Munitionibus Castrorum* (Leipzig: Hildesheim, 1887), 52.

16. Hyginus, *Cast. mun.* 16.

17. *CIL* 3.14; see Domaszewski, *Hygini Gromatici*, 10 n. 16.

18. Hyginus, *Cast. mun.* 16.

The commander of an ala was the *praefectus alae*, ἔπαρχος ἴλης, the highest military position in the equestrian career. A *decurio* was in charge of each turma, and there were the usual subordinate officers, *optio*, *armorum custos*, *librarius*, etc.

The numbers of cohorts and alae levied probably varied somewhat from time to time as need arose for light-armed troops and cavalry. Apart from special instances, such as the Thracians, whose qualifications as bowmen made them useful on every frontier, large numbers of auxiliary troops continued to live during their term of service in the province in which they were levied. It is questionable how far even Vespasian after the revolts and unrest of the years A.D. 68–70 carried out any deliberate policy of crushing the national feeling of the auxiliary units by transferring them to distant regions or mingling the soldiers with levies from other lands.[19] It is certain that cohorts were transferred, e.g. an *ala Sebastenorum* which had previously been in Palestine was changed to Mauretania,[20] while an *ala I Thracum Mauretana* appears in Palestine in a diploma of A.D. 86. We find, however, that many transferred cohorts soon begin to be recruited from the region to which they have been transferred.[21] Other cohorts such as *the II Italica Civium Romanorum* and the *II Classica* which were in Syria in the first century remained there long into the second.

From the military *diplomata*[22] little can safely be inferred as to the total number of alae and cohorts in any province. They are strict evidence only for the presence of particular alae and cohorts at a particular time. Some inference may be made from the number of legions, as the number of cohorts of which we have evidence in any province ranges from five to eight to a legion. The instance of the *cohors I Vindelicorum miliaria*, (*CIL* 16.107 [[=*DMIPERP* §296]]) A.D. 157, Dacia Superior, for which Conrad Cichorius ("Cohors") assumes a previous stay in Palestine from the presence in the cohort of a Jew from Caesarea named Bar Simso, shows how incomplete our evidence must be.

19. See Cheesman, *Roman Auxilia*, 67–72.

20. See *CIL* 8.9358, 8.9359, 8.21044; Theodor Mommsen, *Gesammelte Schriften* (Berlin: Weidmann, 1910), 6.553.

21. Cheesman, *Roman Auxilia*, 67–72.

22. *Diplomata* were certificates of honourable discharge given to soldiers in the Roman auxiliary forces at the end of their service. These usually contain not only the name and unit of the recipient but the names of other units serving in the province. These are published in *CIL* 16 [[see now the *Roman Military Diplomas* series edited by Margaret Roxan and Paul Holder]].

THE ROMAN ARMY IN SYRIA AND PALESTINE

At the end of the Mithridatic war it was evident that the Roman occupation of Syria was a necessity for the preservation of peace and order in the east. Rome was now for the first time in direct contact with the Parthians, who controlled Mesopotamia and continually interfered in the affairs of the various client-kingdoms of Armenia and of Syria. Pompey's aggressions beyond the Euphrates left a heritage of intermittent warfare, which was relieved by dissensions in the Parthian royal household and by the difficulty of securing united action from a large body of semi-independent Parthian chieftains. Within the province the client-princes of northern Syria, Sampsiceramus of Emesa, Alchaudonius of Rhambae, and others required the backing of Roman forces to offset Parthian influence upon them, and the presence of Roman troops was everywhere demanded to prevent dynastic quarrels and ensure internal peace.[23] But peace was difficult to ensure. The raids of the Bedouins of the Arabian desert were a continual source of trouble, and the Jews resented the Roman yoke. To meet the needs of external and internal defence the Roman governor of Syria was given merely the resources usual to provincial governors, the legions voted him by the senate, and the right of levying in case of need both Roman citizens and provincials within his province.[24]

An estimate of the normal garrison of Syria between 62 B.C. and the outbreak of the civil wars is hardly possible. Gabinius as governor, 57 B.C., gathered forces for an invasion of Parthia but was prevented by insurrections of the Jews,[25] and by his mission to restore Ptolemy of Egypt to his throne.[26] The province was taken over in 55 B.C. by Crassus, who invaded Parthia with a force of 7 legions, 4000 horse, and about 4000 light-armed men, probably allied troops.[27] Not 10,000 of this army escaped from Carrhae, and Cassius, after quelling a Jewish insurrection with the help of Antipater

23. See Theodor Mommsen, *The History of Rome* (trans. William Purdie Dickson; 1st ed.; London: Bentley & Son, 1866), 4.428–431; E. S. Bouchier, *Syria as a Roman Province* (Oxford: Blackwell, 1916), is a simple and abbreviated account.

24. Joachim Marquardt, *Römische Staatsverwaltung* (2nd ed.; Leipzig: Hirzel, 1881), 1.536; cf. Cicero, *Att.* 5.18.2; *Fam.* 15.1.5.

25. Josephus, *A.J.* 14.99–100.

26. Dio Cassius 39.56.3; Josephus, *J.W.* 1.175–177; Plutarch, *Ant.* 3.

27. Plutarch, *Crass.* 20.

of Idumea, could muster but two weak legions to face the Parthian invasion of 51 B.C.[28]

Similarly, during the period of the civil wars, Syria, from the military point of view, was in a quite abnormal condition. Pompey, Cassius, and Antony in succession levied troops on Syrian soil, while the Parthians took advantage of the confusion to overrun the province. Syrian detachments assisted Pompey in the earlier portion of the civil war,[29] but after the battle of Pharsalia the province supported Caesar, and an army of Jews, Arabs, and Syrians under Mithridates of Pergamum and Antipater of Idumea came to relieve Caesar in Alexandria.[30] Judaea became an ethnarchy with Hyrcanus as high priest and Antipater as actual governor.[31] In northern Syria the single legion which Caesar left under the command of his kinsman Sextus Caesar was corrupted by the Pompeian, Caecilius Bassus, who managed to resist the troops sent against him until Cassius returned to the east in 44 B.C. Cassius won all the forces there to his command[32] and levied troops in Syria for the campaign of Philippi.[33] During the confusion following Philippi, the Parthians overran Cilicia, much of Asia, and the whole of Syria except Tyre, and placed their own nominee in the high-priesthood at Jerusalem, but they were driven out by Antony's lieutenant, Ventidius Bassus. Sosius, appointed by Antony to protect Syria, aided Herod to regain Jerusalem, which was finally captured in 37 B.C. The total strength of the two armies was 11 battalions of infantry, 6000 cavalry, about 30,000 in all, exclusive of the Syrian auxiliaries who were no inconsiderable number.[34] For his Parthian campaign in 36 B.C. Antony mobilized about 100,000 men, of which 60,000 were Roman legionaries among whom Orientals had been recruited.[35] 10,000 were Spanish and Gallic auxiliaries, and 30,000 more came from Syria and Asia Minor as contingents of the allied kings.[36] Of

28. Cicero, *Att.* 5.20.3; *Fam.* 15.14.2; Josephus, *A.J.* 14.119–122; *J.W.* 1.180.

29. Appian, *B.C.* 2.49; 2.71.

30. Josephus, *A.J.* 14.127–136; *J.W.* 1.187–192.

31. Josephus, *A.J.* 14.137–139; *J.W.* 1.202–203.

32. Josephus, *J.W.* 1.216–217; Dio Cassius 47.26–27; Cicero, *Att.* 14.9.3.

33. Josephus, *A.J.* 14.271–272; *J.W.* 1.225.

34. Josephus, *A.J.* 14.468–469; *J.W.* 1.345–346. τέλος, here translated "battalion," means "legion" in Appian, *B.C.* 5.87, but it is unlikely that it means "legion" in Josephus' passages.

35. Josephus, *A.J.* 14.449; *J.W.* 1.324.

36. Plutarch, *Ant.* 37.3.

this army more than 30,000 were lost.[37] Before Actium, Antony increased his army to 30 legions, two-thirds of whom were orientals,[38] and perhaps seven of these remained in Syria and Egypt.[39] During these years Syria was the prey of invaders and of rival claimants for power in Rome, and the people of the province, pressed into service in large numbers and heavily taxed, passively obeyed whatever power was in command. An extensive orientalization of the Roman army in the east resulted from the levies of Cassius and of Antony, and a large supply of auxiliary forces, light-armed troops, and bowmen was raised locally by the princes of the client kingdoms. These probably maintained armies for the most part raised from their own kingdoms, but sometimes had detachments of Roman soldiers stationed in their realms; for instance, at the time of Caesar's death the garrison of Damascus, which was then at least within the kingdom of the Nabatean Arabs, was composed of Roman soldiers.[40] In 29 B.C. Herod had a Roman legion to guard Jerusalem,[41] but in general used troops raised within his kingdom. The best portion of the garrison at Jerusalem at the time of the deposition of Archelaus was a body of some 3000 Sebastenians of the royal forces.[42] Herod also had mercenaries,[43] and was followed to his mausoleum by his guards, Thracians, Germans, and Gauls.[44]

Augustus rightly considered Syria the point of greatest strategic importance in the east. It controlled the natural routes to and across the Euphrates, and since the province of Asia was without a garrison, was the only eastern province with an army. The defence, therefore, of the whole Roman east, and the support for the client-princes of Galatia, Armenia, Cappadocia, and of Syria itself, depended upon the Syrian army, and Augustus made it an imperial province under a legate of proconsular rank

37. Plutarch, *Ant.* 50.1, 51.1.

38. Johannes Kromayer, "Kleine Forschungen zur Geschichte des Zweiten Triumvirats," *Hermes* 33 (1898): 1–70 (68); cf. Josephus, *A.J.* 14.449.

39. Kromayer, "Kleine Forschungen," 65.

40. Josephus, *A.J.* 14.295.

41. Josephus, *A.J.* 15.72.

42. Josephus, *J.W.* 2.52: τὸ μέντοι πολεμικώτατον μέρος, Σεβαστηνοὶ τρισχίλιοι Ῥοῦφός τε καὶ Γρᾶτος ἐπὶ τούτοις, ὁ μὲν τοὺς πεζοὺς τῶν βασιλικῶν ὑπ᾽ αὐτὸν ἔχων, Ῥοῦφος δὲ τοὺς ἱππεῖς . . . προσέθεντο Ῥωμαίοις.

43. Josephus, *J.W.* 1.301: ἔχουσαι καὶ μισθοφόρους μιγάδας.

44. Josephus, J.W. 1.672: καὶ περὶ τὴν κλίνην οἵ τε υἱεῖς καὶ τὸ πλῆθος τῶν συγγενῶν, ἐφ᾽ οἷς οἱ δορυφόροι καὶ τὸ Θρᾴκιον στῖφος Γερμανοί τε καὶ Γαλάται διεσκευασμένοι πάντες ὡς εἰς πόλεμον.

with legions under his command. It appears that at first there were only three legions under the command of the Syrian legate, since in 4 B.C. Varus left one of the three Syrian legions in Jerusalem to preserve order while Archelaus presented to Augustus[45] his claim to succeed his father Herod, but the number was later increased to four, perhaps at the time of Gaius Caesar's expedition to the east, by the transference of the *legio XII Fulminata* from Egypt to Syria.[46] There certainly were four legions in Syria in A.D. 23.[47] The comparatively peaceful conditions within and without the province after 27 B.C. until the time of Nero necessitated no larger force.

The four regular legions in Syria during the first century A.D. were the *X Fretensis, III Gallica, VI Ferrata*, and *XII Fulminata*.

The *legio X Fretensis* was Caesar's tenth legion, re-levied after his death. It gained the title Fretensis from the campaign under Octavian against Sextus Pompey at the Sicilian straits.[48] Veterans from the legion were settled in colonies in Italy during the triumvirate.[49] The legion was sent to Syria, probably before A.D. 6,[50] certainly by A.D. 17,[51] when it was encamped at Cyrrhae. Veterans of the legion shared in the Claudian colony of Ptolemais. It was in Corbulo's army in A.D. 58.[52] A detachment from this legion went under Cestius Gallus against Jerusalem in A.D. 66.[53] After the campaign in Galilee in A.D. 67 it was with *V Macedonica* at Caesarea.[54] In A.D. 69 it came to Titus before Jerusalem by way of Jericho,[55] and at the end of the war became the permanent garrison of Judaea, encamped on the then desolate site of Jerusalem.[56]

45. Josephus, *J.W.* 2.40: ἓν τῶν τριῶν ἀπὸ Συρίας ταγμάτων; cf. *J.W.* 2.66–67; *A.J.* 17.286.

46. Strabo 17.1.12, 17.1.30 (still three legions in Egypt); Kubitschek and Ritterling, "Legio," 1235, 1243, 1706; Parker, *Roman Legions*, 92.

47. Tacitus, *Ann.* 4.5: *dehinc initio ab Suriae usque ad flumen Euphraten, quantum ingenti terrarum sinu ambitur, quattuor legionibus coercita.*

48. Mommsen, *Res Gestae*, 69.

49. *CIL* 5.4191; 5.4987; 10.3887.

50. Kubitschek and Ritterling, "Legio," 1235.

51. Tacitus, *Ann.* 2.57.

52. Tacitus, *Ann.* 13.40.

53. Josephus, *J.W.* 2.499–500.

54. Josephus, *J.W.* 3.110–111, 3.233–234, 3.409–412.

55. Josephus, *J.W.* 5.42–46.

56. Josephus, *J.W.* 7.5–17; *Life* 422. Mention of a veteran of this legion, enrolled in A.D. 68 and discharged in A.D. 94, and therefore a soldier of the army of Titus before

The *legio III Gallica* had probably been *XV* of Caesar's Gallic army, and when handed over to Pompey in 53 B.C. became Pompey's *III*. It retained this number under Caesar at Munda.[57] It was part of Antony's Parthian army,[58] and when taken over by Augustus after Actium was stationed in Syria where it remained, and shared in the Claudian colony of Ptolemais about A.D. 45. With *VI Ferrata* it was important in Corbulo's army in Armenia, and in A.D. 64 built the castellum of Zialta there.[59] It sent a detachment under Cestius Gallus against Jerusalem in A.D. 66, and must have fought under Vespasian in Galilee. It was, however, moved to Moesia, where it repelled the inroads of the Roxolani, and was important in the movement that brought Vespasian to the throne, marching to Italy in his interest.[60] After a winter at Capua[61] it was sent back to Syria, where it remained a long time with its headquarters perhaps at Raphaneae, which *XII Fulminata* vacated on being moved to Melitene.[62]

The *legio VI Ferrata* was originally part of Caesar's army,[63] and in the campaigns of Caesar in Egypt and Pontus was reduced to an effective of 1000 men,[64] who were finally settled at Arelate. The name remained and *VI Ferrata* after Philippi was one of Antony's veteran legions in Syria.[65] After Actium the legion was stationed in Syria by Augustus, perhaps also at Raphaneae.[66] After the defeat of Paetus it fought in Armenia under Corbulo.[67] Returning to Syria it sent a detachment against the Jews with

Jerusalem, is found in the diptych of Marcus Valerius Quadratus, discovered in 1909 at Philadelphia in the Fayum [[=*DMIPERP* §150]]. See Adolf Deissmann, *Light from the Ancient East: The New Testament Illustrated by Recently Discovered Texts of the Graeco-Roman World* (trans. Lionel R. M. Strachan; 4th ed.; New York: Harper & Brothers, 1922), 442, n. 2, for further literature.

57. Caesar, *bell. Gall.* 8.54; *bell. Civ.* 3.88.2; Pseudo-Caesar, *bell. Hisp.* 30.7.

58. Plutarch, *Ant.* 42.

59. *CIL* 3.6741, 3.6742, 3.6742a.

60. Tacitus, *Hist.* 2.74, 2.85; Suetonius, *Vesp.* 6.

61. Tacitus, *Hist.* 4.3.

62. Josephus, *J.W.* 7.18.

63. Caesar, *bell. Gall.* 8.4.3.

64. Aulus Hirtius, *bell. Alex.* 69.1.

65. Appian, *B.C.* 5.3.

66. *CIL* 3.14165.13 [[=*DMIPERP* §387]]; Henry Cohen, *Description historique des monnaies frappées sous l'Empire Romain* (2nd ed.; Paris: Rollin & Feuardent, 1880), 1.307, nos. 431–432.

67. Tacitus, *Ann.* 15.26; *ILS* 9108.

Cestius Gallus.[68] In A.D. 69 it went to Europe under Licinius Mucianus in Vespasian's interest.[69] It returned to Syria after the return of *III Gallica*,[70] and two years later reduced the kingdom of Commagene.[71] It remained in Syria and took part in Trajan's eastern expedition,[72] and after the Jewish war under Hadrian was moved to Palestine where it made its camp at Caparcotna in Galilee.[73]

There was a *legio XII* under Octavian's command at Perugia, 41–40 B.C.,[74] which probably had been Caesar's twelfth legion.[75] This legion was probably stationed in Egypt during the earlier years of Augustus, since there were three legions each in Egypt and in Syria at that time,[76] but by A.D. 23 at the latest Syria had four legions.[77] The title Fulminata appears on the epitaphs of veterans of the twelfth legion settled in 16 B.C. at Patrae.[78] The legion shared in the Claudian colony of Ptolemais. Corbulo left it in Syria during his advance into Armenia in A.D. 58, but it took part in the unfortunate Armenian campaign of Paetus in A.D. 62,[79] and was returned to Syria by Corbulo.[80] It then had its camp at Raphaneae.[81] It was led by Cestius Gallus against Jerusalem in A.D. 66.[82] Suetonius, *Vesp.* 4, says it lost an eagle on this expedition, but Josephus, *J.W.* 2.540–555, is silent on this point. In A.D. 69 Titus increased the army before Jerusalem from three to four legions using *XII Fulminata*,[83] but it did not retrieve the disgrace of

68. Josephus, *J.W.* 2.499–500.
69. Tacitus, *Hist.* 2.83.
70. Tacitus, *Hist.* 4.39.
71. Josephus, *J.W.* 7.219–228.
72. *ILS* 9471.
73. *CIL* 3.6814–6816; *AE* 1920.78.
74. *CIL* 11.6721.28–30.
75. *CIL* 11.6721.29; the Paterna of 27 B.C., *CIL* 11.1058.
76. Strabo 17.1.12; 17.1.30; Josephus, *A.J.* 17.286; *J.W.* 2.40, 2.67.
77. Tacitus, *Ann.* 4.5.
78. *CIL* 3.504, 3.507, 3.509.
79. Tacitus, *Ann.* 15.6.
80. Tacitus, *Ann.* 15.26.
81. Josephus, *J.W.* 7.18.
82. Josephus, *J.W.* 2.500.
83. Josephus, *J.W.* 5.39–41.

its former defeat, and was transferred to Cappadocia, where it served as garrison for a hundred years.[84]

In addition to these four regular legions in Syria, during the reign of Nero *V Macedonica* was brought from Moesia, *XV Apollinaris* from Pannonia, and *IIII Scythica* probably also came from Moesia to assist Corbulo's campaign in Armenia; all these were stationed in Syria. After the Jewish war *V Macedonica*, which had encamped at Emmaus and had been prominent in the operations about Jerusalem,[85] was brought back to Moesia. *XV Apollinaris*, which had been active in the Jewish war at Jotapata and Gamala,[86] and in the siege of Jerusalem,[87] was returned to Pannonia in A.D. 71.[88] *IIII Scythica* was sent to Syria in the early years of Nero[89] and served in Paetus's unfortunate campaign in Armenia,[90] returning to Syria after its defeat.[91] It sent a *vexillatio* of 2000 men with Cestius against Jerusalem in A.D. 66.[92] In A.D. 69, while one portion of the army lay before Jerusalem and the other was moving on Rome to secure the Principate for Vespasian, this legion was for a few months the only garrison toward the Euphrates border. After the Jewish war it remained a long time in Syria with its headquarters probably in the north near Antioch.[93]

The evidence for the auxiliary troops in Syria in the first century is scanty: a diploma, *AE* 1927.44 [[=*DMIPERP* §225]], A.D. 88, mentions three alae and seventeen cohorts; a second, *ILS* 2724 [[=*DMIPERP* §188]], which probably dates from the Parthian expedition of Trajan, or perhaps from the expedition of Verus (see Dessau's discussion in *ILS*), names five alae and fifteen cohorts; while another, *ILS* 9057 [[=*DMIPERP* §259]], A.D. 157, names four alae and sixteen cohorts. Some scattered inscriptional and literary evidences also occur. Regarding the following list of alae and

84. Josephus, *J.W.* 7.18; *CIL* 8.7079; [[=DMIPERP §187]] Dio Cassius 55.23.5. On these particular legions see Kubitschek and Ritterling, "Legio," 1376–80.

85. Josephus, *J.W.* 5.67–68, 5.467, 6.68–80, 6.237.

86. Josephus, *J.W.* 3.324–325.

87. Josephus, *J.W.* 5.467.

88. Josephus, *J.W.* 7.117.

89. Tacitus, *Ann.* 13.35, and see the discussion in Kubitschek and Ritterling, "Legio," 1558.

90. Tacitus, *Ann.* 15.6–17.

91. Tacitus, *Ann.* 15.26; Dio Cassius 67.22.4.

92. Josephus, *J.W.* 2.500.

93. See Kubitschek and Ritterling, "Legio" on the particular legions and their history.

cohorts which were in Syria in the first and second centuries A.D., the reader is referred to Cichorius, "Ala" and "Cohors," to the indices of the *Année epigraphique*, and the appendices of Cheesman, *Roman Auxilia*.

[[Note: the following section of Broughton's chapter is the most egregiously out-of-date; for an updated study with more detail and recent references to specifically *Judaean* military forces, see Christopher B. Zeichmann, "Military Forces in Judaea 6–130 CE: The *status quaestionis* and Relevance for New Testament Studies," *Currents in Biblical Research* 17 (2018) 86–120. Consequently, I have not provided *DMIPERP* cross-references for this section, as a more complete record with such references can be found in the aforementioned article.]]

Alae

II Flavia Agrippiana, ILS 2724; *CIG* 2.3497.

Augusta Syriaca, ILS 2724.

**I Flavia Civium Romanorum, AE* 1927.44.

**Bosporana, AE* 1922.109, A.D. 54; *CIL* 3.6707.

Colonorum, AE 1895.78.

I Ulpia Dromadariorum Miliaria, ILS 9057.

I Flavia Gaetulorum, ILS 2724; in Moesia A.D. 99, *CIL* 16.45.

**Gallica, AE* 1927.44.

**Thracum Herculiana Miliaria, ILS* 2724, 9057; *CIL* 12.1357, on Euphrates in the first century.

**Miliaria*, in Syria in first century, Pliny, *Ep.* 7.31.

**II Pannoniorum, AE* 1927.44; used in Trajan's Dacian war, *IGRR* 1.824.

VII Phrygum, AE 1899.177; cf. *CIL* 2.4201, first century; *CIL* 16.171, in Palestine A.D. 139.

Praetoria, ILS 2724; in Pannonia A.D. 80, *CIL* 16.31.

I Ulpia Singularium, ILS 2724, 9057; *CIL* 10.6426; *AE* 1911.161.

**Sebastenorum*, first century, Josephus, *A.J.* 19.365; 20.122; *J.W.* 2.263.

**III Augusta Thracum Veterana Gallica, AE* 1927.44; *CIL* 2.4251.

Cohortes

**I Ascalonitanorum, ILS* 2724; *AE* 1927.44; cf. Josephus, *J.W.* 3.12.

* *I Augusta, ILS* 2683, after A.D. 6; *IGRR* 3.1136, Agrippa II; and perhaps Acts 27:1.

**IV Bracaugustanorum, AE* 1927.44; in Palestine A.D. 139.

I Flavia Chalcidenorum Sagittariorum equitata, ILS 2724; *ILS* 9057, n. 9.

II Ulpia Equitata Civium Romanorum, ILS 2724, 9057.

I Flavia Civium Romanorum Equitata, ILS 2724; in Palestine A.D. 139.

**II Classica Sagittariorum, ILS* 2683, after A.D. 6; *AE* 1927.44; *ILS* 9057.

**IV Callaecorum, AE* 1927.44.

**I Flavia Canathenorum, CIL* 8.2394, 8.2395, 8.17904; in Raetia, A.D. 166, *CIL* 3.6001; 16.94, 16.117, 16.183; probably in Palestine during the first century although Canatha was under Agrippa II, Mommsen, *Gesammelte Schriften,* 6.101.

I Ulpia Dacorum, ILS 9057; in Syria until late Empire, *Not. Dig.* 33.33.

III Dacorum Equitata, ILS 2724.

IV Gallorum, ILS 9057.

VII Gallorum, ILS 9057; in Moesia earlier, *ILS* 1999.

**II Miliaria Italica Civium Romanorum Voluntariorum, ILS* 9168, A.D. 69; *ILS* 9057; *AE* 1927.44, and probably in Palestine early in the first century; see below.

**I Ituraeorum, AE* 1927.44.

**Lucensium*, AE 1927.44.

**I Lucensium Equitata, AE* 1927.44; *ILS* 2724; in Pannonia A.D. 80, *CIL* 16.35.

IV Lucensium Equitata, ILS 2724.

I Miliaria, AE 1927.44; Denis Fossey, “Inscriptions de Syrie,” *Bulletin de correspondance hellénique* 21 (1897) 39–65 (45).

Musulamiorum, AE 1897.44.

I Numidarum, AE 1897.44; in Lycia Pamphylia A.D. 178, *CIL* 16.128.

**I Augusta Pannoniorum, AE* 1927.44; *ILS* 9057; in Egypt A.D. 83, *CIL* 16.35, 16.106.

II Pannoniorum, AE 1927.44.

II Ulpia Paflagonum Equitata, ILS 2724, 9057.

III Ulpia Paflagonum Equitata, ILS 2724, 9057.

I Ulpia Petraeorum Miliaria Equitata, ILS 2724, 9057; *AE* 1911.161.

V Ulpia Petraeorum Miliaria Equitata, ILS 2724, 9057.

I Ulpia Sagittariorum Equitata, ILS 2724.

**I Sebastenorum, AE* 1927.44, perhaps in Palestine A.D. 139.

I Sugambrorum Equitata, ILS 2724, but from Moesia.

I Claudia Sugambrorum, ILS 9057; in Moesia A.D. 134, *CIL* 16.22, 16.106.

**IV Thracum Syriaca Equitata, AE* 1927.44; *CIL* 2.1970.

I Thracum or *II Thracum*, see Dessau’s comments in *ILS* 9057, n. 9; *ILS* 2724; cf. *CIL* 3.8261, 3.8262; *ILS* 2733, in Moesia.

**II Thracum Syriaca Equitata, ILS* 9057; *AE* 1927.44.

III Augusta Thracum Equitata, ILS 9057; *CIL* 6.31856, 10.6100; *AE* 1888.66, 1911.161.

III Thracum Syriaca Equitata, AE 1911.161.

* denotes alae and cohorts present in Syria and Palestine during the first century A.D.

The following alae and cohorts were in Judaea in A.D. 86, according to *CIL* 16.33 [[=*DMIPERP* §202]]:

Alae: *Veterana Gaetulorum, I Thracum, I Thracum Mauretana, II Thracum*

Cohortes: *I Augusta Lusitanorum, II Cantabrorum*

None of these is original with Syria, but the possibility of Syrian recruits is not excluded. In A.D. 139 the following appear in Syria Palaestina, according to *CIL* 16.87 [[=*DMIPERP* §211]]:

Alae: *Gallorum et Thracum, I Galatarum, Antoniniana Gallorum, II Galatarum, VII Phrygum, III Bracarum*

Cohortes: *I Thracum miliaria, IV Bracarum, I Sebastenorum miliaria, IV Petraeorum, I Damascenorum, VI Petraeorum, I Montanorum miliaria, V Gemina Civium Romanorum, I Flavia Civium Romanorum*

Note that while many of these are from the eastern portion of the empire, only one is from Judaea itself, and three are from Syria. The two cohorts of Roman citizens were probably originally freedmen, one of Flavian foundation and the other the result of the union of two previously existing cohorts.[94]

It will be observed that there is evidence for the presence of many of these cohorts in Syria in the first century A.D. Cohorts such as the *Petraeorum* were not formed before the time of Trajan, and several of the cohorts above noted are known to have been in Moesia and Pannonia during the first century. The Jewish wars, the formation of the province of Cappadocia, and the expeditions of Trajan and of Verus, demanded fresh alignments of troops, but a few cohorts, e.g. *II Italica C.R.* and *II Classica*, are known to have been in Syria before Vespasian's day and to have continued there afterwards. Many other auxiliary cohorts were used in Palestine and Syria during the first century, as auxiliary forces were gathered by various governors, Varus,[95] Petronius,[96] Cestius,[97] Vespasian,[98] and Titus,[99] to

94. See Eric Birley, "A Note on the Title 'Gemina,'" *JRS* 18 (1928) 56–60, on the meaning of *Gemina*.

95. Josephus, *J.W.* 2.66: τὰ λοιπὰ δύο τάγματα καὶ τὰς σὺν αὐτοῖς τέσσαρας ἴλας ἱππέων.

96. Josephus, *J.W.* 2.186: σὺν τρισὶ τάγμασι καὶ πολλοῖς ἐκ τῆς Συρίας συμμάχοις.

97. Josephus, *J.W.* 2.500: πεζῶν τε ἓξ σπείρας καὶ τέσσαρας ἴλας ἱππέων, πρὸς αἷς τὰς παρὰ τῶν βασιλέων συμμαχίας.

98. Josephus, *J.W.* 3.66: τούτοις εἵποντο ὀκτωκαίδεκα σπεῖραι· προσεγένοντο δὲ καὶ ἀπὸ Καισαρείας πέντε καὶ ἱππέων ἴλη μία, πέντε δ' ἕτεραι τῶν ἀπὸ Συρίας ἱππέων; also large forces from the client kings.

99. Josephus, *J.W.* 5.42: πρὸς οἷς αἵ τε τῶν βασιλέων συμμαχίαι πολὺ πλείους καὶ συχνοὶ τῶν ἀπὸ τῆς Συρίας ἐπίκουροι συνῆλθον; Tacitus, *Hist.* 5.1.

meet disturbances and revolts among the Jews, but their names have not come down. A general survey, however, of the auxilia shows that in the first century the basis of recruitment in the auxilia was largely local, that the majority of the auxiliary units served in the province in which they were raised, and that despite later changes the system of local recruitment and service was never abandoned completely. Whatever the people from which the various units drew their names and origin, a goodly proportion of the soldiers recruited belonged both in the first century and later to the province in which the unit served.[100]

The legions which formed the garrison of Syria were divided between northern and the central regions of the province, near the cities of Antioch and Emesa. Legionary soldiers were not regularly used in Judaea unless on special occasions. It is true that a legion was stationed at Jerusalem to keep order while the succession to Herod was being decided,[101] and that the legions could always be called upon in case of need. The garrison of Judaea under the procurators was regularly composed of Syrian auxiliary cohorts. Among the royal troops under Herod and Archelaus were 3000 Sebasteni, characterized by Josephus[102] as the most warlike portion. The inclusion of these Sebasteni among the Roman auxiliary cohorts upon the reduction of the ethnarchy may be the origin of the *cohortes* and *ala Sebastenorum* which later appear.

Caesarea, not Jerusalem, was the military headquarters for Judaea. The soldiers there were mainly Syrians,[103] many from Caesarea itself and Sebaste (Samaria),[104] and readily took the part of their countrymen against the Jewish community. Of the troops at Caesarea there are mentioned

100. See Cheesman, *Roman Auxilia*, 57–60; Mommsen, *Gesammelte Schriften*, 6.20–24.

101. Josephus, *J.W.* 2.40: ἓν τῶν τριῶν ἀπὸ Συρίας ταγμάτων, ὅπερ ἄγων ἧκεν, ἐν τῇ πόλει καταλείπει.

102. Josephus, *J.W.* 2.52.

103. Josephus, *J.W.* 2.268: τὸ γὰρ πλέον Ῥωμαίοις τῆς ἐκεῖ δυνάμεως ἐκ Συρίας ἦν κατειλεγμένον.

104. Josephus, *A.J.* 20.176: μέγα δὲ φρονοῦντες ἐπὶ τῷ τοὺς πλείστους τῶν ὑπὸ Ῥωμαίοις ἐκεῖ στρατευομένων Καισαρεῖς εἶναι καὶ Σεβαστηνούς; 19.356–357: Καισαρεῖς καὶ Σεβαστηνοὶ τῶν εὐποιιῶν αὐτοῦ λαθόμενοι τὰ τῶν δυσμενεστάτων ἐποίησαν . . . καὶ ὅσοι στρατευόμενοι τότε ἔτυχον, συχνοὶ δ᾽ ἦσαν, οἴκαδε ἀπῆλθον . . .; 19.364–366: πρὸ πάντων ἐπιστεῖλαι τῷ Φάδῳ Καισαρεῦσιν καὶ Σεβαστηνοῖς ἐπιπλῆξαι τῆς εἰς τὸν κατοιχόμενον ὕβρεως καὶ παροινίας εἰς τὰς ἔτι ζώσας, τὴν ἴλην δὲ τῶν Καισαρέων καὶ τῶν Σεβαστηνῶν καὶ τὰς πέντε σπείρας εἰς Πόντον μεταγαγεῖν, ἵν᾽ ἐκεῖ στρατεύοιντο, τῶν δ᾽ ἐν Συρίᾳ Ῥωμαϊκῶν ταγμάτων ἐπιλέξαι στρατιώτας κατ᾽ ἀριθμοὺς καὶ τὸν ἐκείνων ἀναπληρῶσαι τόπον. οὐ μὴν οἱ κελευσθέντες μετέστησαν.

an *ala Sebastena* and five cohorts of infantry,[105] which were there under Agrippa I. Later appear four cohorts and one ala,[106] among which Mommsen conjectures were a *cohors I Sebastenorum*, *I Ascalonitanorum*, and *I Canathenorum*.[107] In Acts 10:1 mention is made of a *cohors Italica* which must have been present about A.D. 40. No *cohors Caesariensium* is known.

The garrison of Jerusalem itself was probably not as large as the turbulent population required. The Roman government (perhaps mistakenly) tried to conciliate the Jews. In response to Jewish demonstrations[108] Pilate sent back to Caesarea the standards of the garrison, which were offensive to the Jews on account of the images of Caesar on them. It is possible that there were some legionary soldiers in the garrison of Jerusalem, since Josephus, *J.W.* 2.260–263 speaks of the hoplites, heavy-armed soldiers, whom Felix used to disperse the following of the false prophets and of the Egyptian impostor, but hoplite does not necessarily mean a legionary soldier.[109] Since any additions to the garrison of Jerusalem were brought from Caesarea it is probable that like the garrison there it was in the main composed of Syrians whose contempt for Jewish religious practices was the cause of serious tumults in both places.[110] We cannot estimate the number of soldiers in the garrison, which must have varied from time to time, but Claudius Lysias could detach 200 soldiers, 70 horse, and 200 δεξιολάβοι to accompany Paul to Caesarea.[111] The unrest and brigandage of the years preceding the out break of war in A.D. 66 doubtless necessitated increased garrisons both

105. Josephus, *A.J.* 19.365.

106. Josephus, *A.J.* 20.122: ἀναλαβὼν τὴν τῶν Σεβαστηνῶν ἴλην καὶ πεζῶν τέσσαρα τάγματα (=cohorts?); *J.W.* 2.236: Κουμανὸς δὲ ἀναλαβὼν ἀπὸ τῆς Καισαρείας μίαν ἴλην ἱππέων καλουμένην Σεβαστηνῶν ἐξεβοήθει τοῖς πορθουμένοις. Cf. *J.W.* 3.66: προσεγένοντο δὲ καὶ ἀπὸ Καισαρείας πέντε (σπεῖραι) καὶ ἱππέων ἴλη μία, when Vespasian was collecting forces to advance into Galilee.

107. Mommsen, *Gesammelte Schriften*, 6.533.

108. Josephus, *J.W.* 2.174: ὑπερθαυμάσας δὲ ὁ Πιλᾶτος τὸ τῆς δεισιδαιμονίας ἄκρατον ἐκκομίσαι μὲν αὐτίκα τὰς σημαίας Ἱεροσολύμων κελεύει; *A.J.* 18.59: καὶ Πιλᾶτος θαυμάσας τὸ ἐχυρὸν αὐτῶν ἐπὶ φυλακῇ τῶν νόμων παραχρῆμα τὰς εἰκόνας ἐκ τῶν Ἱεροσολύμων ἐπανεκόμισεν εἰς Καισάρειαν.

109. The 1500 soldiers which Varus hastily levied from Berytus when on his march to relieve Sabinus in Jerusalem, Josephus, *J.W.* 2.67, are termed ὁπλῖται. Although Berytus was a Roman colony these were not their regular legionary soldiers.

110. Josephus, *J.W.* 2.224–226, 2.266–270.

111. Acts 23:23. See the variations in the text and the difficulty of interpreting in this case.

in Jerusalem and in places of the region such as Jericho,[112] but the additional forces sent to Jerusalem in the time of Floras were merely a matter of cohorts,[113] and, in fact, Florus agreed[114] to leave the city, adding to the garrison but a single cohort of the forces he had brought from Caesarea. Ascalon apparently, like Sebaste, left undefended in A.D. 65,[115] was garrisoned in A.D. 67 by one cohort of infantry and one cohort of cavalry.[116] Joppa remained ungarrisoned in A.D. 66.[117]

THREE PASSAGES IN ACTS OF SPECIAL DIFFICULTY

(a) Acts 10:1—This refers to Cornelius at Caesarea as a centurion Acts *ἐκ σπείρας τῆς καλουμένης Ἰταλικῆς* that is of the cohort called Italian. Probably this was the *cohors II Italica Civium Romanorum*,[118] which must have been in Syria before A.D. 69, for a certain Proculus of this cohort was an *optio* in the *vexillatio* of the Syrian army which accompanied Mucianus to Italy to win the principate for Vespasian.[119] This is shown by an inscription published by Dessau (*ILS* 9168 [[=*DMIPERP* §147]]) which says:

> Proculus | Rabili f(ilius) Col(lina) | Philadel(phia) mil(itavit) |
> optio coh(ortis) II | Italic(ae) c(ivium) R(omanorum) Ɔ Fa[us-]

112. Josephus, *J.W.* 2.484: *οἱ δὲ στασιασταὶ καταλαβόμενοί τι φρούριον, ὃ καλεῖται μὲν Κύπρος, καθύπερθεν δ' ἦν Ἱεριχοῦντος, τοὺς μὲν φρουροὺς ἀπέσφαξαν.*

113. Josephus, *J.W.* 2.296: *ὁ δὲ μετὰ στρατιᾶς ἱππικῆς τε καὶ πεζικῆς ἐπὶ Ἱεροσολύμων ὥρμησεν*, but from 2.332 it appears he came with but one cohort, which was followed by two more from Caesarea, 2.318: *παρεγίνοντο δὲ δύο σπεῖραι*, of which he left one, since the people asked him not to leave the one which fought, i.e. which had accompanied him.

114. Josephus, *J.W.* 2.332: *τῶν δὲ πάντα περὶ ἀσφαλείας καὶ τοῦ μηδὲν νεωτερίσειν ὑποσχομένων, εἰ μίαν αὐτοῖς καταλείποι σπεῖραν, μὴ μέντοι τὴν μαχεσαμένην.*

115. Josephus, *J.W.* 2.460: *ἀντέσχον δὲ οὔτε Σεβαστὴ ταῖς ὁρμαῖς αὐτῶν οὔτε Ἀσκάλων.*

116. Josephus, *J.W.* 3.12: *ἡ δὲ Ἀσκάλων . . . ἐφρουρεῖτο γὰρ ὑπό τε σπείρας πεζῶν καὶ ὑπὸ μιᾶς ἴλης ἱππέων, ἧς ἐπῆρχεν Ἀντώνιος.*

117. Josephus, *J.W.* 2.507: *ὁ δὲ Κέστιος . . . αὐτὸς μὲν εἰς Καισάρειαν ἀφικνεῖται, μοῖραν δὲ τῆς στρατιᾶς προέπεμψεν εἰς Ἰόππην, προστάξας, εἰ μὲν καταλαβέσθαι δυνηθεῖεν τὴν πόλιν, φρουρεῖν.*

118. On the Italian cohort see William Mitchell Ramsay, *Was Christ Born at Bethlehem? A Study on the Credibility of St. Luke* (2nd ed.; London: Hodder & Stoughton, 1898), 260–269; Emil Schürer, "Die *σπεῖρα Ἰταλική* und die *σπεῖρα Σεβαστή* (Act. 10,1. 27,1)," *ZWT* 18 (1875) 413–25. *Italica* as a cognomen for other auxiliary cohorts is attested by a passage of Arrian, *Ect.* 13 (Cappadocia) and *CIL* 6.3654 (Rome); a *cohors I Italica civium Romanorum voluntariorum* is mentioned in a *cursus honorum* at Ostia, *CIL* 14.171.

119. Tacitus, *Hist.* 2.83.

| tini, ex vexil(atione) sa- | git(tariorum) exer(citus) Syriaci | stip(endiorum) VII, vixit an(nos) | XXVI, | Apuleius frate(r) | f(aciendum) c(uravit).

[[Proculus the son of Rabilius, of the tribe Collina, from Philadelphia saw military service as an *optio* of *cohors II Italica c.R.* in the century of Faustinius, being part of a detachment of archers forming part of the army of Syria, served 7 years and lived 26 years. His brother Apuleius saw to the making of this monument. (Trans. Fred Baxter)]]

This cohort is also mentioned in *CIL* 6.3528, referring to a tribune of the cohort in Rome, but no date can be ascertained for this inscription. The full name of the cohort is found by comparing *CIL* 11.6117 and the inscription cited above, *cohors II Miliaria Italica Civium Romanorum Voluntariorum quae est in Syria*, while the persons to whom dedication in the former was made, L. Maesius Rufus, Maria, and Maesia, were probably of Syrian origin.

Mommsen[120] thought that *cohortes civium Romanorum voluntariorum* began in the enrolment of freedmen in the auxiliary cohorts.[121] Only in periods of great stress were freedmen enrolled in the legions, and such soldiers were termed *voluntarii*, or *volones*.[122] Augustus made use of such troops in the legions on only two occasions, during the Pannonian revolt and after the defeat of Varus.[123] In addition, Macrobius[124] says that Augustus enrolled in Germany and Illyricum several cohorts of freedmen which he termed *voluntariae*. The *cohors II Italica* was probably a corps of freed men and similar in origin, but the title *Italica* shows some connexion with Italy, and it is not itself one of these cohorts, since it is found only in the east. It is possible, as Cheesman suggests,[125] that the remainder of the four thousand Oriental freedmen, votaries of Egyptian and Jewish cults, who were enrolled in the army A.D. 19 by way of removing votaries of these cults from Italy, and sent to Sardinia to reduce the brigands there, where the pestilential

120. Mommsen, *Res Gestae*, 72.

121. Cf. Cheesman, *Roman Auxilia*, 65.

122. Livy 22.57.11; 23.35.6; Wallace M. Lindsay (ed.), *Sexti Pompei Festi De verborum significatu quae supersunt cum Pauli epitome* (Leipzig: Teubner, 1913), 511; HA *Vita Marci* 21.

123. Suetonius, *Aug.* 25; cf. Dio Cassius 55.31–32.

124. Macrobius, *Sat.* 1.11.33.

125. Cheesman, *Roman Auxilia*, 66.

climate might soon complete their ruin,[126] were finally transported to Syria. Like the *cohortes voluntariorum* in Dalmatia,[127] and other auxiliary cohorts in general,[128] this cohort came to be composed of local recruits of peregrine status. At any rate it appears in A.D. 69 in the inscription above cited as a regiment of archers, and its *optio*, though a Roman citizen, was a native of Philadelphia (Rabbat Ammon), and, as the name shows, certainly not of Roman stock. So also the *cohors II Classica*, which was in Syria in A.D. 6,[129] appears in A.D. 88 as *II Classica Sagittariorum*.[130] The *cohors II Italica* remained in Syria for a consider able period after the Jewish war.[131] Of its presence in Caesarea at the time of the reference in Acts 10:1 there is no proof, but it seems probable that it is the cohort meant.

On the person of Cornelius the centurion little can be added. As a centurion he was certainly a Roman citizen, but as he served in an auxiliary cohort we cannot decide whether he was born free or not. He cannot have obtained his citizenship by purchase in the manner of Claudius Lysias,[132] who, despite his non-Roman origin, rose to the still higher military position of χιλίαρχος or tribune,[133] since his gentile name, Cornelius, is not that of any of the emperors. He may have belonged to one of the families liberated by Sulla (see note on Acts 10:2). He was not of Jewish stock, although interested in the Jewish religion, but a Gentile, and had won the respect of the Jewish community by his acts of charity. The presence of his family and household in Caesarea suggests that he had settled there at the end of his term of service, but such suppositions are conjectural, since he might well have connexions in Caesarea if the unit with which he served was garrisoned there for a considerable period.

126. Tacitus, *Ann.* 2.85: *actum et de sacris Aegyptiis Iudaicisque pellendis factumque patrum consultum, ut quattuor milia libertini generis ea superstitione infecta, quis idonea aetas, in insulam Sardiniam veherentur, coercendis illic latrociniis et si ob gravitatem caeli interissent, vile damnum; ceteri cederent Italia, nisi certam ante diem profanes ritus exuissent.*

127. Cheesman, *Roman Auxilia*, 67.

128. Mommsen, *Gesammelte Schriften*, 6.77–80.

129. *ILS* 2683 [[=*DMIPERP* §201]].

130. *AE* 1927.44 [[=*DMIPERP* §225]].

131. *AE* 1927.44 [[=*DMIPERP* §225]], in A.D. 88, and *ILS* 9057 [[=*DMIPERP* §259]], in A.D. 157.

132. On the purchase of citizenship under Claudius see Dio Cassius 60.17.

133. Acts 23:22.

(b) Acts 27:2—This describes Paul at Caesarea as given to the custody of Julius, a centurion of the σπεῖρα Σεβαστή.

This σπεῖρα Σεβαστή has been interpreted[134] as referring to the *cohorts Sebastenorum*, i.e. auxiliary cohorts of Samaritans such as had formed part of Herod's garrison in Jerusalem.[135] These, with an *ala Sebastenorum*, were probably the main portion of the garrison of Agrippa I in Caesarea,[136] and were incorporated into the Roman army and used in the Jewish war.[137]

The objection to this ingenious explanation is that σπεῖρα Σεβαστή means *cohors Augusta*, not *cohors Sebastenorum*. Conceivably there has been a confusion in the Greek either of Luke or of the text of Acts, but there is no evidence of this. Moreover there is sure evidence that there was a *cohors Augusta* in Syria in the first century, for Dessau[138] mentions a Quintus Aemilius Secundus who in the time of Augustus served under Quirinius in Syria as prefect of the *cohors Augusta I*, also of the *Cohors II Classica*. The displacement of the numeral may be merely a stone-cutter's error. The same cohort perhaps reappears in the time probably of Agrippa II at Eitha in Batanea, σπείρης Αὐ[γούστης][139] As a *cohors III Augusta*[140] is known in the early Empire, one must admit *cohors I Augusta* as a possible identification for the σπεῖρα Σεβαστή in Acts.

It is perhaps surprising that a centurion of a Syrian auxiliary *cohors Augusta* should have been given charge of an important prisoner on the road to Rome, for we should expect at least a legionary centurion or else

134. On the Augustan cohort see Schürer, "σπεῖρα Ἰταλική"; Theodor Mommsen and Adolf Von Harnack, "Zu Apostelgeschichte 28,16 (στρατοπεδάρχης = *princeps peregrinorum*)," *Sitzungsberichte der Berliner Akademie* 1895: 492–503 = Mommsen, *Gesammelte Schriften*, 6.546–554; Eduard Meyer, *Ursprung und Anfänge des Christentums* (Stuttgart: Cotta, 1923), 3.480.

135. Josephus, *J.W.* 2.52, 2.58.

136. Josephus, *A.J.* 19.365–366.

137. Josephus, *A.J.* 20.122; *J.W.* 3.65–66.

138. *ILS* 2683 [[=*DMIPERP* §201]]: Q(uintus) Aemilius Q(uinti) f(ilius) | Pal(atina) Secundus, [in] | castris divi Aug(usti) s[ub] | P(ublio) Sulipi[c]io Quirinio le[gato] | C[a] esaris Syriae honori- | bus decoratus, pr[a]efect. | cohort(is) Aug(ustae) I, pr[a]efect, | cohort(is) II Classicae, etc.

[[Quintus Aemilius Secundus son of Quintus, of the Palatine tribe, decorated with honours in the service of the deified Augustus under Publius Sulpicius Quirinius, legate of Caesar in Syria. He was prefect of *cohors I Augusta* and prefect of *cohors II Classica*, etc. (Trans. Fred Baxter)]]

139. *IGRR* 3.1136 = *OGIS* 421 [[=*DMIPERP* §30]].

140. *CIL* 6.3508.

one of the *frumentarii* to perform this duty. In the absence, however, of evidence that these were organized as cohorts, or given the cognomen *Augusta*, the question must be left open.

(c) Acts 28:16—According to Western text (see James Hardy Ropes, *The Beginnings of Christianity 3. The Acts of the Apostles: Text of Acts* [New York: Macmillan, 1926], 253 n. 16) the centurion Julius, upon reaching Rome, gave Paul and his companions over to the στρατοπέδαρχος, or camp commander.[141] This is the reading which appears in the Latin Codex Gigas as *princeps peregrinorum*. Mommsen has conjectured[142] that this official, who when Mommsen wrote was only known to have existed in the third century as head of the *castra peregrina*, was also existent in A.D. 62, and is referred to here. A recently discovered African inscription of the time of Trajan[143] which proves the existence of the *princeps peregrinorum* at that time lends great support to this conjecture. The *castra peregrina*, was a centre for legionary officers on furlough in Rome, and was a base for the *milites peregrini* or *frumentarii*. These officials, probably originally charged with business relating to the supply of food for the armies, fulfilled other functions also the bearing of important messages, imperial secret police, etc., and were general liaison officers between the legions in the provinces and legionary centurions on furlough at Rome.[144] Mommsen and Harnack, "Apostelgeschichte 28,16," and in Mommsen's *Römisches Strafrecht* (Leipzig: Duncker and Humblot, 1899), 316, basing his argument, however, chiefly on this passage of Acts, suggests that the *frumentarii* had the care during transport of prisoners who were to be tried at Caesar's court. The *frumentarii* and all the officials of the *castra peregrina*, including even *the*

141. Acts 28:16.

142. Mommsen and Harnack, "Apostelgeschichte 28,16." The view, however, that the person to whom prisoners thus brought to Rome were entrusted was not the *princeps peregrinorum* but the prefect of the praetorian guard finds support in Pliny, *Ep. Traj.* 57. In this passage Trajan directs Pliny to send a certain Julius Bassus, who had been condemned to banishment and who had not within the two years allowed him either appealed his case or left the province, in chains to the prefects of the praetorian guard. Paul at Rome may have been in the hands of the praetorians, Phil 1:13: ὥστε τοὺς δεσμούς μου φανεροὺς ἐν Χριστῷ γενέσθαι ἐν ὅλῳ τῷ πραιτωρίῳ, but the interpretation of this verse and its connexion with Rome are very doubtful.

143. *AE* 1923.28.

144. See "Frumentarii," in *Paulys Realencyclopädie der classischen Altertumswissenschaft* (ed. Georg Wissowa; Stuttgart: Metzler, 1910), 13.122–25; Mommsen and Harnack, "Apostelgeschichte 28,16"; and see especially P. K. Baillie Reynolds and T. Ashby, "The Castra Peregrinorum," *JRS* 13 (1923) 152–67.

princeps peregrinorum, were of centurial rank.[145] Nevertheless it must be remembered that *princeps peregrinorum* is an interpretation, not an accurate rendering, of στρατοπέδαρχος which may refer to the head of the Praetorium (see Hardy, *Beginnings*, 3.253 n. 16).

145. Domaszewski, *Rangordnung*, 28, 104, 267.

2

The Roman Army in Judaea under the Procurators

The Italian and the Augustan Cohort in the Acts of the Apostles

Michael P. Speidel

THE ITALIAN COHORT

Acts 10 report that in in about A.D. 40 the apostle Peter converted in Caesarea a certain "Cornelius, a centurion of the Italian cohort" (Κορνήλιος, ἑκατοντάρχης ἐκ σπείρης τῆς καλουμένης Ἰταλικῆς). Obviously, a citizen cohort originally raised in Italy, a *cohors Italica civium Romanorum*, must be meant here. The accuracy of this repot has been subject to considerable controversy, for it entails a crucial question concerning the military forces of the prefects and procurators in Judaea: did the provincial army consist only of local Sebasteni regiments or was there a variety of auxiliary units, some of them brought in from abroad?

One of the opposing views in this controversy derives from Theodor Mommsen, who knew the Roman army better than any other scholar. The other derives from Emil Schürer, whose *History of the Jewish People in the Age of Jesus Christ* after more than a century of useful service has now been overhauled and reedited and continued to serve as the standard work for the history of that period. We will argue here that documentary evidence vindicates Mommsen's view and reveals some passages of the Acts to be more accurate and reliable than has often been admitted.

There is general agreement that from the reign of Herod the Great to the destruction of the Jerusalem temple in A.D. 70 the garrison of Judaea comprised one cavalry regiment of Sebasteni (*ala I Sebastenorum*) and five cohorts of infantry, among them at least one cohort of Sebasteni (*cohors I Sebastenorum*). The dispute is whether the other four cohorts were also Sebasteni regiments inherited from the army of Herod the Great, or whether the Romans had brought in outside troops when they took the country under direct rule.[1]

Schürer and his new editors insist that all the cohorts of the prefects or procurators were *cohortes Sebastenorum*, units originally raised in the city-territory of Samaria-Sebasete which made them useful against the refractory Jews because of the hatred between the Jews and the Sebasteni. Schürer's view has been widely accepted.[2] It rests in good part on Josephus' report that during the upheaval at the death of Herod the best part of his army sided with the Romans, namely 3000 Sebasteni, cavalry as well as infantry.[3] That number would indeed perfectly fit six standard-sized regiments of five hundred men (i.e., one *ala* and five *cohortes Sebastenorum*).

1. T. Mommsen, "Zu Apostelgeschichte 28,16 (στρατοπεδάρχης = *princeps peregrinorum*)," *SBA* 1895 (1895) 495–503 = *Gesammelte Schriften* (Berlin, 1910) 4.546–54; T. Mommsen, "Die Conscriptionsordnung der römischen Kaiserzeit," *Hermes* 19 (1884) 1–79 and 210–34 (esp. 217–19) = *Gesammelete Schriften*, 4.20–117 (esp. 101–3); E. Schürer, *The History of the Jewish People in the Age of Jesus Christ (175 B.C.—A.D. 135)* (revised and edited by G. Vermes and F. Millar; Edinburgh, 1973), 1.363–65. The best general account of the Roman army in Palestine in the early period is still that by T. R. S. Broughton, "Additional Note XXXIII: The Roman Army," in *The Beginnings of Christianity, Part I: The Acts of the Apostles* (ed. F. J. F. Jackson and K. Lake; London, 1933), 5.427–45 [[= present volume, 1–25]], which we follow in many points concerning *cohors II Italica*.

This article has been researched with the help of a grant by the National Endowment of the Humanities, Research Materials Division. The views presented here are not necessarily those of the Endowment. I am much obliged to G. Bowersock (Harvard) and B. Isaac (Tel Aviv) for valuable suggestions.

2. See, e.g., C. H. Kraeling, "The Episode of the Roman Standards at Jerusalem," *HTR* 35 (1942) 263–89 (esp. 266); M. Avi-Yonah, "Newly Discovered Latin and Greek Inscriptions," *QDAP* 12 (1946) 84–102; E. M. Smallwood, *The Jews under Roman Rule* (Leiden, 1976), 176–77; R. Mellor, "A New Roman Military Diploma," *Bulletin of the J. Paul Getty Museum* 6–7 (1978–79) 173–84; A. Momigliano, *Ricerche sull' organizzazione della Giudea sotto il domino romano* (Amsterdam, 1967), 71.

3. *J.W.* 2.53.

Yet Herod's death was in 4 B.C. and it would seem likely that the Romans brought in some units of their own either then, or when they established the provincial administration in A.D. 6. Moreover, only one *ala* and *cohors Sebastenourm* are known from inscriptions, both with the serial number I.[4] True, Josephus describes the garrison of Caesarea in A.D. 59 as consisting mainly of Caesareans and Sebasteni, yet it was a Roman recruiting practice from the beginning of the empire to enrol local recruits in auxiliary regiments no matter where the unit had been raised originally.[5] Hence some of the other four cohorts of the Caesarea garrison could well have had different names and yet be gradually replenished with trustworthy Palestinian recruits. Besides, still other units may haven stationed elsewhere in the province.[6]

The Italian cohort of the Acts thus stands a fair chance of being authentic. Yet Schürer and his new editors deny this with the subsidiary argument that a true citizen cohort (i.e., a unit of Roman citizens), could not have served under mere equestrian governors and even less so under Agrippa I (A.D. 41–44).[7] But the opposite is true, for in a quite similar case the procurators of Raetia during the Julio-Claudian period had a *cohors I civium Romanorum ingenuorum* under their orders.[8]

4. For *ala I Sebastenorum* see now Mellor, "New Roman Military Diploma" [[= *DMIPERP* §232; cf. §§233–245]]. Avi-Yonah, "Newly Discovered," nos. 11–12 (= *AE* 1948.150–151) [[= *DMIPERP* §§131–132]] discerns in a fragmented text from Samaria-Sebaste a *cohors V Sebastenorum*, but there is no support for this restoration, as he himself points out. Perhaps *cohors VIII Raetorum* is mentioned in his no. 11 (= *AE* 1948.150) [[= *DMIPERP* §131]], for other troops of Dacia and Upper Moesia had come to Samaria in the campaign of Septimius Severus against Pescennius Niger; See M.P. Speidel, "The Rise of Ethnic Units in the Roman Imperial Army," in *ANRW* (1975) 2.3.202–31 (esp. 213–14).

5. Josephus, *A.J.* 19.176; cf. *J.W.* 2.268: τὸ γὰρ πλέον Ῥωμαίοις τῆς ἐκεῖ δυνάμεως ἐκ Συρίας ἦν κατειλέγμενον. For Roman recruitment policy with regard to the *auxilia*, see K. Kraft, *Zur Rekrutierung der Alen und Kohorten an Rhein und Donau* (Bern, 1951), esp. 43–68.

6. Schürer, *History of the Jewish People*, consistently speaks of the garrison of Caesarea, but Mommsen, "Conscriptionsordnung," 217, refers to "die Besatzung des Landes."

7. Schürer, *History of the Jewish People*, 1.365. For citizen cohorts see M.P. Speidel, "Citizen Cohorts in the Roman Imperial Army," *TAPA* 106 (1976) 339–48.

8. For *cohors I civium Romanorum ingenuorum* in Raetia, see *CIL* 5.3936 (A.D. 47) and C. Cichorius, "Cohors," in *Realencyclopädie der classischen Altertumswissenschaft* (ed. G. Wissowa; Munich, 1900) 4.1.231–356 (esp. 303); E. Stein, *Die kaiserlichen Beamten und Truppenkörper im römischen Deutschland unter dem Prinzipat* (Vienna, 1932), 198; H. J. Kellner, "Exercitus Raeticus," *Bayerische Vorgeschichtsblätter* 36 (1971) 206–15 (esp. 215).

The governors of Judaea are even more likely to have commanded such a unit, for epigraphic evidence shows that in the Orient, different from the West, citizen units were filled up with native recruits already during the Julio-Claudian period. This is known for some of the legions and it is evidence for *cohors II Italica* by a gravestone found at Carnuntum in Austria:

> Proculus
> Rabili f(ilius) Col(lina)
> Philadel(phia) mil(itavit)
> optio coh(ortis) II
> Italic(ae) c(ivium) R(omanorum) (centuria) Fa[us-]
> tini, ex vexil(atione) sa-
> git(tariorum) exer(citus) Syriaci
> stip(endiorum) VII vixit an(nos)
> XXVI.
> Apuleius frate(r)
> f(aciendum) c(uravit).[9]
>
> [[Proculus the son of Rabilius of the tribe Collina, from Philadelphia, saw military service as an optio of *cohors II Italica c.R.* in the century of Faustinius, being part of a detachment of archers forming part of the army of Syria, served 7 years and lived 26 years. His brother Apuleius saw to the making of this monument. (Trans. Fred Baxter)]]

Proclus seems to have been a citizen, as suggested by his *tribus*, yet his father's Arab name shows that he was born a non-citizen (and that the Philadelphia concerned is Amman in Jordan). His cohort, therefore, included local soldiers already during the period of the procurators, for the date of the gravestone is generally agreed to be A.D. 69/70, when a task force of the Syrian army came to conquer the empire for Vespasian. Since the deceased had been in service for seven years, he will have enrolled in the cohort in about A.D. 63, at a time when other recruits from Amman-Philadelphia

9. *CIL* 3.13483a (cf. p. 2328.32) = *ILS* 9168 = *CSIR*, Österreich 1.4.553 [[= *DMIPERP* §147]]. Kraft, *Rekrutierung*, 196 doubts the man's citizenship despite the *tribus*, yet the *tribus Collina* makes sense here: as one of the four old urban *tribus* it was not given to provincial towns, hence Proculus received it personally (i.e., when he was given citizenship); cf. G. Forni, "Le tribù romane nelle province balcaniche," in *Pulpudeva* (Plovdiv, 1976), 99–118 (esp. 114).) For *legio XV Apollinaris*, then in the East, see *CSIR*, Österreich 1.4.379; for the legions in Egypt, see J. Lesquier, *L'armée romaine d'Égypte d'Auguste à Dioclétien* (Cairo, 1918), 203–25. In the West such recruitment for citizen units apparently does not predate the Flavian period; see Kraft, *Rekrutierung*, 82–105.

were also enrolled in the *auxilia*,[10] very likely because of the Parthian campaigns of Cn. Domitius Corbulo. If the Italian cohort was recruited locally, Schürer's argument that such a unit could not have been under the procurator's orders collapses.

The Carnuntum gravestone describes the task force of the second Italian cohort as belonging to the Syrian army. Does that exclude this cohort from the Judean army? Hardly, since Syria was the most important command in the Orient and various other armies contributing to its bowmen taskforce could be subsumed under its name. More specifically, Tacitus and Josephus state that after the death of Agrippa I in A.D. 44, Judaea became an annex of Syria, a fact that will have applied to the Judaean army as well, if only in a general sense.[11] Hence *cohors II Italica* could well have been stationed in Palestine even though one of its soldiers on the Carnuntum gravestone is subsumed under the *exercitus Syriacus*. Certainly, after Titus' Jewish War the Flavian emperors revamped the Judaean army, and at the same time *cohors II Italica* seems to have been transferred north into Syria as were *ala* and *cohors I Sebastenorum* of the same provincial army,[12] yet for the time of the procurators there is no reason to doubt the accuracy of Acts 10.

The presence of the centurion Cornelius at Caesarea does not necessarily imply that the cohort was stationed at the provincial capital—the centurion may have been seconded to headquarters duty while the cohort itself was garrisoning another town. Such, at any rate, was the case of the second unit mention by the Acts, the Augustan cohort.

10. *CIL* 16.159 [[= *DMIPERP* §295]] (A.D. 88, diploma): cohort(is) II milliariae (Syriorum) sagittar(iorum) ... equiti Domitio Domiti f., Philadelphia.

When *cohors Italica* came to Palestine it will, of course, have had a high percentage of Roman citizens in its ranks, yet that is not incompatible with its being under the orders of an equestrian governor: many Egyptian legionaries, too, were originally Italians nevertheless under equestrian command; cf. Lesquier, *L'armée romaine*. For the Decapolis of which Philadelphia was a part, see the paper by B. Isaac, "The Decapolis in Syria," *ZPE* 44 (1981) 67–74, where he argues that the Decapolis was under a Roman procurator.

11. Tacitus, *Ann.* 12.23: Ituraei et Iudaei defunctis regibus Sohaema atque Agrippa provinciae Suriae additi; Josephus, *A.J.* 18.1: Ἰουδαίαν προσθήκην τῆς Συρίας γενομένην. H.G. Pflaum, *Les procurateurs équestres sous le Haut-Empire romain* (Paris, 1950), 146–148, discusses this attribution of Judaea to Syria and sees it valid above all in the military sphere. When in A.D. 69 Tacitus (*Hist.* 1.76) speaks of *exercitus Iudaicus* he means the expeditionary army of Vespasian, not the regular provincial army.

12. *CIL* 16.35 [[= *DMIPERP* §225]] of A.D. 88 and the new diploma of the same date *RMD* 1.3 [[= *DMIPERP* §232]]. Cf. Josephus, *A.J.* 19.366. *Cohors I Italica* (*AE* 1974.226) is less likely, but also possible.

THE AUGUSTAN COHORT

The last third of the Acts of the Apostles, from chapter 20 onwards, dealing with the arrest of St. Paul in Jerusalem, his trial at Caesarea, and his passage by sea to Rome, is an eyewitness account that has the compelling ring of historical truth. Its detailed observations are a first-class source for ancient sea travel and shipwreck and no less for the police duties of the Roman army.

Now, Acts 27.1 report that in about A.D. 60, after a hearing by the procurator Festus and king Agrippa II, the apostle was to be transferred from Caesarea to Rome: "They handed Paul and some other prisoners over to a centurion named Julius of the Augustan cohort" (*παρεδίδουν τόν τε Παῦλον καί τινας ἑτέρους δεσμώτας ἑκατοντάρχῃ ὀνόματι Ἰουλίῳ σπείρης Σεβαστῆς*). The name of the cohort, in Latin, must have been *cohors Augusta*. But what was its identity?

Schürer, in order to reconcile the report of the Acts with his preconceived notion that the entire infantry garrison of Caesarea consisted of *cohortes Sebastenorum* resorts to an airy hypothesis: amongst those five cohorts one had been decorated with the honorific epithet *Augusta* and thus among its five sister cohorts, all of the same name, it was not known as *cohors Augusta Sebastenorum* but simply as *cohors Augusta* (σπεῖρα Σεβαστή).[13] The hypothesis, even if farfetched, is not demonstrably wrong, but loses much of its appeal if, as we have shown above, there were units of different names at Caesarea.

Schürer is undeniably wrong, though, when he says the Acts report the Augustan cohort as having been stationed in Caesarea. The Acts do not imply Caesarea was the garrison place of the cohort. In fact, the cohort may have been stationed in quite a different region. A hint about the cohort's tur garrison area comes from a building inscription found in the Hauran mountains near the present-day border of Syria and Jordan. The text, broken off at the beginning and at the end, but otherwise not in doubt, runs as follows:

σι......... ιος ....

13. Schürer, *History of the Jewish People*, 1.363–65, followed, e.g., by Momigliano, *Ricerche*, 71. Mommsen, "Zu Apostelgeschichte," considered that Acts 27:1 mistook the Augustan cohort for the imperial *frumentarii*, but we know now that auxiliaries could be sent abroad on various missions, see e.g., British Museum papyrus 2851 (= *RMR* 63); see also for this question P. K. Baillie Reynolds, "The Troops Quartered in the Castra Peregrinorum," *JRS* 13 (1923) 168–89 (esp. 185–86).

Λούκιος Ὀβούλνιος
ἑκατοντάρχης σπίρης
Αὐγούστης παρηκολού-
θησα τῷ ἔργῳ
(ἔτους) ηκ' τοῦ ϛι'
Ἔτους ηκ' βασιλέως με-
γάλου Μάρκου Ἰουλίου Ἀγρίπ-
πα κυρίου Φιλοκαίσαρος Εὐ-
σεβοῦς καὶ Φιλορωμαίου τ[οῦ
......

Lucius Obulnius, centurion of the cohors Augusta, took care of this work. Year 28. Year 28 of the great king Marcus Julius Agrippa, the lord, friend of the emperor, pious friend of the Romans, ...[14]

The inscription is dated to the year 28 of Agrippa II (i.e., A.D. 84 or 89), and it is paralleled by a similar text from the Dushara precinct at Seeia, also in the Hauran mountains.[15] The two inscriptions mention the Augustan cohort in a context that will explain the circumstances of its providing an escort to the apostle Paul.

This cohort obviously served Agrippa II in his northern Transjordanian client kingdom. It may have been a regular Roman army unit, for we know some of the careers of its commanders, proceeding to the command of other regular Roman cohorts.[16] Certainly, though, this cohort was

14. M. Dunand, *Le Musée de Soueida: Inscriptions et monuments figurés* (Paris, 1934), no. 168 (with an inferior reading in *AE* 1925.121) [[= DMIPERP §§12+13]]. A second inscription from the area (*IGLS* 2112 = *OGIS* 421 = *IGR* 3.1136 [[= *DMIPERP* §30]], from el Hit) also mentions a prefect of the Augustan cohort under Agrippa II and has actually been related to the cohort of Acts 27.1 by Waddington (*IGLS*) and Cichorus ("cohors," 249–50), only its text is very fragmentary, mentioning no more than]σπείρης Αὐ[.

15. For the date see Schürer, *History of the Jewish People*, 1.480 n. 43. For the text of the inscription from Seeia see B. Haussoullier and H. Ingholt, "Inscriptions grècques de Syrie," *Syria* 5 (1924) 316–41 (esp. 325–26; whence *SEG* 7.1100 [[= *DMIPERP* §14]]): [Διὶ] κυρί[ῳ] | [Λούκιος] Ὀβούλ- | νιο[ς] | ἑκατοντ[άρχης] | σπίρης Αὐ[γούστης]. Unfortunately, Haussoulier and Ingholt, too, consider the *cohors Augusta* of the Acts as stationed in Caesarea and therefore not identical with one of the Hauran inscriptions.

16. *CIL* 3.6687 = *ILS* 2683 [[= *DMIPERP* §201]]; cf. Cichorius, "cohors," 249–50; H. Devijver, *Prosopographia Militarum Equestrium* (Leuven, 1976), no. A90. See also *AE* 1967.525 [[= *DMIPERP* §148]], where the career is perhaps descending rather than ascending. For irregular forces under Agrippa II, see e.g., *AE* 1966.493 = *OGIS* 425 = *Princeton Exp.Inscr.IIIA* 797.1 [[= *DMIPERP* §23]].

structured along Roman lines with Roman citizens as centurions.[17] Roman troops stationed in client states, side by side with native irregulars, are not unusual: they are known, for instance, in the Bosporanian kingdom and in Palmyra. Indeed, the very army of the procurators must have remained in Palestine when the country was given over to the king Agrippa I from A.D. 41–44. Client states were considered integral parts of the Roman empire, and Agrippa II is known to have been especially subservient.[18]

The reason why *cohors Augusta*—or part of it—was present at Caesarea during the hearing of the apostle Paul is readily apparent form a previous chapter of the Acts where Agrippa II and his sister Berenice are said to have come to meet the new procurator Festus (Acts 25:13). Festus, considering Agrippa an expert in Jewish-Christian 'superstition,' asked him to join in the hearing of the apostle, and we are told that the affair took place with great pomp (μετὰ πολλῆς φαντασίας). Even the regimental commanders (χιλίαρχοι) were present, the height of military splendor in a procuratorial province. Agrippa, naturally, will have had is own share in such pomp, and for that reason, if not for security, he will have brought along some of the troops of his kingdom, including officers and men of the Augustan cohort.[19]

Why was Paul handed over to a centurion of the Augustan cohort rather than to an officer of the Caesarea garrison? For one thing, the centurion Iulius, as his Roman family name shows, was a Roman citizen; hence

---

There is a possibility that our cohort is identical with *cohors I Augusta Thracum equitata*, for which see M. P. Speidel, "The Roman Army in Arabia," in *ANRW* (1977) 2.8.687–730—the cohort is later found precisely in the Hauran area. If so, the cohort, under Agrippa's orders, could nevertheless have been part of the Syria regular army, as evidenced by the diploma *RMD* 1.3 [[= *DMIPERP* §232]]. Because there were so many Thracian cohorts in the area, the title *Thracum* was frequently omitted (To mention only units on the diploma just cited: *ala Gallorum et Thracum Constantium* drops the ethnic in *ILS* 9488, *CIL* 14.5351, *ala Gallorum et Thracum Antiana* drops the ethnic in *CIL* 16.87 [[= *DMIPERP* §211]] and in the diploma *RMD* 1.69 [[= *DMIPERP* §224]]. There are many more such cases.)

17. Both Lucius Obulnius of the Hauran inscription and Iulius of Acts 27.1 are Romans. See also *AE* 1966.493 [[= *DMIPERP* §23]], perhaps referring to this very cohort.

18. Suetonius, *Aug.* 48: nec aliter universos quam membra partisque imperii curae habuit. For Agrippa II, see Schürer, *History of the Jewish People*, 1.471–83. The king had, for example, to contribute his troops (regular or irregular) to Nero's Parthian campaign in A.D. 54: duosque veteres reges Agrippam et Antiochum expediere copias, quis Parthorum fines ultro intrarent (Tacitus, *Ann.* 13.7).

19. For ceremonial functions of auxiliary guards see M. P. Speidel, *Guards of the Roman Armies* (Bonn, 1978), 42–53. Members of the guards could be used as messengers to the capital, cf. *CIL* 6.3339, 6.3614.

even in the unlikely case that *cohors Augusta* was not a fully regular unit, Iulius was still of a position and of a status that enabled him to deal with Roman officialdom in the capital. Secondly, Iulius may have had the confidence of Agrippa, and, like his king, the requisite knowledge of matters of 'superstition' to act as a witness in the forthcoming trial of Paul in Rome. Agrippa's involvement is indeed borne out by a passage of the text that until now has baffled commentators. Acts 27:1 report: "They handed Paul over to a centurion . . ." (παρεδίδουν). Who are "*they*"? Is not Festus, the procurator, alone in charge of the judicial and military matters at Caesarea?[20] The passage takes on meaning if Paul as the prisoner was in the governor's charge and if the centurion of the Augustan cohort was under orders of the king, so that both were involved in handing Paul over, just as they had joined in the hearing of the apostle.

Our study thus suggests factual accuracy of the Acts in a point where it had been doubted the most (i.e., with regard to the Italian cohort). With the help of inscriptions and by making sense of a hitherto obscure passage of the text, the Acts are further shown to report with great reliability the name, the officer and the escort duty of the Augustan cohort. We thereby gain valuable new insight into the journey of the apostle Paul and into the history of the Roman army in Palestine.

20. Jackson and Lake, *Beginnings of Christianity*, 4.325.

ADDENDA (2019)

See the discussion of this article in *AE* 1985.828. This article was also reprinted in Michael P. Speidel, *Roman Army Studies* (Mavors Roman Army Researches 8; Stuttgart: Steiner, 1992) 2.224–31, with addenda from 1992 on page 232. Those addenda are updated here.

Karl Strogel, *Die Donaukriege Domitians* (Abhandlungen zur alten Geschichte 38; Bonn: Habelt, 1989) 20–21, may be right in dating Proculus' gravestone to the years AD 89–92 and in denying the man's Roman citizenship (no conclusive arguments are put forward)—it makes not much difference for this paper. Multiple new inscriptions of Lucius Obulnius (and in one instance, a rereading of an old inscription) have been published since the original article. All of them were discovered at Seeia in Syria, which—as noted in the article—was within Agrippa II's kingdom.

(DMIPERP §15) Text: [ὑπὲρ τ]ῆς σωτηρία[ς . . .] | [. . .] βασι[λ]έως Ἀ[γρίππα . . .]

Translation: For the salvation of King Agrippa [. . .]

(DMIPERP §16) Text: Λούκιος Ὀβούλνιος ἑκατοντάρχη(ς) | σπείρης Αὐγούστης ἀνήθηκ(εν).

Translation: Lucius Obulnius, centurion of *cohors Augusta*, erected this.

(DMIPERP §17) Text: [...] Διὶ Κυρίῳ [. . .] | [. . . Ὀβουλ]νίου (ἑ)[κατοντάρχου] | [σπειρῆς Αὐγούστης . . .]

Translation: To Zeus Kyrios [. . .] Obulnius, centurion of *cohors Augusta* [. . .]

(DMIPERP §18) Text: Θεᾷ κυρίᾳ Ἀταργά- | τει | Λούκιος Ὀβ- | ούλνιος ἑκα- | τοντάρχης | σπείρης Αὐγο- | ύστης ἀνά- | θ[ηκεν].

Translation: To Atargatis Kyria. Lucius Obulnius, centurion of *cohors Augusta*, erected this.

None of these have a substantial effect on the argument of the original article. See also the discussion in *SEG* 33.1306 and M. H. Gracey's objections in *SEG* 35.1321–1322. As a final note, *AE* 1925.121 (=*DMIPERP* §12+§13) has been recently argued to comprise two distinct inscriptions by Lucius Obulnius; see the discussion by Maurice Sartre in *IGLS* 16.197. In short, *DMIPERP* §12 is argued to have been erected in 69 CE.

(DMIPERP §12) Text: στ[ρατοπε]δάρχο[. . .] | Λούκιος Ὀβούλνιος | ἑκατοντάρχης σπ(ε)ίρης | Αὐγούστης παρηκολού- | θησα τῷ ἔργῳ | ∟ ακ' τοῦ ϛι'.

Translation: [. . .] Lucius Obulnius, centurion of *cohors Augusta*, oversaw this work in the 21st year, which is also the 16th year.

DMIPERP §13 was added to the same stone in either 76 or 81 CE, depending on how one enumerates Agrippa II's regnal years.

(DMIPERP §13) Text: ἔτους ηκ' βασιλέως με- | γάλου Μάρκου Ἰουλίου Ἀγρίπ- | πα κυρίου Φιλοκαίσαρος Εὐ- | σεβοῦς καὶ Φιλορωμαίου τ[οῦ] | [ἐκ βασιλέως μεγάλου] | [. . .]

Translation: The 28th year of the great king Marcus Julius Agrippa: lord, friend of Caesar, pious, and friend of Rome from the great king [. . .]

3

The Beginning of the Roman Defensive System in Judaea

Israel Shatzman

More than fifty years ago, A. Alt published an article in which he argued that a defensive system of forts and fortlets, manned by adequate forces and connected by a road, was established by the Romans between Raphia (on the Mediterranean Sea) and the Dead Sea in the period following the quelling of the First Jewish Revolt and before the annexation of the Nabataean Kingdom in 106 CE.[1] In an article published in 1958, M. Avi-Yonah, who had earlier accepted Alt's dating of this system, questioned that dating and put forward arguments for a Diocletianic date for its beginning.[2] Four years later, some of Avi-Yonah's points were answered by

1. I am grateful to the anonymous readers of the Editorial Committee and especially Prof. E. Badian, whose comments have helped me to avoid errors of fact and expression. I am indebted to Dr. A. Kempinski of Tel Aviv University who gave me valuable advice on the archaeological evidence. They are not responsible for the views expressed here or any errors that remain.

A. Alt, "Limes Palaestinae," *Palästinajahrbuch* 26 (1930) 43–82; 27 (1931) 75–84; for the dating see (1930) 60–64.

2. M. Avi-Yonah, "The Date of the 'Limes Palaestinae,'" *Eretz-Israel* 5 (1958) 135–37; M. Avi-Yonah, *The Holy Land: From the Persian to the Arab Conquests 536 B.C. to A.D.*

Sh. Applebaum, who tried to support Alt's dating. He concluded his article with the observation that "there is a limit to what a discussion of the literary sources and a topographical analysis as well as analogies from other provinces can contribute towards the clarification of the point at issue; only the shovel can give a definite answer to the question of date."[3] Since then, M. Gichon [=Giḥon] has been publishing various studies in which he has tried to present archaeological support of the dating of the *limes Palaestinae* to the Flavian Period.[4] His account of the working of the system as been accepted by G. Webster in what is probably the best text-book on the Roman army in English, and it partly helped E. Luttwak to reconstruct the new strategy allegedly introduced by the Flavians.[5] Some doubts have been expressed as to the date, and G.W. Bowersock even claimed that the Palestine *limes* existed only in the southern part of the Hashemite Kingdom of Jordan, contesting the application of the term to describe what in his view was merely a fortified road across the northern Negev.[6] No serious attempt,

---

640 (1966) 118–21; for his earlier opinion, see M. Avi-Yonah, *Historical Geography of the Land of Israel* (3rd ed.; 1962) 69–70.

3. Sh. Applebaum, "The Initial Date of the Limes Palaestinae," *Zion* 27 (1962) 10 (in Hebrew, my translation).

4. M. Gichon, *The Limes of the Negev from Its Establishment to Diocletian* (1966); also M. Gichon, "The Origins of the Limes Palaestinae and the Major Phases of Its Development," in *Vorträge des 6. Internationalen Limes-Kongressus in Süd-deustschland* (1967) 175–93; Sh. Applebaum and M. Gichon, *Israel and Her Vicinity in the Roman and Byzantine Periods* (1967) 35–64; M. Gichon, "Das Verteidungssystem und die Verteidiger des flavischen Limes in Judäa," in *Provinciala: Festschrift für R. Laur-Belart* (1968) 317–34; M. Gichon, "The Site of the *Limes* in the Negev," *Eretz-Israel* 12 (1975) 149–66; M. Gichon, "The Military Significance of Certain Aspects of the Limes Palaestinae," in *Roman Frontier Studies 1967*, ed. Sh. Applebaum (1971) 191–200; M. Gichon, "Towers on the Limes Palaestinae," in *Actes du IXe congrès international d'études sur les frontiers romaines*, ed. D.M. Pippidi (1974) 513–44; etc.

5. G. Webster, *The Roman Imperial Army* (2nd ed.; 1979) 64; E.N. Luttwak, *The Grand Strategy of the Roman Empire from the First Century A.D. to the Third* (1st ed.; 1976) 78 and n. 67. Luttwak's account of Roman tactics in the Flavian period (ibid. 61–67) accords with Gichon's views.

6. Webster, *Roman Imperial Army*, thinks that there is no "sound evidence" for ascribing the system to the Flavian period. For arguments against the application of the term "Palestinian *limes*" to the northern Negev zone, see G. W. Bowersock, "*Limes Arabicus*," *HSCP* 80 (1976) 219–29; G.W. Bowersock, "Old and New in the History of Judaea," *JRS* 65 (1975) 183. A confused concept of the nature of the *limes* is presented in K.C. Gutwein, *Third Palestine* (1982) 309–11. He seems to accept Bowersock's negation of a *limes* in the central Negev zone, and yet ignores his demonstration that there was no arrangement of inner and outer defensive zones. B. Rothenberg mainly accepts Avi-Yonah's dating of the Palestine *limes*, but suggests that the first works of defence were

however, has been made to discus the problem in detail. The implications of the operation of such a defensive system in this area, and of its existence at the dates advocated by Alt, Applebaum and Gichon, for the understanding of the development of Roman strategy as well as for the history of Judaea in the imperial period justify a detailed presentation of a dissenting view.

I

It will be useful to briefly recapitulate the political history of the region in question. The Negev south of Beersheba and the Sinai peninsula belonged to the Nabataean Kingdom, though the exact demarcation line between it and the Herodian Kingdom, and later the Roman province of Judaea, is not sufficiently clear and agreed upon.[7] After the annexation of the Nabataean Kingdom in 106 CE, which was a peaceful action, the Negev and Sinai were included in the Roman province of Arabia.[8] Under Diocletian a territorial reorganization took place, as a result of which the southern part of the province Arabia—namely, the Sinai and Negev sections, as well as the area south of the Zered and east of the 'Araba valley—were added to the province Syria Palaestina.[9] From *ca.* 358 these parts of the old Nabataean Kingdom were organized as the province Palaestina Salutaris, which became Palaestina Tertia with the organization of three Palestinian provinces shortly after 400.[10] The organization lasted to the end of Byzantine rule in Palestine.

---

constructed as early as Hadrian. See his *Negev: Archaeology in the Negev and the Araba* (1967) 166–67. A Diocletianic date is also accepted Y. Tsafir, "The Provinces of Eretz Israel," in *Eretz Israel from the Destruction of the Second Temple to the Muslim Conquest*, ed. Z. Baras et al. (1982) 365–69. Some arguments against a Flavian date for the Palestine *limes* are presented by D. Gera in his unpublished M.A. thesis, *The Roman Government and the Army in Judaea AD 70–132* (1977) 47–49, to which I am indebted.

7. Compare, for instance, the map in Avi-Yonah, *Historical Geography*, 103 with that in A. Negev, "The Nabataeans and the Provincia Arabia," *ANRW* 2.8 (1977) 550.

8. See G.W. Bowersock, "A Report on Arabia Provincia," *JRS* 61 (1971) 219–42; Negev, "Nabataeans," 640–45, with a map of the province on p. 641, which should be corrected to include northwest Saudi Arabia, as argued by G. W. Bowersock, "The Greek-Nabataean Bilingual Inscription at Ruwwāfa, Saudi Arabia," in *Le monde grec. Hommages à Cl. Préaux*, ed. G. Cambier *et al.* (1975) 513–22.

9. For this reorganization and its date see R. E. Brünnow and A. v. Domaszewski, *Die Provincia Arabia* 3 (1909) 273–76.

10. For Palaestina Salutaris see Libanius, *Ep.* 337; P. Rohden, *De Palaestina et Arabia provinciis Romanis quaestiones selectae* (1885) 22–29. For Palaestina Tertia see *Cod.*

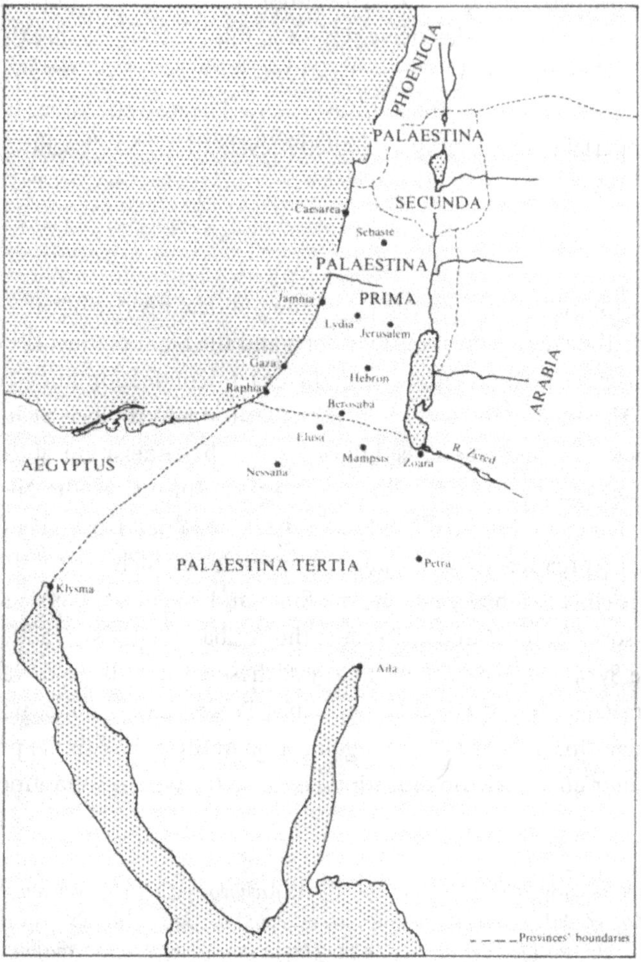

I shall first present the written sources related to the above-mentioned Roman defensive system. The term *limes Palaestinae* appears in a Christian Greek inscription, probably of the 6th century, whose exact provenance is unknown, but is said to have been southern Palestine.[11] The two verses

Theod. 7.4.30, 16.8.29; *Not. Dig. Or.* 22; Brünnow and Domaszewski, *Provincia*, 277–80; Avi-Yonah, "Initial Date," 121, with a map on p. 125; M. Avi-Yonah, "Palaestina," in *Realencyclopädie der classischen Altertumswissenschaft Supplementband*, ed. G. Wissowa (1973) 13.417–18.

11. The inscription was first published by F.-M. Abel, "Épigraphie du Sud palestinien," *RBi* 29 (1920) 120–22 no. 13. See also A. Alt, *ZPalV* 46 (1923) 64 no. 19. Abel included this inscription in the section "Autres inscriptions du Négeb"; all these inscriptions came

of the inscription record that "when Dorotheos left the divine land of the *limes Palaestinae*, he did not lose honours given by the king" (my translation). The deceased Dorotheos, as suggested by Abel and Alt, probably held some position associated with the administration of the *limes Palaestinae*, but not much more can be inferred from the inscription.[12] Be that as it may, the inscription does testify to the existence of a *limes* somewhere in the Negev, unless we assume that Dorotheos served far away from the place where he was buried, which is unlikely.[13] However, no clear understanding of the geographical limits and military functions of this *limes* can be deduced from such evidence.

The Palestine *limes* is mention in an edict of the emperor Anastasius I, known to us from fragments of an inscription found at Qaṣr el-Ḥallābāt in Transjordan.[14] I quote the relevant passage because of its importance to our discussion:

> *ὥστε τοὺς ἄρχοντας τῶν ἐπ[α]ρχηειῶν,*
> *εἰ μὴ τ[ὰς δίκας (?) κα]θ' ὃ διετυπώ[θ]η συστήσωνται ἢ τ[ὰ]ς ἀνα-*
> *φορὰς [ποιήσωσι]ν πρὸς τοὺς [δ]οῦκας, ἐν μὲν τῷ Πα[λ]αιστί-*
> *νης κ[αὶ Εὐφρατη]σίας λιμίτῳ αὐτοὺς εἴκοσι [χ]ρυσίου*
> *λίτρας [καὶ τὰς τ](ά)ξις τὰς αὐτῶν ἀνὰ τριάκο[ν]{α}τα, {ἐν}*
> *ἐν δὲ [τοῖς ἄλλ]οις λιμίτοι[ς] τοὺς ἄρχοντας [ἀ]νὰ δέκα*
> *καὶ τὰ[ς αὐτῶν τ]άξις ἀνὰ εἴκοσι προστίμ(ου) λόγῳ κα[τ]ὰ πάν-*
> *τα τρό[πον—16?—]αν δι[ὰ ἀν]α[φο]ρᾶς το[ῦ] δουκό[ς]*

---

from the ruined cities of this region, though the precise places of origin could not be ascertained.

12. *οὐδὲ λιπὼν λιμιτοῖο Παλαεστ(ίνης) χθόνα δῖαν* | *Δωρόθεος γεράων πέλεν ἄμμορος ἐκ βασ[ι]λῆος*. See Abel, "Épigraphie," no. 13; Alt, "Limes Palaestinae" (1930) 43–44.

13. Bowersock, "Limes," 229 argues that the Palestine *limes* means the fortified part of the Palaestina Tertia from 'Aqaba into Syria. He also cites this inscription, but he does not explain how a person buried in the Negev can be associated with a fortified zone some 100 km away.

14. B. Littman, D. Magie, and D. R. Stuart, *Publications of the Princeton University Archaeological Expeditions to Syria, in 1904–1905 and 1909: III Greek and Latin Inscriptions in Syria. 2. Southern Ḥauran* (1910) no. 20, pp. 24–41. A few years ago several new fragments of the inscription were discovered during two quite different explorations of the fort site. The new additions to the inscription, however, do not bear upon the reading of this passage. See J. Mareillet-Jaubert, "Recherches au Qasr el Hallabat," *ADAJ* 24 (1980) 121–124; D. L. Kennedy, *Archaeological Explorations of the Roman Frontier in North-East Jordan* (1982) 43–47.

According to the editors, the edict is of the same general type as the edict of the same emperor found at Ptolemais in Cyrenaica.[15] Still, a difference is to be noted in that the latter edict is probably confined to Cyrenaica.[16] At any rate, the present edict's regulations apply to Roman officials in general and not only those of the province Arabia, and indeed it seems that there are fragments of copies of the edict from other sites.[17] Thus the fact that this copy of the edict was found in Qaṣr el-Ḥallābāt in Transjordan has no bearing on the meaning of the Palestine *limes* mentioned in it; as the content shows, it is only the variation of fines in different administrative districts that occasioned the specific mentioning of the Euphrates and Palestine *limites*. Furthermore, the omission of Arabia in this connection means that this variation has nothing to do with the eastern frontier as a whole. On the other hand, the reference to Klysma, a town that was situated on the northern point of the Gulf of Suez and is mentioned as belonging to Palestine in the opening sentences of the edict, led the editors of the inscription to conclude that the frontier extended from that fortress "along the eastern short of the Red Sea."[18]

In thus equating the *limes*, in this edict, with a narrow, specific strip of land, the editors seem to miss the real importance (from our point of view) of this text, which in other respects they do not fail to notice in their commentary on fragments 15–19: "The *praesides* and their *officia* are thus rendered liable to the payment of penalties in case they fail to settle cases according to statutory prescriptions, or neglect to submit to the *duces* those questions which fall under the jurisdiction of the military governor."[19] Since the *dux Palaestinae* was responsible for the Palestine limes, it follows that in this context the *limes Palaestinae* is not a fortified zone along the border, but that territory wherein the *dux Palaestinae* has jurisdiction over

15. For this edict see *IGLS* 1906a (= *SEG* 9.346, 9.414). Cf. Littman, Magie, and Stuart, *Publications*, 24.

16. See Waddington's commentary (*IGLS* 1906a) to lines 1–3 of the edict.

17. See *IGLS* 1906 (Boṣrā) and *IGLS* 2033 (Imtān) and cf. Littman, Magie, and Stuart, *Publications*, 24.

18. Littman, Magie, and Stuart, *Publications*, 30–31. In fact Klysma is supplemented from other copies (*IGLS* 1906, 2033). They rightly reject the supposition of Kirchhoff and Waddington that the phrase ἐν Μεσοποταμίᾳ καὶ ἀπὸ τοῦ Κλύματος, κτλ. Refers to a *limes* that extended from Mesopotamia to the Red Sea. Still, there is some difficulty in their interpretation of lines 3–7 of the inscription, but this goes beyond the present discussion. See Ptolemy *Geog.* 4.5.14; Lucian, *Alexandros* 44; L. Moritz, "Klysma," in *Realencyclopädie der classischen Altertumswissenschaft*, ed. G. Wissowa (1921) 21.881.

19. Littman, Magie, and Stuart, *Publications*, 33.

in certain cases. We shall presently see another text which imply this wider territorial meaning.[20]

A third source is a passage in Rufinus' *Historia Ecclesiastica*, written in the early fifth century: "Mavia Sarracenorum gentis regina, vehementi bello Palaestini et Arabici limitis oppida atque urbes quatere, vicinasque simul vastare provincias coepit."[21] It is not easy to identify the geographical location of the Palestine *limes* in this passage. The Saracens were originally a nomad tribe of the Sinai peninsula, attested in the 2nd century CE by the geographer Ptolemy, but the name was also employed to designate tribes of north Arabia and the Syrian desert.[22] It follows that Mavia could have invaded the Palestine province from the south, i.e. from Sinai, which implies a *limes* in the Negev, or from the east, which means that the references is to a *limes* east of the 'Araba. The fact that Mavia negotiated with the Roman authorities in Egypt, including Lucius the bishop of Alexandria, to receive the hermit Moses as a bishop for her tribe, and that this Moses lived on the border between Egypt and Palestine, may indicate her base was in the Sinai peninsula.[23] On the other hand, the alleged range of the military operations, which necessitated the intervention of the *magister militiae pedestris et equestris in oriente*, suggests that the incursions spread over large parts of the provinces, and hence Rufinus may have had in mind both the Negev and the Transjordan sections of Palestine.[24] On balance, the notice seems

20. This wider meaning may be compared to that of the *limes Aegypti* whose military units were deployed throughout Egypt, and whose *comes*' authority extended over this territory. See *Not. Dig. Or.* 27, and for a discussion and a map, see R. M. Price, "The limes of Lower Egypt," in *Aspects of the Notitia Dignitatum*, ed. R. Goodburn and Ph. Bartholomew (1976) 147–49, 155.

21. Rufinus *HE* 2.6.

22. Ptolemy *Geog.* 5.17.3. See L. Moritz, "Saracen," in *Realencyclopädie der classischen Altertumswissenschaft*, ed. G. Wissowa (2nd series; 1920) 2.2388–2389. For recent discussions of the term "Saracen" see D. Graf and M. O'Connor, "The Origin of the Term Saracen and the Ruwwāfa Inscription," *Byzantine Studies* 4 (1977) 52–66; D. Graf, "The Saracens and the Defense of the Arabian Frontier," *BASOR* 229 (1978) 14–15.

23. Rufinus *HE* 2.6; Socrates *HE* 4.36; Sozomenos *HE* 6.38; Theodoret *HE* 4.20. That Mavia's incursions reaches the confines of Egypt is explicitly said by Sozomenos. For installing the Lucius in Egypt after Athanasius' death in 373 see A. H. M. Jones, *The Later Roman Empire* (1964) 1.152. Jones apparently thought that Mavia reigned over a tribe in the Syrian desert (942), but he did not argue the case.

24. Bowersock, "*Limes*," 223, 226 argued at first that there was a connection between the works of fortifications in Transjordan ca. 367–375 and the revolt of Mavia. But such works were carried out at the same time at 'En Boqeq in the Negev/Judaean zone (see *infra* n. 90). I may also add that a chain of forts with observation posts along a road

to refer to a *limes* in the Negev, but one cannot be sure of the geographical implication.

M. Avi-Yonah thought that there is a reference to the *limes Palaestinae* in the *Chronicon Paschale*. The reference is to a defensive measure taken against the Saracens by the emperor Decius, who sent lions and lionesses εἰς τὸ λίμιτον ἀνατολῆς ἀπὸ Ἀραβίας καὶ Παλαιστίνης ἕως τοῦ Κιρκησίου κάστρου.[25] Strictly speaking, this text does not mention the Palestine *limes*, only an *orientis limes*, but does imply a defensive policy along the eastern frontier of the provinces Arabia and Palestine, which in this context does not seem to refer to the Negev. An important text for our problem, which I shall only discuss briefly here, is a letter of Honorius and Theodosius II of 23 March 409: "Limitanei militis et possessorum utilitate conspecta, per primam, secundam, et tertiam Palaestinam, huiuscemodi norma processit ut, pretiorum certa taxatione depensa, specierum intermittatur exactio: sed ducianum officium sub Versamini et Maenaeni castri nomine salutaria statuta conatur evertere."[26] The letter specifically deals with the *limitanei* associated with the forts of Birsama and Menois, which means that a *limes* system did exist in this part of the Negev. But the opening sentence indicates that such soldiers could also be found in other parts of Palestine, for otherwise there would be no point in mentioning Palaestina Prima and Secunda. This is an interesting piece of evidence because it seems to show

on the eastern ridge of Mount Ḥebron has recently been observed. Trial excavations at several sites suggest that this defensive line was constructed at the end of the fourth or beginning of the fifth century. See Y. Hirschfeld, "A Line of Byzantine Forts along the Eastern Highway of the Ḥebron Hills," *Qadmoniot* 12 (1979) 78–84. However, in a recent article Bowersock has corrected the date of Mavia's revolt to 378; see G. W. Bowersock, "Mavia, Queen of the Saracens," in *Studien zur antiken Sozialgeschichte. Festschrift Friedrich Vittinghoff* (1980) 477–95, esp. 485–87. Consequently the works of fortification in Transjordan are irrelevant to Mavia's area of operations. At any rate Bowersock, "*Limes*," 229 (cf. "Mavia," 484) is not aware of the difficulties involved in the passage when he asserted that Rufinus means the frontier territory from 'Aqaba into Syria. His conclusion is that in fact based on his assumption that there was not a *limes* in the Negev—clearly a *petitio principii*. Moreover, Graf's interpretation of the term "Saracens" (see n. 22) has no bearing on the whereabouts of these tribes; hence Bowersock's conjecture ("Mavia," 484) that Mavia was a successor of Imru'l-qais finds no support in this interpretation. A sceptical approach to the accounts concerning Mavia is advocated by Ph. Mayerson, "Mauia, Queen of the Saracens—A Cautionary note," *IEJ* 30 (1980) 123–31. He has no conclusion to offer for the geographical location of the base of Mavia. On Mavia see also W. Ensslin, "Mavia," in *Realencyclopädie der classischen Altertumswissenschaft*, ed. G. Wissowa (1930) 28.2230.

25. *Chronicon Paschale* 504.

26. *Cod. Theod.* 7.4.30.

that the Palestine *limes* is not to be understood as merely a linear defensive system, but as a military system to which various forces were attached, regardless of their position in the country. Finally, mention should be made of a letter of Jerome, of the year 411, which may or may not refer to a *limes* in the Negev.[27]

Several written sources record the presence of Roman army units in the Negev in the late Roman period and Byzantine times. A Roman unit was already stationed in Nessana in the mid-fifth century and was still there in the sixth century, according to papyri found there.[28] The *Notitia Dignitatum* records Roman units in six places, which may have belonged to a defensive system established along a line between the Dead Sea and Raphia: Zoara, Moleatha, Berosaba, Birsama and Menois, with Chermula some distance in the rear.[29] It also mentions more units in other places, some (but not all) of which may be identified, and at any rate not all of which can be part of the same line of defence.[30] Finally, the *Onomasticon* of Eusebius of the early 4th century and its Latin version by Jerome mention garrisons in Carmel (Chermula), Beersheba (Berosba), Zoara, Thaiman, Thamara, Adomim, Mephaath and Aila.[31] Only the first three may belong to the same line of defence.

27. Jerome, *Ep.* 126.2: "Hoc autem anno cum tres explicassem libros, subitus impetus barbarorum, de quibus tuus dicit Virgilius, *lateque vagantes Barcaei* et sancta Scriptura de Ishmael, *contra faciem omnium fratrum suorum habitabit*, sic Aegypti limitem, Palaestinae, Phoenicis, Syriae percurrit ad instar torrentis cuncta secum trahens, ut vix manus eorum misercordia Christi potuerimus evadere."

28. The presence of a Roman unit in a camp at Nessana is known from a number of papyri, 17 of which are regarded as "the soldiers' archive"; see C. J. Kraemer, *Excavations at Nessana 3. Non-Literary Papyri* (1958) 5.1–23. The unit was the *numerus Theodosiacus* established at Nessana before 450 (*ibid.* 41–45; see also nos. 36–37 (pp. 111–17)).

29. *Not. Dig. Or.* 34.18–20; 34.22; 34.26; 34.45. The location of Thamara, i.e., Tarba (according to *Not. Dig. Or.* , ed. O. Seeck (1876) at 34.40), is disputed. Y. Aharoni, "Tamar and the Roads to Elath," *Eretz-Israel* 5 (1958) 129–34 proposed to identify it with 'Ain Ḥussub, some 30 km south of the Dead Sea. But even if any of the other proposals is accepted (see A. Alt, "Aus der 'Araba," *ZPalV* 58 (1935) 33–35; B. Rothenberg, "The 'Arabah in Roman and Byzantine Times in Light of New Research," in *Roman Frontier Studies 1967*, ed. Sh. Applebaum (1971) 215, they all indicate places south of the line of defence suggested.

30. For suggestions see Alt, "'Araba," esp. 19–29. But see also Aharoni, "Tamar," 129–134. At any rate, the units seem to have been stationed along the roads to Elath (Aila).

31. Eusebius *Onomasticon*, ed. E. Klostermann (1904), Carmel: 118–19; Beersheba: 50–51; Zoara: 42–43; Thaiman: 96–97; Adommium: 24–25; Mephaath: 128–29; Aila: 6–7. Three more forts are mentioned by Eusebius, but they are all in Transjordan: Amona: 10–11; Carcaria: 116–17; Roboth: 142–43.

The discussion so far shows that, contrary to Bowersock's opinion, the term *limes Palaestinae* was applied not only to the southern part of the Hashemite Kingdom of Jordan—that is, of the old Nabataean Kingdom turned into a Roman province under Trajan—but also to a part of the Negev, whose exact geographical location cannot be accurately ascertained on the basis of written sources. As none of the above-mentioned sources is earlier than the early fourth century, those who want to date the establishment of the defensive system, whatever this may have been, prior to the reforms of Diocletian are faced with some difficulty. Following an observation of Alt, however, Applebaum argued that the list of Idumaean towns given by Ptolemy indicates that Idumaea was organized as a special military zone after the First Jewish Revolt.[32] But the support sought from Ptolemy cannot sustain closer examination. Ptolemy does not seem to have described contemporary administrative conditions, as Philadelphia and Gerasa are included in Syria in his account, whereas in his day they belonged to Arabia.[33] That he used an earlier source follows from his remark about Jerusalem, "which is now called Aelia Capitolina."[34]

But Ptolemy's account presents some difficulties. He divides Palestine into four regions: Galilee, Samaria, Judaea and Idumaea, a division not attested in any other source.[35] Neapolis is included in Samaria, but Sebaste belongs to Judaea, an arrangement not recorded elsewhere and which is highly implausible.[36] Thamara is ascribed to Judaea and Maliatha (Moleatha) to Arabia, a very complicated territorial disposition if the last place is to be identified with Tel el-Milḥ (see below).[37] Beit Gubrin (Eleutheropolis) is in Judaea and not in Idumaea, but the quite unknown Gemmaruris is enumerated as one of the towns of Idumaea, although it was in the territory

32. Alt, "*Limes*," (1930) 60–62; Applebaum, "Initial Date," 6–8. Alt, "*Limes*," (1930) 63 n. 1, however, is puzzled by Ptolemy's inclusion of Elusa in Idumaea before 106, as this town was part of the Nabataean Kingdom.

33. Ptolemy, *Geog.* 5.14.18. See Brünnow and Domaszewski, *Provincia Arabia*, 250.

34. Ptolemy, *Geog.* 5.15.5.

35. Ptolemy, *Geog.* 5.15.3. The only division that comes close to it is the one ascribed by Avi-Yonah (*Historical Geography*, 63–64; *Holy Land*, 98–99) to the Herodian administration, which included Galilee, Samaria, Judaea, Peraea and Idumaea. But see the objections of A. Schalit, *König Herodes* (1969) 214 n. 252.

36. Ptolemy, *Geog.* 5.15.5.

37. Ptolemy, *Geog.* 5.15.5, 5.16.4. Applebaum insists on this identification, which is also suggested by C. Müller in his edition (with commentary) on Ptolemy's *Geography*.

of Beit Gubrin.[38] Finally, let us give the complete list of Idumaean towns according to Ptolemy: Birsama, Kaparorsa, Gemmaruris, Elusa and Mampsis.[39] There is no doubt that Elusa and Mampsis were Nabataean towns, and hence it is inconceivable that they were annexed to the Roman Empire before 106.[40] But geographically, Ptolemy's account now becomes very difficult, even impossible. A glance at the map shows that if Thamara, Mampsis and Elusa belong to the province Syria Palaestina, Maliatha must be an enclave within this province: Nabataean, if this list is supposed to reflect conditions prior to the annexation of 106, or part of another Roman province after the formation of Arabia. In either case, such a territorial arrangement strains credulity and is due to some confusion. One may escape the difficulty by accepting Ptolemy's location of Maliatha further to the south, but if so, it is the only record of such a town in Arabia.

Now, we do not know how Ptolemy compiled his list. He may have used the map of Marinus of Tyre, as was once suggested,[41] but obviously with additions or changes based on other sources or information about later conditions. Clearly his account cannot be taken as a description of the administrative reorganization of Judaea under the Flavian emperors. And there is another point. Contrary to Applebaum's suggestion, it seems

38. Ptolemy, *Geog.* 5.15.5. For Gemmaruris see also A. Saarisalo, "Topographical Researches in the Shephelah," *Journal of the Palestine Oriental Society* 11 (1931) 100–101.

39. Ptolemy, *Geog.* 5.15.7. Caparorsa may be identified with Ὀρήσᾳ, the suggested reading of Josephus, *A.J.* 14.361, instead of the MSS Θρήσᾳ. For Mampsis and Elusa see Negev, "Nabateans," 631–635; A. Negev, "Mampsis, eine Stadt im Negev," *Antike Welt* 3 (1972) 13–28; A. Negev, "Survey and Trial Excavations at Ḥalusa (Elusa), 1973," *IEJ* 26 (1976) 89–96. He suggests that Elusa was the most important Nabatean town in the Negev.

40. Cf. *supra* n. 32. Applebaum, "Initial Date," 7–9 takes this as an indication that the Roman government established a special military zone after the First Jewish Revolt. But this is obviously pure guesswork, and it is implausible that Vespasian turned against the Nabataeans who had helped him in the Jewish War. One could counter this by arguing that Vespasian did indeed annex Commagene (Josephus, *J.W.* 7.219–243), whose king had supported him (*J.W.* 3.68) and his son Titus (*J.W.* 5.460–465). In this case, however, Josephus' silence is telling. He exceeds the limits of his subject to report events in Commagene, in Gaul (*J.W.* 7.75–88), in the Danubian provinces (*J.W.* 7.89–95), the invasion of Media by the Alani (*J.W.* 7.244–251), and the Roman measures taken against Jews in Egypt and Cyrene (*J.W.* 7.443–446). He would not have failed to report the annexation of such a territory as envisaged by Applebaum.

41. Brünnow and Domaszewski, *Provincia*, 250. It should be noted that Marinus probably composed his work after the Trajanic annexation of the Nabataean Kingdom. See E. Honigmann, "Marinus," in *Realencyclopädie der classischen Altertumswissenschaft*, ed. G. Wissowa (1930) 28.1767.

that there is nothing in Ptolemy's account to suggest that it has any military significance. He first gives a list of the eight Palestinian ports. Then he enumerates the provincial towns: four in Galilee, two in Samaria, twenty in Judaea west of the Jordan, five in Judaea east of the Jordan, and five in Idumaea. Many of these towns were naturally situated along roads and can be shown to have had Roman garrisons for some time, but in this respect nothing differentiates Idumaea from the other three regions.[42] It appears, then, that Ptolemy's account does not help in understanding the Roman military deployment in the Negev.

II

Now the archaeological evidence. Alt's article was associated with an archaeological survey carried out by F. Frank in 1932–1934 and published in 1934.[43] One of Avi-Yonah's arguments is that, in so far as Roman fortresses were examined in the 'Araba and west of the Dead Sea, they show characteristics shared with the fortresses of Diocletianic times, or even of a later period, to be found in Syria and the northern part of the *limes Arabiae*.[44] Applebaum did not contest this argument, but expressed his hope that further archaeological excavations would bring forward new evidence. In the meantime, B. Rothenberg carried out a prolonged archaeological survey of the 'Araba, on the basis of which he concluded that there never was a second, or even a third, line of defence, from north to south, along the 'Araba as assumed by Alt and accepted by Avi-Yonah.[45] The supposed existence of such a line of defence is outside the scope of the present discussion, but this state of affairs may serve as a warning about the uncertainty of conclusions based on finds observe in archaeological surveys.

42. *Contra* Alt, "*Limes*," (1930) 60 n. 1. A. Schulten, "Eine neue Römerspur in Westfalen," *BJ* 124 (1917) 89–103 (esp. 91–93), referred to by Alt, shows that in his account of Germany Ptolemy reports the Roman camps distinguished in the wars Augustus and Tiberius, which is altogether a different case.

43. F. Frank, "Aus der 'Araba I," *ZPalV* 57 (1934) 191–280. For an earlier description of the same area see A. Musil, *Arabia Petraea* (1907–8); for the Roman remains see Musil's index s.vv. Römische Bauten, Römerstrauße. There are no suggestions of a defensive system and no precise dating of the remains in these surveys.

44. M. Avi-Yonah, "The Date of the 'Limes Palaestinae,'" *Eretz-Israel* 5 (1958) 136.

45. Rothenberg, "'Arabah," esp. 214 and 220; *contra* Alt, "'Araba"; Avi-Yonah, *Holy Land*, 119.

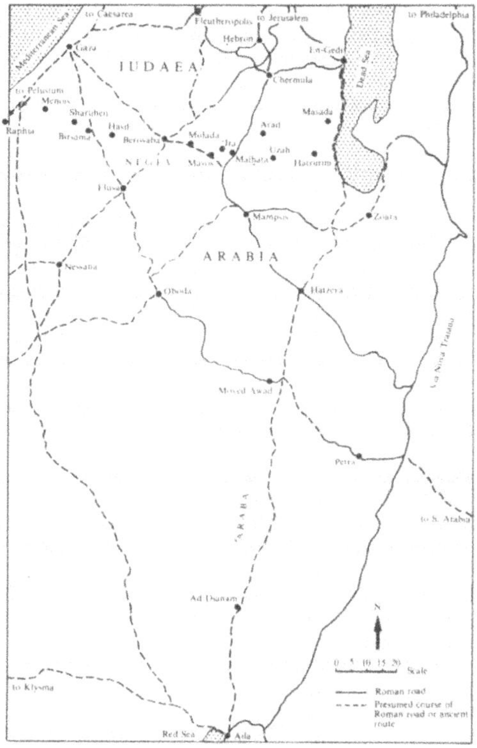

As regards roads, this map is based on that of B. Isaac, "Trade Routes to Arabia and the Roman Army," in *Roman Frontier Studies 1979*, ed. W. S. Hanson and L. J. F. Keppie (1980) 890–91, who mainly follows the Roman road-system prepared by I. Roll of the Israel Milestone Committee. It should be noted that according to these maps, these scholars do not presume the existence of a road connecting Raphia with the Dead Sea along the forts of the Negev (*contra* Gichon, "Research," 851, 853). It is also well to bear in mind that the existence of an ancient road through the 'Araba to Aila is denied by Rothenberg ("'Arabah," 211–14).

M. Gichon has not so far published the long-awaited complete presentation of his archaeological study of the fortifications and structures of the Palestine *limes*. Yet one of his articles is detailed enough to allow a close analysis of the evidence at his disposal and the methods of his work.[46] He claims that he has identified 161 sites belonging to the Palestine *limes*, of which those south of the line Odoba-Moyet 'Awad as well as the settlements

46. M. Gichon, "The Sites of the *Limes* in the Negev," *Eretz-Israel* 12 (1975) 149–66. Although this article is listed in the bibliography, Gutwein, *Third Palestine*, 321–36 does not take its data into consideration in his account of the military role of Palaestina Tertia.

near Elusa are excluded from the discussion.[47] The remaining 114 are classified according to functional criteria: a) *castella*—major forts; b) *castella parva*—forts; c) *burgi* (πύργοι)—fortlets; d) *turres*—towers; e) *mansiones, mutationes, stationes*—various servicing buildings along the roads. The corresponding tables give various details including the periods of occupation of each site and the evidence on which the dating is based. There are fifteen *castella*, fourteen *castella parva*, forty-eight *burgi*, twenty-six *turres* and eleven *mansiones*. Of these, 68 sites are dated on the basis of pottery finds, 11 on the basis of pottery finds and coins, 5 on the basis of pottery and architectural designs, 1 on the basis of pottery and excavations and 7 on the basis of excavations. 2 sites are surprisingly dated without any supporting evidence. 20 sites are not dated and one may wonder whether they belong to the subject under consideration.[48] When one tries to check and understand the dating system, one gets into trouble, as the nomenclature is hopelessly confused. Some 25 sites are dated "from the Roman period to the Byzantine period" (or "to the Moslem conquest"), which seems to suggest continued occupation from the first century to the seventh century. But when it is noticed that more than a dozen sites are dated "from the Flavian period (or "from the 1st–2nd century") to the Byzantine period" (or "to the Moslem conquest") one comes to suspect there are no firm criteria or evidence for dating the beginning of the Roman occupation of these sites. One can also ask why a fort that is dated to the "Nabataean period" is included in the list.

These dating notices betray the weakness of the dating system which is overwhelmingly based on potsherds discovered in an archaeological survey.[49] That such a dating is often unreliable may be illustrated by the following examples. As early as Alt, Tel Masos (Khirbet el-Meshāsh), located some 12 km east of Tel Beersheba, was considered as a Roman fort of the Flavian period, and the dating and classification of the site were commonly

47. This is rather curious, as it may imply that some fortifications were well inside the Sinai peninsula, unless the reference "south of Oboda-Moyet 'Awad" is to such sites as Ad Dianam and Aila. For Moyet 'Awad, identified with Moa, see now R. Cohen, "Negev Emergency Survey," *IEJ* 32 (1982) 164–65.

48. No evidence is given for the dating of the fortlet Beer Bor to the Nabataean period (Gichon, "Sites," 159) and of the tower Khirbet Ma'aravim "from the Roman period to the Byzantine period" (Gichon, "Sites," 163).

49. The uncertainty of Gichon is reflected in the many question marks and variations he adds to his dating notices as well as in notices like "from the Nabataean period (2nd century)," "from the Nabataean period to Hadrian's time (the Byzantine period)" (*sic*!), etc.

accepted.[50] The site was excavated in three seasons of work, 1972, 1974, and 1975. The account of the first season of excavations at the site reports the following discovery: "It was ascertained that the Roman fort was merely a private structure of the Roman period, evidently an unfortified villa. Fragments of measuring cups and remains of Herodian stone tablets suggest a 1st-century CE date for its construction."[51] During the excavations of the same area in the second season surprising remains were discovered, showing, at last definitely, that what had at first been considered a Roman fort and then a villa of the first century CE was in fact a Nestorian monastery, built in the seventh or eighth century CE. It is worth while quoting the explanation given for the new dating:

> The identification of the building as a Roman villa in the first season was reached by the excavated parts of Rooms 601 and 602 and a few pieces of Roman pottery. The *terminus post quem* given by this pottery led to an incorrect dating that had to be corrected in the light of the pottery found *in situ* and of the Syrian inscriptions in a datable type of script. The Roman pottery of the second season is very scanty, which points to periodic presence on the tel rather than a permanent settlement. No architectural activity in this period can as yet be attested, probably the tel had not been settled in the Roman period.[52]

No further comments are needed.[53]

Beersheba is considered one of the major fortresses of the Palestine *limes*, of which, according to Gichon, there were three more (Menois,

50. Alt, "*Limes*" (1931) 81; Avi-Yonah, *Historical Geography*, 169; M. Gichon, "Origin," 177, 185, 187 (maps); Applebaum and Gichon, *Israel*, 44: "Today only very few vestiges are left of Ḥasif and Zuḥban, whereas at Molada and Mashosh the outline of the buildings is clearly discernable, one to two courses of masonry being above ground."

51. Y. Aharoni, V. Fritz, and A. Keminski, "Excavations at Tel Masos (Khirbet El-Meshâsh). Preliminary Report on the First Season, 1972," *Tel Aviv* 1 (1974) 64–74 (esp. 71); Y. Aharoni, V. Fritz, and A. Mekminski, "Vorbericht über die Ausgrabungen auf der Ḥirbet el-Mšāš (Tel Māśôś), 1. Kampagne 1972," *ZPalV* 89 (1973) 197–210.

52. Y. Aharoni, V. Fritz, and A. Keminski, "Excavations at Tel Masos (Khirbet El-Meshâsh). Preliminary Report on the Second Season, 1974," *Tel Aviv* 2 (1975) 97–113 (esp. 110–12). See also A. Kempinsi and V. Fritz, "Excavations at Tel Masos (Khirbet El-Meshâsh). Preliminary Report on the Third Season, 1975," *Tel Aviv* 4 (1977) 136–58 (esp. 154–56).

53. Gichon, "Sites," does not include this tel in his lists of the sites in the Palestine *limes*, but the fort (or fortlet) still appears in the three maps accompanying the article.

Birsama and Moleatha) in the Flavian period.[54] The site of ancient Beersheba has been identified with Tel Beersheba, some 5 km east of modern Beersheba. Annual, systematic excavations of this site started in 1969 under the direction of Y. Aharoni.[55] The specific site of the Roman fortress observed on the tel was latter assigned to V. Fritz, who published a detailed preliminary report in 1973.[56] Fritz states that the pottery remains found in the excavations are too few and fragmentary to allow dating of the fort, besides being out of context. Several coins allow some conjectures. A coin of 94/95 CE is rejected as significant for dating the fort to the first century CE, apparently as being out of context. A Trajanic coin of the year 112 CE, found within an inner wall, is taken to show the *terminus post quem* for the construction of the fort. A silver coin of Neapolis of 251–253 CE indicates a *terminus post quem* for the destruction of the fort, and three coins of the fourth century, found outside the fort, make it probable that the fort still existed then.[57] Fritz's caution and hesitation in precisely dating the fort are noteworthy. He apparently does not consider the architectural design and building material as datable indications. He states that pottery that does not come from clear contexts is of no help in dating the fortress. In contrast, Gichon asserts that an earlier building was constructed on the site under the Flavians, when the *limes* was allegedly established, and that the Trajanic coin slipped into it. Clearly these are mere speculations.[58]

54. Applebaum and Gichon, *Israel*, 39: "No surface remains beyond a few blocks of flint and ashlar, and a large amount of pottery, testify to the existence of a fortress on the talus of Birsama. On the mounds of Beersheba and Malhata, on the other hand, the outlines of the forts can still clearly be made out, their curtains projecting one course above ground-level." See also Alt, "*Limes*," (1930) 50–51.

55. For the first report, see Y. Aharoni, "Tel Beersheba," *IEJ* 19 (1969) 245–47.

56. V. Fritz, "Vorbericht über die Ausgrabung des römischen Kastells auf dem *Tell es-Seba*," *ZPalV* 89 (1973) 54–65; V. Fritz, "The Roman Fortress," in Y. Aharoni, *Beer-Sheba* (1973) 1.83–89.

57. Fritz, "Vorbericht," 60 and *apud* Aharoni, "Tamar," 86–87.

58. Gichon, "Sites," 152 n. 21. On p. 153 n. 24 he suggests that the Herodian fortress was inherited by the Romans in the Flavian period, which is not compatible with his contention for a Flavian construction. He wrongly reports that Fritz found a Hadrianic coin. In his recent article ["Research on the *Limes Palaestinae*: A Stocktaking," in *Roman Frontier Studies 1979*, ed. W. S. Hanson and L. J. F. Keppie (1980) 845], Gichon does not repeat these suggestions. But there he wrongly argues that "numismatic evidence from within the *castellum* proves its existence in A.D. 112." The Trajanic coin of 112 proves that the building was constructed not earlier than that year; it could have been constructed in that year, in the next generation or even later. Gichon's attempt to dissociate the inner walls of the fortress from the outer walls is not cogent.

According to Aharoni, the excavations have shown that the Roman fortress was built atop a Hellenistic bath-house belonging to a Herodian fortress, which preceded the Roman one.[59] As for dating, Aharoni at one time took the Trajanic coin as "indicating the fortress was constructed after the second century,"[60] and at another wrote that the fortress was built in the second half of the second century at the earliest.[61] At any rate, to anyone without a prejudiced approach, it is now clear that the Roman fort of Tel Beersheba cannot be dated to the Flavian period, or to the early second century CE, on the basis of archaeological evidence. Finally, it should be noted that Tel Beersheba may perhaps not be identical with the late Berosaba of the *Notitia Dignitatum*. The fort on the tel is too small to accommodate a Roman cohort, and is considered by Fritz as an intermediate fort between Berosaba and Moleatha; the first of these is supposed to have been situated in the old quarter of modern Beersheba.[62]

'Ira is one of the sites considered to be "excellent examples of the continuity of border-defence from biblical times to the Roman occupation of Judaea. . . . Roman and Byzantine pottery attests to 'Ira's incorporation in the Limes defence system."[63] Thus Gichon in 1967. A rescue excavation of the site began in March 1979, concentrating on two areas in the northwestern part of Tel 'Ira. The finds discovered show that the site was occupied in the Israelite, Herodian and Byzantine periods. In one area (*M*), part of a tower and the city wall was unearthed; the upper courses, belonging to the Byzantine period, were built on remains of the Israelite period. Some remains indicate that the Israelite city wall was re-used, with some additions, in the Herodian and Byzantine periods. The same picture emerges from the finds of the second area (*L*) excavated. The Byzantine upper course of the wall was built on top of the Israelite wall and there

59. Aharoni, "Tel Beersheba," (1969) 246; Y. Aharoni, "Tel Beersheba," *IEJ* 22 (1972) 170.

60. "Tel Beersheba," (1972) 170. Gichon, "Sites," 153 (with n. 24) is misleading in giving this reference as authority for his dating of Tel Beersheba to the Flavian period.

61. Y. Aharoni, "Tel Beersheba," *Qadmoniot* 6 (1973) 73–84, esp. 78. See also Y. Aharoni, "Beersheba," in *Encyclopedia of Archaeological Excavations in the Holy Land*, ed. M. Avi-Yonah (1976–78) 1.88; Y. Aharoni, "Excavations at Tel Beer-Sheba, Preliminary Report on the Fourth Season, 1972," *Tel Aviv* 1 (1974) 42; Aharoni, *Beer-Sheba*, 1.7–8.

62. See Fritz, "Vorbericht," 63 with n. 18, who rejects Gichon's assumption ("Verteidigungssystem," 321; "Research," 845) that Roman command was first centred on Tel Beersheba and only in the fourth century was transferred to Berosaba (= old quarter of modern Beersheba). See also Gutwein, *Third Palestine*, 329–30.

63. Applebaum and Gichon, *Israel*, 45.

are also architectural remains of the Herodian period. No remains of the Roman period are reported, even among the relatively large number of vessels.[64]

Two more seasons of excavations, in which work was carried out in the eastern and southern parts of the site, have revealed basically the same results. The fortifications on the eastern extremity of the mound, belonging to the Israelite period, were destroyed at the end of the seventh century BCE. In the same area, ruins of structures were found and dated as Roman and Byzantine on the basis of the sherds collected in their vicinity. When they began to unearth the main structure, however, the excavators realized that it was a Byzantine monastery of the late fourth or early fifth century. A chapel was excavated above the gate of the Israelite town. The houses uncovered in the southern part of the tel are dated to the Israelite, Hellenistic and Byzantine periods. Finally, a large structure was uncovered on the hill nearest to Tel ʻIra. In the surveys of the 1950s it was considered to be a Hellenistic fortress, but the excavation has now shown it to be a civilian building of the Byzantine period, probably of the fifth century.[65] Thus three seasons of archaeological excavations have disproved the assumption that Tel ʻIra was occupied by the Romans after the First Jewish Revolt, and there is no evidence of military presence at the site during the Roman and Byzantine periods.

I have discussed these three examples (Tel Masos, Tel Beersheba and Tel ʻIra) at length to demonstrate that a dating system mainly based on an archaeological survey and pottery collected from the surface may prove wrong in many of the sites, once they are excavated. It should be stressed that there are not a few uncertainties in the chronology of the pottery remains. Since the life spans of the pottery types is of two, three, four and even more centuries, one should proceed with the utmost caution in trying to define periods of occupation.[66] And there is another problem. As we

64. A. Biran and R. Cohen, "Tel ʻIra," *IEJ* 29 (1979) 124–25.

65. I. Beit-Arieh, "Tel ʻIra 1980," *IEJ* 31 (1981) 243–45.

66. In his article, "Migdal Tsafit, A Burgus in the Negev (Israel)," *Saalburg-Jahrbuch* 31 (1974) 16–40, Gichon admits the uncertainty involving the pottery remains. He claims that "the pottery analysis [of the finds at Tsafit] provides further proof of the Roman character of many wares and forms that continued the former local tradition and were apt to mislead investigators as to the period of their production" (p. 24). He may be right in saying "that any insight gained will be applicable not only to the ceramic history of the Roman Negev, but to that of the entire Provincia Palaestina" (p. 32), but one may become sceptical when one reads that "the overwhelming majority of our finds is not from the stratified layers in the tower, but from the surrounding surface finds and

have seen, remains of structures supposed to be part of fortifications on the basis of archaeological surveys may turn out to be civilian buildings after they have been unearthed. Obviously this need not be the case every time, but it may be quite often. Hence, the mere presence of pottery—be it Herodian, Nabataean, Roman or Byzantine—is no proof the military character of the site.

Let us now examine the evidence for the fortifications of the alleged Flavian *limes* in the Negev. In 1967 they were grouped by Gichon according to the following classification: a) main forts: Menois, Birsama, Berosaba and Malḥata (Moleatha); b) smaller fortifications: Mesad Sharuḥen, Khasif, Abu Ṣukhban, Molada, Tel Masos, Rujm Zohar and Mesad Ḥatrurim; c) forts inherited from earlier periods: ʿUza, ʿIra, ʿArad and ʿEn-Gedi.[67]

Of group (a), the Roman occupation of Tel Beersheba has been proven to be of post-Flavian date, as we have seen, and there is no clear archaeological or other evidence for the stationing of a Roman unit at Tel Beersheba prior to Diocletian. The exact site of Menois (Maʿin of Khirbet Maʿan) has not been located. The remains of a civilian settlement indicate a late date, not earlier than the fourth century, and it is admitted that there are no archaeological grounds for dating the fort earlier.[68] The location of Birsama is in doubt. Alt at first sought to identify it with Tel Farʿah (Beit Pelet), excavated by Sir Flinders Petrie.[69] He realized, however, that the Roman fort on the north hill of this tel is too old and too small to be identified with Birsama; actually, the coin evidence indicates that the fort was abandoned shortly after 58/59 CE.[70] He then proposed to identify Birsama with Ḥdirbet

the slopes of Tsafit hill" (p. 35). His discussion and attempt at reaching a chronology (pp. 34–38) should be compared with the detailed description of the stratified sherds (pp. 25–30). See also the reservations expressed by Kennedy, *Archaeological Explorations*, 313, 325 about the dating of ceramics on *limes Arabicus*.

67. Applebaum and Gichon, *Israel*, 39–45; Gichon, "Verteidigungssystem," with the map on p. 318. A few more sites are apparently assigned to the Flavian period in Gichon, "Sites," but the confusing nomenclature debars me from taking them into account.

68. For an account of the remains see Musil, *Arabia Petraea*, 1.223–24. Cf. Alt, "*Limes*," (1931) 53–54; Applebaum and Gichon, *Israel*, 40–41. Musil does not designate the remains "Roman," contrary to what Gichon ascribes to him. At any rate, Gichon admits there is no archaeological evidence for dating Menois to the Flavian period.

69. See F. Petrie, *Beth-Pelet* (1930) 1.20–21, and for a preliminary report, *Ancient Egypt* (1929) 8. See also A. Alt, "Birsama," *ZPalV* 52 (1929) 110–15 (= *Kleine Schriften* (1959) 3.468–72); Alt, "*Limes*" (1930) 55–56.

70. Alt, "*Limes*," (1931) 82–83, with a rejection of his other proposal to identify Birsama with E-Shallale. Petrie, *Beth-Pelet*, 1.20–21 came to a wrong conclusion in asserting

el-Far, some 7 km southeast of Tel Far'ah.[71] Here were noticed remains of a civilian settlement and a fort. The first was dated to the Roman-Byzantine period by Alt on the basis of potsherds, but he proposed no date for the latter.[72] Gichon dates the fort as occupied "from the Flavians to the Moslem conquest," citing coins and pottery as evidence.[73]

Moleatha, long ago identified with Tel el-Milḥ, was dated to the Roman-Byzantine period by Alt; according to Gichon it was occupied "from the Flavians to the Moslem conquest," again on the basis of coins and pottery.[74] Earlier, Woolley had been able to find only "Semitic" and Byzantine pottery at the site both on the surface and in a hole dug near the wall, and the only question for him was whether the fort was Byzantine or dated to the 2nd millennium BCE.[75] But in the meantime M. Kochavi excavated the tel, including the fort, for two seasons. More recently, several salvage excavations have been carried out at the site, one of them by Gichon himself. Unfortunately the results seem inconclusive for the point at issue. While accepting the theory that the fort at Tel el-Milḥ was part of the *limes* system, M. Kochavi has not been able to suggest a more precise date than "Roman period."[76] Gichon excavated the civil settlement at the tel, but he reports surface finds only. He writes they "cover the Hellenistic-Herodian

---

the Vespasianic date of this fort. Three coin-hoards found in the debris of the fort, containing coins not later than 58/59 CE, indicate that the site was abandoned shortly after this date and had been constructed at an earlier period. The absence of any later remains corroborates this inference. The "Roman" houses on the main hill are civilian and, according to Petrie, contemporary with the fort.

71. Alt, "*Limes*," (1931) 83–84, accepted by F.-M. Abel, *Géographie de la Palestine* (1938) 2.51, 180; Avi-Yonah, *Historical Geography*, 108, but with some doubt in Avi-Yonah, *Holy Land*, 163.

72. Alt, "*Limes*," (1931) 83. According to Musil, *Arabia Petraea*, 2.63, the ruins of Khirbet el-Far spread over an area of about 400x150 m. The fort was a square with a side of 65 m, according to Alt.

73. Gichon, "Sites," 153.

74. Alt, "*Limes*," (1930) 48–50; Alt, "*Limes*," (1931) 80; Gichon, "Sites," 153.

75. C. L. Woolley and T. E. Lawrence, *The Wilderness of Zin* (1914–15) 50–51.

76. M. Kokhavi [=Kochavi], "Tel Malḥata," *IEJ* 17 (1967) 272–73; M. Kochavi, *RBi* 75 (1968) 392–95. His report in *Qadmoniot* 3 (1970) 22–24 adds nothing on this point and the report in *Ḥadashot Archeologiot* 40 (1971) 34–36 does not mention the Roman fort at all (cf. *RBi* 79 (1972) 593–96). Kochavi's final report is "Tel Malhata," in Avi-Yonah, *Encyclopedia*, 3.771–775. I may single out two points. First, Kochavi was the only one who excavated the fort himself. Secondly, there is no mention of Hellenistic finds, let alone of Hellenistic building activity, in Kochavi's final report, though the first report did mention "two Hellenistic building phases" (*not* fortifications).

and early-to-late Roman period."[77] On the other hand, the other excavators, concentrating their work on the west side of the tel and to the south of it, have uncovered late Roman and Byzantine finds only, including buildings, graves, pottery and a coin.[78] Obviously the finds of these salvage excavations do not necessarily affect the dating of the fort.

Thus of the four major forts adduced by Gichon for a Flavian *limes*, one (Tel Beersheba) is post-Flavian, one (Menois) offers no archaeological support for a Flavian date, and two (Birsama and Moleatha) offer only doubtful archaeological support for possible occupation in the Flavian period.

Of group (b), Tel Masos, as we have seen, has to be eliminated. Sharuḥen is dated by Gichon "from the Flavians to the Severan period" on the basis of excavations (claiming it to be of Herodian origin), with reference to Petrie's *Beth-Pelet*. This is unacceptable, since evidence indicates that the fort (=Tel Far'ah) was abandoned soon after 58/59 CE; therefore the site has to be excluded from the list.[79] Molada and Mesad Ḥatrurim are dated by Gichon himself, in his 1975 article, "from the Severan period to the Moslem conquest."[80] The ruins of Rujm Zohar are admitted by Gichon to date from the fourth century, but he assumes, on the basis of early Roman potsherds, that earlier fortifications had existed. Clearly there is little ground for keeping it on the list.[81] Of the remaining two, one is dated on the basis of pottery alone and the other, Khasif, on the basis of pottery and coins.[82]

77. Gichon, "Research," 847. I must point out that Kochavi (see previous note) never reported "The existence of a Hellenistic fortification beneath the Roman site," as Gichon asserts. For Gichon's work in the civil settlement, see also his report in *Ḥadashot Archeologiot* 69–71 (1979) 10–12. There he admits that "although pre-Byzantine pottery has been found in all the areas that have been examined, we cannot ascribe any remains in these areas to a pre-Byzantine period" (my translation).

78. I. Eldar and D. Naḥlieli, "Tel Malḥata," *Ḥadashot Archeologiot* 80–81 (1982) 39–41; J. Baumgarten, "Malḥata," *Ḥadashot Archeologiot* 80–81 (1982) 41–42.

79. Gichon, "Sites," 155 with n. 1. See nn. 69 and 70 *supra*, with text. M. Gichon, "Idumaea and the Herodian limes," *IEJ* 17 (1967) 36–37, discusses Tel Sharuḥen, without suggesting that the fort was occupied until the Severan period. But he is mistaken in stating that the latest coins found in the three coin hoards are of Agrippa I. Petrie, *Beth-Pelet*, 1.21 explicitly writes, "The latest of these [coins] was of the Vth year of Nero, A.D. 58–59."

80. Gichon, "Sites," 155.

81. Applebaum and Gichon, *Israel*, 43.

82. Applebaum and Gichon, *Israel*, 43. A short account of Khasif and Abu Sukhban is given by Musil, *Arabia Petraea*, 2.64. Both sites have been destroyed. Rujm Zohar is dated by Gichon on the basis of pottery, but with a question mark.

Of group (c), ʿIra now has to be excluded. The case of Tel ʿArad is very doubtful. No Byzantine pottery was found, "only Roman sherds of approximately the first century CE," to quote the official report. According to Aharoni, who was the director of the excavations, the fort was probably constructed before the annexation of the Nabataean Kingdom and abandoned in the second century.[83] This is not a necessary conclusion, for since sherds are the only evidence, it is equally possible that the fort was abandoned in the first century. But it is quite surprising to find that Gichon, who was responsible for the excavation of the Roman fort in Tel ʿArad, admits that the fort may be dated either to the Herodian or to the Flavian period. Under the spell of the Flavian *limes* theory, he postulates that it was reoccupied under the Flavians.[84] There is not a shred of evidence for such a reoccupation. The simple truth is that what I called "the Roman fort" at Tel ʿArad cannot be dated. It may have been constructed at any time from the late 1st century BCE to the second century CE, and it may have been abandoned soon after 70 CE, or after the annexation of the Nabataean Kingdom, or after the Bar Kochba war. For whatever reasons, the excavations at the fort have not clarified the dating problem.[85]

Next, ʿEn-Gedi. The settlement there suffered destruction in the First Jewish Revolt, but it was economically too important to be left deserted. There is ample archaeological evidence that it was soon reoccupied. However, there is no evidence for Flavian fortifications, although the site has been extensively excavated.[86] The presence of a centurion of the *cohors I*

83. Y. Aharoni, "Excavations at Tel Arad: Preliminary Report on the Second Season," *IEJ* 17 (1967) 242–43. At the time of this report the Roman fort was "almost completely cleared." See also Y. Aharoni, "Tel Arad," in Avi-Yonah, *Encyclopedia*, 1.88.

84. Applebaum and Gichon, *Israel*, 46. Obviously the dating of ʿArad "from the Flavian period to the Moslem conquest" in Gichon, "Sites," 153 (with n. 25) is an open contradiction with this conclusion, but both are based on the same evidence.

85. The distinction between finds and inferences seems clear in the Aharoni's final account ("Tel Arad," 1.88): "Stratum III is a Roman fort . . . . On the basis of the scanty material found on its floor, including a Greek ostracon, it has been dated to approximately the first century A.D. It thus appears to have belonged to a network of fortifications of the *limes Palaestinae* and to have gone out of use completely with the annexation by Trajan of the Nabataean kingdom in A.D. 106." Yet in his *Arad Inscriptions* (1981) 8, Aharoni writes that in Stratum III "Almost no material was found which could be ascribed to the stratum within the fortress. Material form the first and second centuries C.E. was found mainly at the foot of the tell and in garbage dumps—apparently from the time of the citadel." The only two Greek ostraca of ʿArad, published by B. Lifshitz *apud* Aharoni, *Arad Inscriptions*, 177, do not offer any chronological clue.

86. For the destruction see Josephus, *J.W.* 4.402–404; Pliny, *NH* 5.15. For the

Thracum milliaria and of a military garrison is attested at 'En-Gedi by a papyrus document of the year 124 CE.[87] Yet it has recently been shown that it was only a detachment of this unit that was stationed at 'En-Gedi, and that the camp of the main force of the cohort should be located at Ḥebron.[88]

Finally, 'Uza; this was dated on the basis of surface sherds alone. Recent excavations show that the fort was indeed occupied in the Roman period, although the evidence does not allow us to establish amore precise date.[89]

It appears, then, that there is at present no clear, sound archaeological evidence for the military occupation of any of these sites in the Flavian period. The archaeological evidence suggests that at least two of the sites of the first group, five of the second group and two of the third group were not garrisoned in the Flavian period; and it is no more than possible that the remaining six were at the time garrisoned. A further observation with regard to the archaeological evidence is apposite. Of the numerous sites allegedly associated with the *limes* system, only eight are said to have been dated on the basis of excavations. Gichon himself dates three of these to post-Flavian periods.[90] The assignment of two of the other five (Sharuḥen and Tel Beersheba) to the Flavian period should be rejected, as we have seen. The

excavations see B. Mazar, T. Dothan and I. Dunayevsky, "En-Gedi. The First and Second Seasons of Excavations 1961 and 1962," *'Atiqot* (English Series) 5 (1966) 1–100; B. Mazar and I. Dunayevsky, "En-Gedi. Fourth and Fifth Seasons of Excavations," *IEJ* 17 (1967) 133–43 (esp. 142–43).

87. H. J. Polotsky, "The Greek Papyri from the Cave of Letters," *IEJ* 12 (1962) 259 [[= *DMIPERP* §43]].

88. M. P. Speidel, "A Tile Stamp of Cohors I Thracum Milliaria from Hebron-Palestine," *ZPE* 35 (1979) 170–72.

89. Gichon, "Sites," 153; cf. Applebaum and Gichon, *Israel*, 45. See now I. Beit Arieh, "Ḥorvat 'Uza, 1982," *IEJ* 32 (1982) 262–63; I. Beit Arieh, "Ḥorvat 'Uza, 1983," *IEJ* 33 (1983) 271–72. The fort had originally been built in the Israelite period and part of it was used again in Hellenistic times. In his recent excavations Beit Arieh found remains of the Roman period in the Hellenistic area of the fort and noticed changes made in the rooms. He kindly informed me that in 1985 season of excavations remains of constructions outside the fort were revealed. These seem to him to indicate occupation by the Roman army. I am grateful to Professor Beit Arieh for this information.

90. See M. Gichon, "Das Kastell En Boqeq: Die Ergebnisse der ersten Kampagne 1968 (Vorbericht)," *BJ* 171 (1971) 386–406—the fort was constructed in the third quarter of the 4th century; M. Gichon, "Excavations at Mezad-Tamar, 1973–74," *IEJ* 26 (1976) 188–94—the fort here was built during the last quarter of the third century; M. Gichon, "Migdal Tsafit, A Burgus in the Negev (Israel)," *Saalburg-Jahrbuch* 31 (1974) 16–40—the building of the tower is dated to the Trajanic period.

case of one other, Tel 'Arad, is inconclusive. The seventh is Ḥatseva ('Ain Ḥussub), identified by Alt with Eiseba, by Aharoni with Thamara.[91] Following Alt, Gichon identifies Thamara with Mesad Tamar (Qaṣr el-Juheiniye) and claims that "recent excavations at Ḥatseva have proved the complete absence of the Byzantine period, which is a *condicio sine qua non* for its identification with Tamar."[92] Now the excavator, R. Cohen, has published a brief communiqué of these excavations, which were conducted on two sites. One is southwest of the fort, in which were found thirty coins from the first to the fourth century CE, and the other is the southwest tower of the fort, where no remains of any archaeological significance are reported to have been found. And yet various Byzantine remains have been reported at Ḥatseva on several occasions.[93] This evidence is obviously not enough to corroborate Aharoni's proposal, but it is sufficient to question Gichon's inference about Ḥatseva. At any rate, Ḥatseva was in Nabataean territory and its supposed military occupation does not affect the discussion of the alleged Flavian *limes*. The same holds true of the last site excavated.[94]

However, to Gichon's list should now be added the excavations at Tel Masos, Tel el-Milḥ Tel 'Ira and 'Uza. Mention should also be made of the excavations at Tel 'Aroer, situated some 18 km southeast of Tel Beersheba. The fortress there, a 38x30 building, constructed apparently in the first century BCE, suffered destruction probably in the First Jewish Revolt. No later remains have been found.[95] Thus, in so far as excavations have been carried out, they have only undermined the theory of a Flavian *limes*.

91. A. Alt, *Die greichischen Inschriften der Palaestina Tertia westlich der 'Araba* (1921) 10; Alt, "'Araba," 31; Aharoni, "Tamar," 129–34.

92. Gichon, "Sites," 154 n. 29; M. Gichon, "Excavations at Mezad Tamar—"Tamara" 1973–1975, Preliminary Report," *Saalburg-Jahrbuch* 23 (1976) 80–81.

93. R. Cohen, *Ḥadashot Archeologiot* 44 (1972) 36–37; But see Rothenberg, "'Arabah," 216–17; *Ḥadashot Archeologiot* 45 (1973) 41; *Ḥadashot Archeologiot* 67/68 (1978) 63.

94. For Ma'ale Miḥmal see now R. Cohen, "Negev Emergency Project," *IEJ* 34 (1984) 203 (with references to earlier work). The dating is based on potsherds found during the excavation.

95. A. Biran and R. Cohen, *IEJ* 26 (1976) 139–40; A. Biran and R. Cohen, *IEJ* 27 (1977) 250–52; A. Biran and R. Cohen, *IEJ* 28 (1978) 197; A. Biran and R. Cohen, *Qadmoniot* 41 (1978) 20–24. Though Gichon accepts the excavators' conclusion that the fortress was destroyed in the First Jewish Revolt, he includes it in his map of the Flavian limes! (See Gichon, "Research," 844, 849.) If this implies that he suggests the fortress was rebuilt, it must be stated that there is no archaeological support for such a suggestion. There is nothing in the recent excavations, which have added much evidence on the Herodian building activity at the site, to indicate that the fortress was rebuilt. See A. Biran and R. Cohen, "'Aroer, 1981," *Ḥadashot Archeologiot* 80–81 (1982) 42–45; A. Biran,

A glance at the map shows that, without Tel 'Ira, Tel Masos, Tel Beersheba, Tel Far'ah and Menois alone, not to mention other sites, the defensive system ascribed to the Flavian period could not possible operate, even if a few sites were indeed garrisoned in this relatively early period.[96] If Roman forces were stationed in Idumaea in several places in the Flavian period, the explanation should be sought in another direction, as I shall presently argue, and is not to be linked with the framework of an imaginary *limes*.

III

A passage of Josephus has at times been cited in support of the theory that Vespasian and Titus realized that there was need to establish a defensive system against the Nabataean Kingdom on the southern frontier of Judaea.[97] As the passage is important for the understanding for the understanding of the whole problem, I give it in full:

> Having reduced the neighbourhood of the province of Thomna, he moved to Lydda and Jamnia; both of these districts already being subdued, he quartered upon them an adequate number of residents from those who had surrendered, and passed to Ammaus. Having occupied the approaches to the capital of this province, he fortified a camp and, leaving the fifth legion there, advanced with the rest of his forces to the province of Bethleptenpha. After devastating with fire this and the neighbouring district and the outskirts of Idumaea, he built fortresses in suitable situations; finally, having taken two villages right in the heart of Idumaea, Betabris and Caphartoba, he put upwards of ten thousand of the inhabitants to death, made prisoners of over a thousand, expelled the remainder and stationed in the district a large division of his own troops,

"Aroer, 1981," *IEJ* 32 (1982) 161–63.

96. See the map in Gichon, "Verteidigungssystem," 325 and note the importance of 'Ira: its "chief merit lay in its skilfully chosen position, which enabled visual contact with nearly all the more important Limes sites, and also with a number of the major forward observation posts and with signal stations linked with Chermela and other near bases" (Applebaum and Gichon, *Israel*, 45).

97. Applebaum, "Initial Date," 8–9; Gichon, "Origin," 183 n. 36: "Applebaum . . . has drawn attention that [sic] the passages 446–8 of Josephus, *Wars* IV, allude to the takeover of the border defences by the Romans, immediately after the conquest of Idumaea"; Gichon, "Verteidigungssystem," 328–33.

> who overran and devastated the whole of the hill country. He then returned with the rest of his forces to Ammaus.[98]

To begin with, it must be said that Applebaum-Gichon's approach to this text is erroneous and reveals misunderstanding of Vespasian's mission in Judaea, which was, as all readers of Josephus know, to crush the Jewish revolt. The suggestion that Vespasian, while the war was still going on, would have started fortifying the southern border of Judaea to protect its Jewish population against incursions by the Nabataeans, who were at that time serving in his army against rebellious Jews, should be rejected.[99] What Vespasian did in Idumaea was part of his strategy, namely, tight, continuous control of the Jewish population by the establishment of garrisons in regions already subdued. This security policy started from the very beginning, as can be inferred from the dispatch of a Roman force to Sepphoris and the garrisoning of Samaria.[100] We have evidence for the garrisoning of Japha, Jamnia and Ashdod along the coast, and the same was done in Gischala.[101] Camps were stationed at Ammaus, Jericho and Adida, as part of the systematic encircling of Jerusalem on all sides;[102] in 69 Bethel

98. Josephus, *J.W.* 4.444–449 (H.St.J. Thackeray's translation in the Loeb edition). Gichon, "Verteidigungssystem," 328–329 interprets this passage as if Vespasian quartered Samaritans in Lydda and Jamnia as part of a policy of securing the frontier with the help of this faithful population. This should be rejected. True, Samaritans expanded to other regions of Palestine in the Roman period, but this expansion, including the settlement in Jamnia, started in the 2nd century CE. In this last respect, Gichon's reference to S. Klein, *Eretz Yehuda* (1939) 175, 188–190, 199 and G. Alon, *History of the Jews in the Period of the Mishna and Talmud* (1955) 2.248–251 is misleading. There is no evidence that the Samaritan expansion was in any way supported by the Roman government, and it is wrong to describe the Jamnia-Lydda area as the hinterland of the *limes*. Vespasian had no reason to trust the Samaritans, and actually sent Cerialis to subdue a Samaritan gathering on Mt. Gerizim (Josephus *J.W.* 3.307–315). Besides, Joḥanan ben Zakkai, the Jewish sage who left Jerusalem when he realized that it was doomed, would not have developed Jamnia as a national centre of learning and religious administration for the Jewish population (and he got Vespasian's permission to go there), had it become as Samaritan town. It is interesting to note that Sh. Applebaum, "Judaea as a Roman Province: The Countryside as a Political and Economic Factor," in *ANRW* 2.8 (1977) 385–86 interprets Josephus, *J.W.* 4.444 as a reference to "Jewish collaborators concentrated at Jamnia and Lydda" by Vespasian.

99. Josephus, *J.W.* 3.68; 5.42; 5.290. For Applebaum's and Gichon's interpretation, see n. 97 above.

100. Sepphoris: Josephus, *J.W.* 3.31–34; *Life* 394; Samaria: *J.W.* 3.309.

101. Japha: Josephus, *J.W.* 3.428–431; Jamnia and Ashdod: *J.W.* 4.130; Gischala: *J.W.* 4.120.

102. Josephus, *J.W.* 4.445.

and Ephraim were garrisoned.[103] Josephus clearly does not enumerate all of the sites garrisoned by Vespasian, as can be inferred from the incidental mention of the garrison at Gophna.[104] Of Vespasian's work in the winter 67/68 Josephus writes: "He employed himself in securing with garrisons the villages and smaller towns which had been reduced, posting decurions in the villages and centurions in the towns; he also rebuilt many places that had been devastated."[105]

Vespasian's garrisoning of Idumaea clearly had nothing to do with threats of incursions into Judaea from Nabataean territory in the Negev. The garrisons were there, as in other parts of the country, to secure Roman control of the rebellious Jewish population. This also points to the right interpretation of the presence of Roman garrisons in Judaea in the period between the First Jewish Revolt and the Bar Kochba War, and probably even later. The legion *X Fretensis* was transferred from Syria to Jerusalem as a result of the First Revolt to secure future roman control over the Jews. A Roman unit was stationed at Masada after its capture by Silva, not to block Nabataean incursions, but to prevent its falling into Jewish hands.[106] The *cohors I Thracum milliaria* was stationed at Ḥebron to ensure tight control over the nearby Jewish population, as did its detachment at 'En-Gedi.[107] Roman garrisons may be attested at a few more sites, but surely our knowledge of the deployment of the Roman army is incomplete.[108] And one more aspect of the period should be mentioned here. The Roman victory brought extensive confiscation of Jewish territory by Vespasian, colonization of veteran soldiers, the distribution of much land to Flavian supporters and other Romans, and the uprooting of a large section of the Jewish population. As

103. Josephus, *J.W.* 4.551. There is a chronological difficulty here; basically I accept W. Weber, *Josephus und Vespasian* (1921) 155–57, who dates the event to 69 CE.

104. Josephus, *J.W.* 5.50; for its conquest by Vespasian, see *J.W.* 4.551.

105. Josephus, *J.W.* 4.445 (Thackeray's Loeb translation).

106. Josephus, *J.W.* 7.407. For the Roman occupation of Masada after 73 see Y. Yadin, "Masada and the Limes," *IEJ* 17 (1967) 44–45.

107. See Speidel, "Tile Stamp."

108. See Sh. Applebaum, *Prolegomena to the Study of the Second Jewish Revolt (A.D. 132–135)* (1976) 28–31. That the garrisoning of Jewish settlements was common is implied in Josephus, *J.W.* 7.163, 7.252. It may perhaps be inferred from the following Jewish source: "(They) station *castra* in the townlets to torture brides, so that no man seeks to wed a wife because of them" (*Megilat Ta'anit* 6). The historical setting of the account, however, is obscure and we cannot confidently apply it to the late first or early second century CE. See H. Lichtenstein, "Die Fastenrolle," *Hebrew Union College Annual* 8–9 (1931–32) 304–5.

a result, the Judaean countryside did not remain at rest, and the Roman administration had much work to execute and was sensitive to signs of rebellious tendencies in the Jewish population. This is no more than the background to the problems that required constant military attention and precautions in the Flavian period.[109] A further argument of Applebaum and Gichon has now to be considered:

> Both authors of this brief survey have maintained that solely on the grounds of the peculiar social and demographic conditions on the desert fringes, the immediate taking over of the Herodian border defences by the Flavians was a *condicio sine qua non* for the maintenance of Pax Romana within the confines of Judaea.[110]

Without denying that a problem of defence of a settled area against desert nomads did sometimes exist, the present writer questions the validity of the argument. Various systems could have been developed to defend the settled population of Judaea against nomad incursions, and the need for defence will have varied according to the nature of the threats and the political conditions on both sides of the border. Were the dictum right, the *limes* should have been constructed earlier, following the establishment of the province of Judaea in 6 CE. True, Josephus reports border skirmishes between Nabataeans and Herod, but the bone of contention was Trachonitis, whose local brigands were given support and shelter by the Nabataean Syllaeus; the Negev region is never mentioned. At any rate, no incursions were recorded after Judaea became a province.[111] Applebaum's attempts to find an allusion to such an occurrence is a complete failure.[112] Apparently

109. See A. Büchler, *The Economic Conditions of Judaea after the Destruction of the Second Temple* (1912); Applebaum, "Judaea," 379–95.

110. Applebaum and Gichon, *Israel*, 37.

111. Josephus, *A.J.* 16.271–299. Later, a war was started between Aretas IV and Herod Antipas, who divorced his wife, the daughter of the Nabatean king. The territorial dispute associated with the war concerned Gabala, in Transjordan and not in the Negev. See Josephus, *A.J.* 18.112–125. For a defence of the reading in *A.J.* 18.113 and hence the view that the invasion was of the territory of Philip, and not that of Herod Antipas, see G. W. Bowersock, *Roman Arabia* (1983) 65–68. This of course does not affect my argument. That Herod established a *limes* in southern Judaea is argued by Applebaum, "Initial Date," 3 and Gichon, "Idumaea and the Herodian Limes," *IEJ* 17 (1967) 27–42. I have tried to show that this theory should be rejected. See "Herodes' Army and Security Problems," in *Studies in Judaism*, ed. I. Gilat (1983) 96–97.

112. Applebaum, "Initial Date," 8 interprets Josephus, *A.J.* 20.5 as if Roman forces had to stay in Nabataean territory during Cuspius Fadus' governorship as part of a military operation against the brigand Ptolemy. This is given as evidence for the suggestion that

the Nabataeans knew the difference between the territory of a client king and that of a Roman province. There was no change in this respect after 70 CE.

IV

The conclusions reached in this article may be summarized as follows:

1. The extant written sources indicate that in the fourth to seventh centuries CE there existed a defensive system in the Negev, with which was associated some kind of economic and administrative organization.
2. Some elements of the *limes* system probably started earlier than Diocletian's period, but the institutional character of the system as a whole, comprehending interrelated military, administrative, juridical and economic institutions, is a phenomenon of the later Roman Empire, viz. form the late 3rd century onward.
3. Historical considerations (namely, the relations between the Roman Government and the Jews as well as the Nabataean Kingdom) and the archaeological evidence show that in the second half of the first century CE it was the problem of internal security that attracted the military attention of the Roman authorities of Judaea and not threats from foreign incursions. This state of affairs lasted at least to the war of Bar Kochba.
4. The development of the Palestine *limes* was naturally linked with the history of that part of the Negev which until 106 CE belonged to the Nabataean Kingdom, from then on to the province of Arabia, and from *ca.* 300 to Palestine. There is still a controversy about what

the alleged unstable conditions that necessitated the deployment of Roman forces along the Raphia-Dead Sea line, against the Nabataean territory, had existed even before 70 CE. However, Josephus leaves little doubt that Ptolemy's base was in Judaea (cf. Applebaum, "Judaea," 385 n. 163). The security problem arose from internal conditions in Judaea and hence the case does not show the need to protect Judaea against incursions from across the border. Applebaum's second suggestion ("Initial Date," 8), that the Syrian governor Cassius Longinus increased the garrison force in Judaea because of the unstable conditions in the south, is likewise a misinterpretation of his text, Josephus, *A.J.* 20.7. The governor came with a strong army to Jerusalem, fearing that the demand of Fadus to store the High Priests' vestments in the Antonia might provoke the Jews to rise against the Romans. It was a temporary measure, irrelevant to conditions on the southern frontier.

happened in this area,[113] but as the main line of the Roman garrisons attested in Eusebius, and especially in the *Notitia Dignitatum*, is to the north of the Nabataean region in the Negev, there does not seem to have been direct connection between the later system and what may have existed in the second century.

5. Recent archaeological surveys and excavations have revealed numerous sites dated to Nabataean, Roman and Byzantine periods. Once the accumulated evidence is properly assessed and more reliable distribution maps of the inhabited sites, chronologically arranged, are arrived at, the duties and functions of the Roman army in the Negev, as well as in the whole of Palestine, may be better understood. However, even at this stage it can be asserted that the idea of the *limes* as a defensive line to protect a civilian population from outward incursions cannot be upheld, as this line would cut across an inhabited area that extended far away in all directions.[114]
6. Since several of the sites attributed to the *limes Palaestinae* can no longer be considered military posts, and since the military character of many more sites may be doubted, the idea of the *limes* as a zone of defence in depth is more than questionable. It appears that a reconsideration of the functions of, and the means deployed by, the Roman military system in the Negev is needed.

113. For the problem see G. W. Bowersock, "A Report on Arabia Provincia," *JRS* 61 (1971) 225.

114. See, however, Negev, "Nabataeans," 620–35, 647–60.

4

The Roman Army in the Galilee

Ze'ev Safrai

It is generally accepted among historians that every province of the Roman empire was responsible for financing and supporting military forces within its borders, both in peacetime and at times of war. This means that the larger the army in a particular province the greater the burden on its inhabitants—a view originally challenged by E. Gren and subsequently a number of other scholars.[1] However, while residents of the provinces were theoretically responsible for maintaining the army, in practice, troops were supported by the central government or treasury. Thus, there was a dual cash flow in the Roman empire; on the one hand, monies were sent from all provinces to the central government, while, on the other, the

1. E. Gren, *Kleinasien und die Ostbalkan in der wirtschaftlichen Entwicklung der römischen Kaiserzeit* (Uppsala, 1941); A. H. M. Jones, *The Roman Economy* (Oxford, 1974), 274–89; A. R. Birley, "The Economic Effects of Roman Frontier Policy," in *The Roman West in the Third Century—Part I*, eds. A. King and M. Hoenig (BARIS 109; Oxford, 1981), 39–53; D. C. Burnham and H. B. Johnson, eds., *Invasion and Response: The Case of Roman Britain* (BARBS 73; Oxford 1979); R. MacMullen, "Rural Romanization," *Phoenix* 22 (1968) 337–41; A. L. F. Rivet, "Social and Economic Aspects," in *The Roman Villa in Britain*, ed. A. L. F. Rivet (New York, 1969), 173–216; T. C. F. Blagg and A. C. King, eds., *Military and Civilian in Roman Britain* (BARBS 136; Oxford, 1985), and dozens of other articles.

wealthy provinces (Gaul, Egypt, Syria, etc.) sent funds to border provinces to support large forces concentrated there. The German provinces and Britain are generally portrayed as having been relatively poor provinces accommodating a large concentration of soldiers and thus receiving a significant amount of funding. Much has been written about the influence of this flow of capital on the economies of these provinces and attempts have been made to analyze the various parts of this process and its economic consequences. In what follows, we shall examine the impact of the Roman army on the small province of Judea. The Roman army in Judea underwent many far-reaching changes. Four our purposes, we shall single out four stages:

1. Until 66 C.E., the Roman army in Judea was rather small. The three–six auxiliary units stationed there were composed, in part, of local militia from Sebaste and Caesarea.[2]
2. During the period from 70–120 C.E. (or perhaps a bit later) the Tenth Legion was stationed in Judea together with a number of auxiliary units. Six–twelve auxiliary units were usually attached to a legion, thereby adding about as many soldiers as in the legion itself. We do not have a complete list of all the forces in Judea at the time; it is possible that there were fewer forces than usual, numbering perhaps 10,000 soldiers.
3. From 120 C.E. to the beginning of the fourth century C.E. there were two legions in Palestine—*Legio X Fretensis* and *Legio VI Ferrata*—to which were attached auxiliary units compose of about 25,000 soldiers.[3] *Legio X Fretensis* was based in Judea proper and had military camps in Jerusalem and Caesarea. *Legio VI Ferrata* was based in the Galilee, with its headquarters in Legio (= Kefar ʿOtnai). Numerous auxiliary forces were sent to Palestine during the Bar-Kokhba revolt, but they were there only for a short period.

2. M. Mor, "The Roman Army in Eretz-Israel in the Years A.D. 70–132," in *The Defence of the Roman and Byzantine East*, eds. P. Freeman and D. Kennedy (BARIS 297; Oxford, 1986), 575–602.

3. B. Lifshitz, "Sur la date du transfert de la Legio VI Ferrata en Palestine," *Latomus* 19 (1960) 109–11; B. Isaac and I. Roll, "Judea in the Early Years of Hadrian's Reign," *Latomus* 38 (1979) 54–66; B. Isaac and I. Roll, "Legio II Traiana in Judaea," *ZPE* 33 (1979) 149–56; B. Isaac and I. Roll, "Legio II Traiana—A Reply," *ZPE* 47 (1982) 131–32; D. L. Kennedy, "Legio VI Ferrata: The Annexation and Early Garrison of Arabia," *HSCP* 84 (1980) 283–309.

4. During the fourth century, *Legio VI Ferrata* was removed from Palestine and *Legio X Fretensis* was transferred to the south of Palestine, along the *limes*, with its headquarters in Aila.[4] There as a relatively small number of soldiers in Palestine at this time, probably no more than 7,000–8,000, The shift of units to the *limes* region was of great economic significance. It was necessary, for instance, to extend supply lines to this desert region from the central areas of the province. The specific problems created by this change, however, are evident in the Byzantine period and are beyond the realm of our present discussion.

The above information shows that during the Roman period (approximation 120–300 C.E.) Judea contained the greatest number of Roman troops of any province of its size (approximately 20,000 sq. km.); half of this army was stationed in the Galilee, the area of which was only 25% that of Judea. It is therefore important to examine the impact of the Roman army on the residents of the Galilee. However, due to the dearth of data in this regard we must supplement what we know with inferences from similar conditions in other provinces.

What do we know of the Roman army in the Galilee? The headquarters of the legion which arrived in the Galilee about the year 120 C.E. was, as noted, near Kefar ʿOtnai (Legio). The site was surveyed by G. Schumacher, who claimed to have discovered a small 2–3 dunam enclosure surrounded by a larger one.[5] He suggested that the smaller enclosure was the legionary camp, although hundreds of soldiers could hardly have been quartered within such a small area. At most, this smaller area was the *principia* of the legionary camp. If the larger enclosure (two sides of which clearly existed) were closed on all four sides it would have measured about 20 dunams, which is the usual size of a camp designated for a cohort (about 1,000 soldiers).

A Roman army unit was stationed at Sepphoris,[6] but this was during the time of R. Eliezer b. Hyrcanus, i.e., before 120 C.E. and the "official" arrival of the Roman army in the Galilee. A Roman military fortress (*castrum*, *qatzrin*) was located on the hill above Tiberias, and, based on a reconstruction of the city, would have measured about 20 dunams or the size of a

4. M. Gichon, "The Origin of the Limes Palestinae and the Major Phases in Its Development," in *Studien zu den Militärgrenzen Roms* (Köln, 1967), 175–93.

5. G. Schumacher, *Tell el-Mutesellin* (Leipzig, 1908), 188–90.

6. T. Shabbat 13 (14):9; J. Shabbat 16.15d and parallels.

camp designated for a cohort.[7] A small fortified enclosure was discovered at Mt. Ḥazon,[8] and a Roman camp measuring about 20 dunams was located at Tel Shalem, about 12 kms. South of Beth Shean. The southern gate of Beth Shean was referred to as the "gate of the camp" (*pilei de-qampon*) since it led to the Roman camp at Tel Shalem. A number of structures have been discovered at this camp, as well as inscription mentioning expeditionary troops (*vexilla*) from *Legio VI* and an impressive statue of Hadrian.[9]

We thus have evidence of three camps for cohorts. The rest of the army was probably stationed in rural outposts. The situation would explain the repeated reports of confrontation between the Roman army and Galilean Jews attested by numerous rabbinic traditions.[10] An encounter with the Roman government at this time probably meant running into a local military unit or troops passing through the region.

As indicated above, the commanders of the Roman army had recourse to the resources available in a specific province as well as to external funds for maintaining their armies. The tax rate was not affected by the presence of military forces in a province, since the tax base in the various provinces was more or less the same. It is known that taxes were particularly high in Judea[11] and that a special tax was levied on the Jews after 70 C.E. If this small province also had to support the military forces stationed there, it would have been an unbearable and indeed unique burden. We have no indication that this was the case. Based on the above and on the somewhat gratuitous assumption that the tax base levied on the provinces was the

7. J. 'Eruvin 5.22b. See also M. Avi-Yonah, *Carta's Atlas of the Period of the Second Temple, the Mishnah and the Talmud* (Jerusalem, 1966), 92, map 42 (Hebrew); M. Avi-Yonah, "Newly Discovered Latin and Greek Inscriptions," *QDAP* 12 (1946), 88; S. S. Miller, *Studies in the History and Traditions of Sepphoris* (Leiden, 1984), 15–46.

8. D. Bahat, "A Roof Tile of the Legio VI Ferrata and Pottery Vessels form Ḥorvat Ḥazon," *IEJ* 24 (1974) 160–69.

9. G. Foerester, "A Cuirassed Bronze Statue of Hadrian," *'Atiqot* [English Series] 17 (1985) 139–57. Eusebius (early fourth century C.E.), in his *Onomasticon* (*Eusebius Werke*, ed. E. Klostermann [Leipzig, 1904], III.1, 152; ed. E. Melamed, *The Onomastikon of Eusebius* [Jerusalem, 1966], no. 813), mentions Shalem but not the military camp there, even thought he was wont to do so in his description of other sites having military camps. Eusebius still refers to the Jezreel Valley as the "Campus Legionis"; perhaps the camp at Shalem was only a temporary one and was abandoned before the end of the third century. This matter relates to the larger issue of sources of the *Onomasticon* and will not be dealt with here.

10. S. Krauss, *Persia and Rome in the Talmud and Midrashim* (Jerusalem, 1948).

11. Appian, *Syr.* 50.

same, it is possible to estimate the inflow of capital needed to support the army in Judea.

K. Hopkins has suggested a method of arriving at cost quantification of the Roman army, whereby the government levied a tax of 10% of the empire's gross national product (GNP).[12] Moreover, about half of Rome's expense went towards support of the army.[13] Hopkins does not include unique or unusual income, such as that due from estates, since this is impossible to calculate. He does, however, take into account the role of the residents of the empire in supporting the corrupt system of tax collection. In economic terms, it has made little difference whether the monies went directly to the Roman fiscus or to the corrupt freedmen collecting the taxes.

Hopkins' calculations of the cost of the army, which is based on the rate of salary paid to its soldiers, are too low. It is known that the Roman soldier had to pay for his food and that of his horses out of his salary. There is no certainty, however, that they were charged realistic prices; there are indications that the prices were lower than market value. If Hopkins' cost estimates are to be raised, then the taxation rates must be changed as well. The figure 10% of the GNP seems to be too low, as the accepted rate of payment in estates was 33.3% in grain fields and up to 50% in orchards and the like.[14] Even in Judea, payment of up to 50% of the produce was customary. This would seem to indicate that the average family had to sustain itself, albeit with difficulty, on half the produce it succeeded in cultivating. Had the rate of taxation been only 10%, the farmer would had about 40% more than his subsistence needs, which could have been marketed at a profit, placing him in a better economic position than we know him to have had. It is possible that the tenant farmer had larger tracts of land at his disposal than the average independent farmer, but the question still pertains. Under the rule of John Hyrcanus II, the Roman empire levied a tax of 12.5% from wheat fields in Judea. Another 10% was the customary percentage handed over to the semi-autonomous rulers and the Temple.[15] Is it possible that when autonomous rule was later abolished the tax rate was lowered?

12. K. Hopkins, "Taxes and Trade in the Roman Empire (200 B.C.–A.D. 400)," *JRS* 70 (1980) 101–25.

13. M. H. Crawford, "Money and Exchange in the Roman World," *JRS* 60 (1970) 40–48.

14. A. C. Johnson, et al., eds, *Ancient Roman Statutes* (Austin, 1971), 173–75.

15. Josephus, *A.J.* 14.203.

Although Hopkins' estimations appear low, it is still impossible to determine the exact tax rate in Judea or the Roman empire in general. We shall, however, use his low estimates in in the course of our discussion, bearing in mind that when the tax burden becomes greater, the support of the army by the residents becomes greater; this, in turn, leads to a larger influx of capital into the province for maintenance of the army.

Judea comprised less than 1% of the entire Roman empire. It would thus seem likely that the tax revenues from that province did not exceed 1%. For the sake of caution, however, we shall assume that the tax income from Judea comprised 1.5% of the empire's total revenue. Approximately 8% of the Roman forces of the empire (25,000 soldiers) were encamped in Judea; the empire would have had to allot 4% of its revenue for the support of these units (assuming that support of the army constituted 50% of Roman expenses). Thus, for every 1.5 dinars which reached the Roman treasury from Judea, it was necessary to allocate an additional 2.5 dinars to support the army there, and an additional amount to maintain the army station in the Galilee. If taxes constituted 10% of the GNP of every province in the Roman empire, the Roman government had to allocate Palestine 16.6% of its GNP for this provinces' military expenses. The tax burden undoubtedly was greater, as well as the expenses for support of the army. The flow of capital to the provinces would have had to have been even higher. Not all this money actually reached the provinces, since some of it was saved for the soldiers' salaries when they left the province. Even if these numbers are somewhat inflated, it is clear that the contribution of the Roman army to the province, especially to the Galilee, was of great importance to the economy of the province and the region.

The land was devastated after the Bar-Kokhba revolt; income from taxes was especially low. During this time, and at least until 130 C.E.,[16] additional legions were stationed in Palestine, thus necessitating a large inflow of capital to support them. In this manner the Roman army unwittingly helped restore somewhat the economy of the province. There is evidence that commodities were transferred from Egypt at this time;[17] during the period of anarchy, when governmental or Imperial support was often delayed, the legions took care of themselves—at the expense of

16. S. Applebaum, *Prolegomena to the Study of the Second Jewish Revolt (A.D. 132–135)* (BARIS 7; Oxford, 1976), 25–27; L. J. F. Keppie, "The Legionary Garrison of Judea under Hadrian," *Latomus* 32 (1973) 859–64.

17. *P.Ryl.* 2.189 [[= *DMIPERP* §189]].

the local residents—thereby adding yet another economic burden to the already existing economic catastrophe.

It is likely that the army based in Judea had at its disposal large sums of money to buy food supplies, clothing, and weapons on a regular basis. Cassius Dio, for example, cites a specific instance when Roman forces bought weapons from local manufacturers in Judea.[18] This was probably the case regarding other army supplies as well. Although there has been much scholarly debate regarding the provision of supplies to the Roman forces,[19] we have no information on this matter for Judea. Since the army was relatively large there, it presumably had relatively greater buying power than in most other provinces.

This seems to have been the case regarding the supply of linen. The army probably received supplies from the Imperial weaveries in Scythopolis, thought some linen, at least, was undoubtedly bought on the open market from other countries that produced flax (e.g., Egypt).[20] The food supplies of the Roman army were naturally dependent upon the customs storehouses, and it clear that taxes in kind or commodities were usually earmarked for the forces regularly garrisoned in the province. It seems likely, therefore, that a good deal of the tax debt in Judea was paid in kind. Talmudic literature contains many halakhic statements concerning taxes in cash and in kind. This relation between the amount of taxes paid in cash and that paid in kind is difficult to determine, however, and the situation in the provinces, perhaps apart from Egypt, is not very clear.

Every province apparently had its own policy. In Judea, it seems likely that the Romans would have been more interested in being paid in kind so that the goods collected could be transferred to the units as part of their food supplies. This, however, was not always the case; a number of Talmudic references indicate that commodities which reached these storehouses were sold to the general public. Two independent traditions specifically

18. Cassius Dio 69.12.2; R. MacMullen, "Inscription on Armor and the Supply of Arms in the Roman Empire," *AJA* 64 (1960) 23–40; R. MacMullen, "Rural Romanization"; R.W. Davies, "The Supply of Animals to the Roman Army and the Remount System," *Latomus* 28 (1969) 429–59; M. Speidel, "The Prefect's Horse Guard and the Supply of Weapons to the Roman Army," in *Roman Army Studies* (Amsterdam, 1984), I, 329–31.

19. P. S. Middleton, "Army Supply in Roman Gaul: An Hypothesis for Roman Britain," in *Invasion and Response*, 81–98; J. Lesquier, *L'armée romaine d'Egypte d'Auguste à Dioclétien* (Cairo, 1918).

20. E. Wipszycka, "Das Textilhandwerk und der Staat im römischen Agypten," *Archiv für Papyrusforschung* 18 (1966) 1–22; J. P. Wild, "Romans and Natives in the Textile Technology," in *Invasion and Response*, 123–31.

mention merchants (from the Galilee) who bought commodities (wheat?) from a storehouse in Jamnia (= Yavneh), which was specifically referred to as government property. One of these traditions dates to the Ushan period (140–180 C.E.);[21] the second involves two sages, R. Judah the Prince and R. Yose b. Judah (180–225 C.E.).[22] A number of laws deal specifically with produce bought from such storehouses,[23] and the purchase of produce there seems to have been a common occurrence. It seems that even in a small province the government preferred to sell commodities collected as taxes and to transfer the money to military units.

Perhaps the structure of the local economy dictated this situation. Units stationed in the plains, such as those at Jamnia, had an abundance of grain at their disposal while others stationed in the Galilee suffered from more limited grain supplies. The surplus of tax revenues in kind, from olive oil or flax, could not compensate for the lack of grain. This was, of course, the result of the trend at the time to cultivate less grain in the Galilee in order to free lands for the cultivation of other crops. Moreover, the Roman soldiers stationed in the provinces usually enjoyed a diet which was much richer in meat that that of the local residents.[24] There was not much meat production in Palestine, nor was pig-meat, a staple of the Roman troops, readily available there. This imbalance between the agricultural system and the commodities paid as taxes on the one hand, and the needs of the Roman army on the other, probably resulted in the sale of local tax commodity surplus in order to purchase the other supplies. A Roman law from the end of the fourth century C.E. provides additional testimony for this economic interaction in Palestine and particularly in the region of the *limes*.[25] We shall return later to the modes of tax collection and their implications.

Based on our above analysis, it appears that the Roman army had an extremely positive influence on the economy of Palestine. Since the support of the standing army there required an inflow of 16.6% of Palestine's GNP,

21. T. Demai 1:12–13.

22. Genesis Rabbah 76:8; J. Theodor and C. Albeck, *Bereschit Rabba* (Berlin, 1912), II, 960.

23. T. Demai 1:11–14.

24. R. W. Davies, "The Roman Military Diet," *Britannia* 2 (1971) 122–42; R. W. Davies, "The Daily Life of the Roman Soldier under the Principate," in *ANRW* eds. H. Temporini and W. Haase (Berlin, 1974), II.1, 299–338; A. King, "Animal Bones and the Dietary Identity of Military and Civilian Groups in Roman Britain, Germany and Gaul," in *Military and Civilian in Roman Britain*, 187–92.

25. *Codex Theodosianus* 7.4.30.

this money was used to buy various supplies from the residents of the province. Moreover, providing supplies for the army encouraged further business activity.

***

The presence of such a large army in a small province undoubtedly had many effects on the country's socio-economic framework. We shall examine the extent to which R. MacMullen's short summary of this matter,[26] as well as those studies mentioned at the beginning of the article,[27] pertain to Palestine.

1. The Roman soldier received a rather good salary. From the period of Diocletian wages wereabout 300 dinars; auxiliary forces received 75% this amount.[28] The soldier set aside a fixed sum to pay the army for his food supplies. He could save some of his money in the camp treasury and withdraw it only upon his release. Another part of his salary, which is impossible to estimate, was used for personal expenses or towards purchasing communal sacrifices. The amount set aside for savings determined the sum which the soldier could spend in the province. Undoubtedly, there was no set rule and each soldier made his own decision in this regard.

   We do not know how much money a soldier spent in his camp. We do know, however, that large civilian settlements (*canaba*) and small ones (*pagi*) that sprang up around the military camps usually housed people who provided services for the military. Soldiers' families lived there as well, even though they were not recognized by Roman law.[29] It is likely that the situation as similar in the Galilee; it might explain why the village of Legio, the civilian settlement next

26. MacMullen, "Rural Romanization."

27. See literature above, n. 1.

28. Speidel, "The Prefect's Horse Guard," 83–90; R. Develin, "The Army Pay Raises under Severus and Caracalla, and the Question of Annona militaris," *Latomus* 30 (1971) 687–95; G. R. Watson, "The Pay of the Roman Army," *Historia* 5 (1956) 332–40; G. R. Watson, "The Pay of the Urban Forces," in *Acta of the Fifth Epigraphic Congress* (Cambridge, 1971), 413–16; H. C. Boren, "Studies Relating to the Stipendium Militum," *Historia* 32 (1983) 427–60; P. A. Brunt, "Pay and Superannuation in the Roman Army," *PBSR* 18 (1950) 50–71.

29. *RMR* 68–70, 77, 83.

to the *Legio VI Ferrata* headquarters, contained a theater,[30] since no other village in Judea or Galilee had one. In the third century C.E. this same village became the *polis* Maximianopolis. It would appear, from the large number of Byzantine inscriptions found at Beer Sheva and from the relatively large size of the town, that this civilian settlement also developed out of a *canaba* of the military headquarters of the *limes*. There were undoubtedly other such settlements throughout Palestine.

2. Since the army camp served as a consumer of services and supplies, it perforce became a merchandising center surrounded by markets. We have no information about this phenomenon in the Galilee, but it seems to have been fairly common in other provinces at the time. An indication of this may be a weight measure of the Fifteenth Legion found in Palestine.[31]

3. The army was a consumer of technology and Roman lifestyle. The soldiers and officers of the legion consumed large quantities of high quality wine and used Roman pottery[32] and other such implements.[33] This encouraged local manufacturers to raise the quality of their goods and local residents to buy them. Tiles stamped with the imprint of *Legio VI Ferrata* have been discovered at Ḥorvat Ḥazon, Kefar Ḥananya, and Legio;[34] however, it is not known whether these finds are indicative of a local factory which produced for the Roman army or for the villages (see below). Another factory for the manufacture of such tiles for the Tenth Legion was found near Jerusalem, although here, too, it is not clear whether this was a civilian or military establishment.[35] Bricks from this factory have been found in Joppa (60 kms. from Jerusalem)

30. See above, n. 5.

31. S. Qedar, *Münz Zentrum Auktion* (Köln, 1981), XLV, 45.

32. P. S. Middleton, "The Roman Army and Long Distance Trade," in *Trade and Famine in Classical Antiquity*, eds. P. Garnsey and C. R. Whittaker (Cambridge, 1983), 75–83; cf. C. R. Tchernia, "Italian Wine Trade in Gaul and in the Republic," in: *Trade in and Ancient Economy*, eds. P. Garnsey, K. Hopkins and C. R. Whittaker (Berkeley, 1983), 87–104; P. Green, "Pottery and the Roman Army," in *Invasion and Response*, 99–106.

33. For example, see King, "Animal Bones," 187–92.

34. Bahat, "A Roof Tile"; D. Adan-Bayewitz, "Kefar Ḥananya 1986," *IEJ* 37 (1987) 178.

35. D. Barag, "Brick Stamp-Impressions of the *Legio X Fretensis*," *Eretz-Israel* 8 (1967) 168–82 (Hebrew).

and at Ramat Rachel south of Jerusalem, the latter site clearly having been civilian.[36]

4. The army manufactured utensils and sold them in civilian markets (see above).
5. The army provided services (such as bath houses) in order to demonstrate to the local population the quality of the Roman lifestyle.
6. The army provided and built services for its own use which also benefited the province itself. It constructed many roads in Judea and the Galilee, such as the road network between Scythopolis and Caesarea, Diocaesarea (i.e., Sepphoris), and Legio.[37] Many sources indicate, however, that the local population often paved these roads or provided for their upkeep through the various *liturgiae* imposed by the Romans.[38] M. Avi-Yonah published an inscription testifying to the contribution of two villages near Ptolemais to the construction of the road from Ptolemais to Tyre.[39] Also sections of local aqueducts, such as those at Caesarea, were occasionally built by Roman troops.
7. The army served as a roving ambassador of Roman culture, religion, and economics. At times, however, the presence of large Roman troops created difficulties for local residents because of the numerous *angariae* imposed on them. During certain seasons of the year, a large military presence could result in shortages of various commodities and rising prices, as once was the case in Antioch.[40] On the whole, however, the presence of the military was beneficial to the economy of the province. This attitude might explain why rabbinic literature generally evinces a positive attitude to the Roman army in spite of the marked hostility towards Roman rule expressed in this same literature.[41]

36. Contra Y. Aharoni, *Excavations at Ramat Rachel* (Rome, 1962–64), I–II.

37. Isaac and Roll, "Judea"; B. Isaac and I. Roll, *Roman Roads in Judea, I: The Legio-Scythopolis Road* (BARIS 141; Oxford, 1982).

38. W. H. C. Frend, "A Third Century Inscription Relating to *Angareia* in Phrygia," *JRS* 46 (1956) 46–56.

39. Avi-Yonah, "Newly Discovered Latin and Greek Inscriptions," 85–86.

40. G. Downey, "The Economic Crisis in Antioch under Julian the Apostate," in *Studies in Roman Economic and Social History in Honor of A. C. Johnson*, eds. P. R. Coleman-Norton, et al. (Princeton, 1951), 312–21; B. Isaac, *The Limits of Empire* (1st ed.; Oxford, 1990), 269–310.

41. S. Safrai, "The Relations between the Roman Army and the Jews of Eretz Israel

> Rabbinic traditions attest to cooperation and reciprocity between the army and local populations of Palestine in matters of everyday life. Thus, for example, soldiers stationed in Sepphoris sought to aid in extinguishing a fire at the house of a senior Jewish official.[42] In spite of the general hostility to Roman rule, good relations with local troops might have developed, at least on a personal level. Undoubtedly, such positive relations had great economic potential.

Another means of providing supplies for the army was through the *territorium legiones*. A legion was given a territory from which it could demand the provision of its supplies, in a manner similar to that of the Roman century or any other sub-unit which received an area that was to provide for its needs. The details of this system are not entirely clear, such as whether the legion received a government estate or whether the army or the soldiers collected the usual taxes from the *territorium*.[43] Interestingly, rabbinic literature contains references to officers functioning as tax collectors.[44] Such a *territorium* might have existed in the Jezreel Valley, near the camp of *Legio VI Ferrata*,[45] since the Jezreel Valley contained government estates; its exact location, however, is unknown. The system, therefore, apparently existed in the Galilee, but, due to insufficient data, it is impossible to determine its economic implications.

after the Destruction of the Second Temple," *Roman Frontier Studies 1967*, ed. S. Applebaum (Tel Aviv, 1971), 224–30; see also D. Sperber, "Angaria in Rabbinic Literature," *L'antiquité Classique* 38 (1969) 164–68.

42. T. Shabbat 3:9, S. Lieberman, *Tosefta Ki-Fshutah: Moed* (New York, 1955), 60; cf. J. Shabbat 16.7.15d; J. Yoma 8.5.45b; J. Dedarim 4.9.38d; B. Shabbat 121a.

43. M. Kandler, "Zum Territorium Legiones von Carnuntum," in *Limes: Akten es XI Internationales Limeskongresses*, ed. J. Fritz (Budapest, 1975), 145–54; A. Schulten, "Das Territorum Legiones," *Hermes* 29 (1984) 481–516.

44. D. Sperber, "The Centurion as a Tax Collector," *Latomus* 28 (1969) 186–88.

45. Contra Isaac and Roll, *Roman Roads I*, 105–6.

5

Jewish Military Forces in the Roman Service

Jonathan P. Roth

INTRODUCTION

Jewish military forces played an important role in protecting Roman Palestine, including a significant contribution to suppressing various anti-Jewish revolt, most notably the Great Revolt of 66–73 CE. Indeed, Jews (in the religious if not the ethnic sense) served in the regular Roman army, and Jews in both senses fought side-by-side with Romans, and provided an important command function, both in peace and war. This role is generally ignored, even by books specifically detailing Roman, and pro-Roman forces.[1]

1. See, e.g., Mordechai Gichon, "Aspects of a Roman Army in War According to the *Bellum Judaicum* of Josephus," in *Defence of the Roman and Byzantine East* (ed. David L. Kennedy and Philip Freeman; BARIS 297; Oxford: BAR, 1986), 287–310; Benjamin Isaac, "Reflections on the Roman Army in the East," in *Defence of the Roman and Byzantine East* (ed. David L. Kennedy and Philip Freeman; BARIS 297; Oxford: BAR, 1986), 383–95; Jonathan T. Price, *Jerusalem under Siege: The Collapse of the Jewish State 66–70 CE* (Brill's Series in Jewish Studies 3; Leiden: Brill, 1992); Adrian Goldsworthy, "Community under Pressure: The Roman Army at the Siege of Jerusalem," in *The Roman Army*

Before discussing "Jews in the Roman Service," however, one needs to consider the meaning of this term. The distinction between "Jews" and "Romans," "Greeks," "Pagans," or "Gentiles" is often exaggerated. In the first place, there was very little physical distinction between the soldiers on either side: Livy famously remarks that if one took the standards and armament away, one could not tell the difference between Romans and Carthaginians (21.43.16). Much of ancient, and modern ethnic terminology refers region or language, but not without ambiguity. When the Romans referred to Syrians, for example, they might mean the inhabitants of Syria, whether Greek, Aramaic or even Latin speaking, or they might mean anyone who spoke Syrian, even in the first century, a common way of referring to Aramaic. Thus, a Jew who lived in Syria or an Aramaic-speaking Jew might accurately be described as a Syrian. Josephus refers to a Syrian centurion in the Roman army named Gallus (*J. W.* 4.37), who can clearly speak Aramaic, but we are at a loss to know what his "ethnicity" is.

The use of religion as an ethnic marker had begun—the terms *Ioudaioi* or *Judei* were sometimes used in this way, but even then it was ambiguous. Jews rejecting modernist tendencies of a Philo or a Paul might refer to their followers as "Greeks." Conversely, the Romans would lump all different sorts of eastern monotheistic God-worshippers as "Jews." Indeed, in the first century the religious distinctions between Jews, Samaritans, and Christians is so slight that all could quite accurately be called Jews in the religious if not ethnic sense of the word. Conversely, "Roman" might be a linguistic or a regional marker, but in the first century, it was also a political appellation. There were many Roman colonies in the east, not to mention half a dozen legions and tens or even hundred of thousands of individual Roman citizens. These individuals may have migrated from Rome, or their ancestors might have done, but many others were non-Latin speakers who had obtained Roman citizenship, either themselves or had inherited it. Paul and Flavius Josephus are famous examples. These individuals may, depending on the context, have been referred to, again quite accurately as "Romans." Just as the Romans "lumped" all Easterners together as Syrians, Jews referred to Greeks and Romans collectively as *kittim*, literally Cretans.[2] It is quite possible that Greek-speaking Jews and particularly

as a Community (ed. Adrian Goldsworthy and Ian Haynes; JRASupp 34; Oxford: BAR, 1999), 197–210. An exception is Menachem Mor, "The Roman Army in Eretz-Israel in the Years A.D. 70–132," in *The Defence of the Roman and Byzantine East* (ed. Philip Freeman and David L. Kennedy; BARIS 297; Oxford: BAR, 1986), 578.

2. Compare the Spanish *gringo* from *griego* (meaning "Greek") and the Arabic *Franj*, from Frank.

those with Roman citizenship may have been called *kittim* in our Hebrew and Aramaic sources.

Despite the fact that Jewish soldiers are commonplace in the modern world, scholars still underplay the role that ancient Jews played in the military forces of Western Asia in the first millennium B.C. The role of Jews in the Persian military is beyond the scope of this paper, but is attested by the famous Elephantine papyri. In his study of the Ptolemaic military, Jean Lesquier identified three basic elements of the Hellenistic military force: military settlers (*katoikoi*), mercenaries, and indigenous inhabitants.[3] We find Jews serving in all of these categories in antiquity. Indeed, by the first century, Jews had had long tradition of military service, both at home and especially in foreign service. Indeed, in this respect they might be called the Scots of the ancient Near East.

The Hellenistic monarchies established after Alexander the Great's conquests used the military settlement system widely, probably taking it over from the Persians. While Jews are not normally associated with the armies of this period, they are in fact very active as soldiers. In fact, the study done by Lesquier of the Ptolemaic army suggests that at some points Jews made up as much as 20% of the its military forces.[4] By the first century, Jews seem to have made up a major part of the officer corps, and we know of two Jews who commanded all Ptolemaic forces. Jewish and Samaritan participation in the Seleucid army is less well attested, but almost certainly existed.

Josephus quotes a letter from Antiochus III ordering the settlement of 2,000 Jews from "Mesopotamia and Babylonia" to Lydia and Phrygia as military settlers.[5] There are inscriptions attesting to the existence of this settlement, which was probably called Ioudda, and lasted for hundreds of years. Indeed, it is quite possible that the "Hellenizing Jews" whom the Maccabees opposed were made up in part of Jewish soldiers and veterans serving the Seleucids. Babylonian Jews were particularly martial in this period, forming at one point their own state in southern Mesopotamia. They may well have served in the Parthian military. There is clearly nothing

3. Jean Lesquier, *Les Institutions militaire de l'Egypte sous les Lagides* (Paris: Leroux, 1911), 11–29. For the term, see the discussion in Bezalel Bar-Kokhba, *The Seleucid Army: Organization and Tactics in the Great Campaigns* (corr. ed.; Cambridge Classical Studies; Cambridge: Cambridge University Press, 1979), 22–26.

4. Lesquier, *Institutions militaire*, 11–29.

5. Josephus, *A.J.* 12.147–153; *CIJ* 2.775; see Bar-Kokhba, *Seleucid Army*, 45 and 114.

about Jewishness that interfered with doing military service for a foreign army.

We know very little about the Hasmonean military, but certainly Jews served in it. It is likely that they used the military settlement system, probably taking over units that had previously served the Seleucids. In addition, there seems to have been some sort of levy. During the revolt of 88 BCE, tens of thousands of Jews fought on both sides, and probably only a small portion were professionals or military settlers. When the Idumeans were forcibly converted, we begin to see them serving in the Jewish army. While probably speaking Arabic rather than Aramaic, the Idumeans appear to have worshipped the Jewish God and so would have been Jews in this sense.

THE HERODIAN ARMY

It is worth noting that from the time Herod took power, all the way down to the time of the Jewish War, it was the Herodian army, the Jewish Royal Army, that provided both internal and external security for the Romans in Palestine. Whatever the make-up of the Hasmonean military, this army did not survive the civil war, the Parthian invasion and the Roman reconquest. Thus, Herod seems to have built his army almost from scratch. While there certainly were some changes, the military forces of the region remained basically the same from the reign of Herod, through his successors Archelaus, Antipas, Philip, Agrippa I and II, down to the end of the Jewish War. Even the so-called Roman garrison was in fact only a number of Herodian units put in Roman service. Most, perhaps all of these soldiers were Aramaic speakers and Jewish (i.e., Israelite), by religion. Conversely, the idea of a Temple Police and the Captain of the Temple arresting and imprisoning people under the authority of the Temple or the High Priest is almost certainly a fiction of the Gospels and Acts.[6]

Although little attention has been paid to it, we are actually remarkably well informed about the organization of the Herodian military forces.[7] The bulk of it can be called Jewish, in the religious if not ethnic sense of the word. It is true that Herod's bodyguard (*somatophylakes*, *doryphoroi*) was

6. See below, pages 87–88.

7. Contra Jonathan Price, "The Enigma of Philip ben Jakimos," *Historia* 40 (1991): 77 n. 2. Cf. M. H. Gracey, "The Armies of Judean Client Kings," in *Defence of the Roman and Byzantine East* (ed. David L. Kennedy and Philip Freeman; BARIS 297; Oxford: BAR, 1986), 311–323.

made up of Gauls, Thracians and Germans.[8] These units, however, were probably relatively small, perhaps a thousand men in total at most, and in any case, we hear nothing of them after Herod's funeral. They were probably disbanded, either by Archelaus, Herod's son, or by the Romans when they took control in 6 CE.

HERODIAN MILITARY ORGANIZATION

Like all Hellenistic forces, the mainstay of the Herodian army consisted of soldiers in military settlements. The first, and most important, of Herod's military settlement was at Sebaste, which initially consisted of 6,000 men.[9] These troops were ultimately absorbed into the Roman army (probably in 6 CE) and formed most, if not all, of the Roman garrison up to the outbreak of the Jewish War. The Samaritans in general considered, and still consider, themselves to be the true Children of Israel. Jewish sources sometimes scornfully refer to them at Cuthaeans or even *kittim*, but there is no reason to think that the Samaritan forces in Herodian service were pagans.

Another significant military settlement was at Bathyra, in Batanaea (Bashan). This unit of Babylonian Jewish horse-archers first entered the country in 20 BCE under their commander Zamaris. He came from Parthia; indeed, he may have been a military commander there and be defecting to the Romans. He approached Sentius Saturninus, but it was Herod who settled them in Batanaea in a military colony called Bathyra. Zamaris was offered freedom from taxation in exchange for military service. Zamaris' settlement consisted of 500 horse archers and 100 "relatives" (Josephus, *A.J.* 17.24). Josephus claims that by the time of Zamaris' grandson, Philip ben Jakimus, the Bathyran unit was as large as the rest of King Agrippa's army combined (*A.J.* 17.3). This is probably an exaggeration, but the force may have numbered several thousand by the mid-first century and been the mainstay of the Herodian army.

There was an Idumaean settlement of 2,000 men, but we do not know of its exact location. These troops revolted on Herod's death (Josephus, *J.W.* 2.55). The Idumeans were forcibly converted to Judaism by the

8. Josephus, *A.J.* 16.198–199; *J.W.* 1.397, 1.672.

9. Josephus, *J.W.* 1.403, 2.55; *A.J.* 15.293, 17.266. Sebaste was a refounding of the colony of Samaria, established as a military colony by Alexander himself. It played an important role in Seleucid resistance to the Hasmoneans and was probably destroyed by Alexander Jannaeus (*A.J.* 13.375–378).

Hasmoneans, but while we are not well-informed, there is no reason to doubt that Jewish belief and ritual was widespread or even ubiquitous, even among the Idumean soldiers in Herodian service.

We hear of three other military settlement: at Esbonitis (Heshbon), east of the Dead Sea in Peraea, an area which apparently was mainly inhabited by Jews, at Gaba (north of Mount Carmel) and at Trachonitis (Hebrew: Argob), located to the east of the Jordan.[10] The latter unit was made up of 3,000 men and was probably stationed at the fort whose remains are at 'Ein Targhuna today.[11] According to Josephus, it was destroyed in the revolt of 10–9 BCE (*A.J.* 16.292), but we hear again of forces from Trachonitis, specifically archers, in the revolt of 4 BCE. This is significant, as it suggests that such military colonies might be re-established when destroyed.

Herod built and renovated a number of fortresses, Masada, Alexandrium, Hyrcania, Cypros and Herodium, in addition to the tower overlooking the Temple, formerly called Baris, and now the Antonia. All had to be garrisoned and were commanded by an official called, in Greek, a *phrourarch*. In addition, there were fortified towers (*pyrgoi*).[12] There is archaeological evidence for forts and towers along the Negev border.[13] We also hear of royal arsenals (*hoplothekai*; Josephus, *J.W.* 2.56). We know very little about the garrisoning of these fortified points. They may have been garrisoned by mercenaries or been satellites of military settlements in the region or represented "mini-settlements."

There is the question of militia, what Lesquier called indigenous forces.[14] During the Jewish War, Simon bar Giora raises his forces, according to Josephus, first from freed slaves and the *poneroi* or plebs (*J.W.* 4.508). Subsequently, however, he draws from the "citizen levy (*demotikon* ... *oligon*) who obeyed him like a king" (*J.W.* 4.510). This may refer to Jewish property-owners subject to military service. When Simon's army, now numbering 20,000 marches on Idumaea, the leaders (*archontes*), mustered (*athroisantes*) a force of 25,000 of the "most warlike" (*machimotaton*; *J.W.* 4.516). The "leaders" are probably the toparch's *strategos* and other military

10. Josephus, *A.J.* 15.294; *J.W.* 2.36. The exact location of Gaba is unknown.

11. Josephus, *A.J.* 16.271, 16.295; Shimon Applebaum, *Judaea in Hellenistic and Roman Times: Historical and Archaeological Essays* (SJLA 40; Leuven: Brill Academic, 1989), 67–68. Applebaum's suggestion that the unit, along with the Bathyran archers, was moved to Libya by Augustus, has little to recommend it.

12. Josephus, *A.J.* 18.147; see Gracey, "Armies of Judean Client Kings," 318.

13. Gracey, "Armies of Judean Client Kings," 318.

14. Gracey, "Armies of Judean Client Kings," 317.

officers, but Gracey is right to doubt that in this case it involves a regular militia.

When Herod died in 4 BCE, Archelaus, his son, oversaw a parade of his soldiers (*stratiotai*) marching in bands or contingents (*kata stiphos*). The same term is used a few lines later to refer to the royal bodyguard (*doryphoroi*) of Thracians, Germans and Gauls who marched in Herod's funerals (Josephus, *J.W.* 1.672). Elsewhere, however, we hear of the *speire* as the basic unit (Josephus, *J.W.* 2.13). At one point, Josephus refers to five Roman cohorts (*speiras*; Josephus, *J.W.* 1.301) and five Jewish ones operating together. Our sources generally use Greek terminology to refer to the titles of officers and the names of military units, but it is usually difficult to say if they are being used as technical terms, in some general sense or translating a Latin term. *Chiliarch* for example, might refer to the Seleucid officer commanding a thousand-man infantry unit, or be a general term for a sub-commander or translate the Latin *tribunus militum*. *Speire* might be the Seleucid unit of 256 men, a general term for unit, or translate *cohors* an Roman infantry unit of 480 men. There is no evidence for the use of any Hebrew or Aramaic military terminology by the Herodians. It is quite likely, however, that it was. Herod had served alongside Romans all through the civil wars and was particularly close to Mark Antony. It is probable that when he built up his forces, he organized, trained and armed them in the Roman fashion, and probably used Roman officers in addition to his own Jewish one. In fact, many of these Jewish officers may well themselves served in the army or the Roman Republic before serving under Herod.

In his discussion of the revolt of 4 BCE, Josephus mentions a general (*strategos*) being sent into the temple to negotiate, Thackeray muses that this might be the *sagan* or Temple Captain, but this is doubtless the commander-in-chief of Archelaus' armies.[15] While the king was technically commander-in-chief, and sometimes actually led the army, there seems to have been a commander of all military forces called the *strategos*. In the course of fighting, Josephus mentions two commanders: Rufus over the cavalry and Gratus over the infantry (*J.W.* 2.52). In the narrative, it becomes clear that they are not merely commanders over the Samaritans, but over the entire army (*J.W.* 2.58). It is likely therefore, that this Gratus is the unnamed *strategos* mentioned above. Under Agrippa II, it is Philip

15. Josephus, *J.W.* 2.9; H. St. J. Thackeray, *Josephus in Nine Volumes* (LCL 203; Cambridge: Harvard University Press, 1927), 2.326 n. a.

ben Jakimos, the grandson of Zamaris, who is the *strategos* of the Jewish army.[16] Since military command was often hereditary in the Near Eastern tradition (and not just), it is possible that his father Jakimos, and perhaps Zamaris himself had held this post under previous Herodians.

The governors of the toparchies, however, were also called *strategoi*, and they may to have been in charge of security within their districts. We hear of Achiab, the king's cousin, who seems to be the toparch of Idumaea commanding troops (Josephus, *J.W.* 2.55). We also hear of Ptolemy, who was a "friend" of both Herod and of Archelaus, commanding troops, but it is not clear if this is a special command due to the revolt (Josephus, *J.W.* 2.64).

There was also an officer named the *hipparchos*, literally cavalry commander. In Seleucid terminology this was either the command of a 500-man cavalry unit—the *hipparchia* or the commander of all of the cavalry. In the Herodian military the term seems to have had this latter meaning. In the army of Agrippa II, the *hipparch* Darius commanded 2,000 cavalry, a force which included the Bathyrans (Josephus, *J.W.* 2.421).

In the description of Herod's funeral, we hear officers called hegemons and taxiarchs (Josephus, *J.W.* 1.673). Elsewhere we hear of a chiliarch commanding a *speire* (Josephus, *J.W.* 2.13). Phrourarchs commanded fortresses, but this is an assignment rather than a rank (Josephus, *J.W.* 2.18). Josephus refers to a number of military officers in Herod's army who have Roman names. Some of may well be Romans who after discharge from Antony's or Octavian's forces, went into service in the Jewish army. There were, however, Jewish Roman citizens, some of whom may have received citizenship exactly because they fought for the Romans in Jewish military units. The origins of Paul's father's citizenship has always been a mystery, and it is not inconceivable that his father had served in Herod's army.

Even putting Jewish Roman citizens aside, we should not immediately assume that a Latin name equals Roman ethnicity. Latin names were used by Jews in the first century: for example, the Justus mentioned by Paul in his letters. We can expect Jewish soldiers and officers to take Latin names or nicknames.[17] An interesting case is Aequus Modius, the grandson of Zamaris (Josephus *Life* 61, 114, 180–81). His name, which at first glance seems to mean "Fair Measure" might be a nickname: he could have served as a quartermaster. Alternatively, it might reflect the Roman nomen Modius

16. Josephus, *A.J.* 17.31; *J.W.* 2.421; Price, "Enigma of Philip."

17. Col 4:11; cf. Acts 1:23, 18:7.

and cognomen Aequus.[18] Modius might also be a calque on a Jewish name such as Omri or Gomer. In any case, this is a clear example of a Jewish soldier with a Latin name. Thus, the Herodian officers such as Volumnius who served as a military tribune (Josephus, *J.W.* 1.535; *A.J.* 16.332), Rufus, who was in charge of the royal cavalry, and Gratus, who commanded the infantry (Josephus, *J.W.* 2.52, 2.74; *A.J.* 17.266; *DMIPERP* §3), may well have been Jews.

Finally, we have the question of the existence of a Temple security force under the authority of the High Priest. In a note, Thackeray suggests that the *strategos* mentioned by Josephus might be the *sagan* or Temple Captain.[19] In fact, Josephus makes no mention of such an official or of any Temple Police either in his description of the Temple or in any other part of his writings.[20] Given Josephus' knowledge and interests, this is a powerful argument from silence.

It is the New Testament that gives the strong impression of a Temple Police functioning as a kind of security force for Jerusalem. The New Testament talks about a *strategos tou hierou* usually translated "Captain of the Temple" although "general" would be more literal. This force does seem to act like police: in Acts 4:1, this individual, along with the "priests" and the Sadducees, arrest Peter and John and place them under guard (*eis teresin).* In the next chapter, Peter is also arrested (5:17–42). The arrest is actually made by the high priest, and the apostle is put in prison (*desmoterion*). "Officers" (*hyperetai*) and "guards" (*phylakes*) find him missing, and the Captain of the Temple among others, is perplexed.

The entire presentation of this religious police force is probably fictional. In the tractate *Middoth*, which concerns the temple (in the order *Kodashim*), the *Mishnah* describes these guards.[21] *Middoth* suggests that this Temple Guard was only formal, made up of three Priests and 21 Assistant Priests, who were stationed at various parts of the Temple as a sort of ceremonial watch. The commander does not have the quasi-military title *sagan* (who is in fact another Temple official, in charge of ritual), but is called only The Overseer of the Temple Mount (*ish har ha-bayit).* The *Middoth* gives the source for its description: Eliezer bar Jacob, who was one of

18. Two soldiers of *legio III Cyrenaica* have relevant names: Modius Priscus (*P.Mich.* 7.444) and Papirius Aequus (*CIL* 3.6628).

19. Thackeray, *Josephus*, 2.326 n. a.

20. See especially *J.W.* 5.22 where one would expect such a reference.

21. Mish. *Ked.* 10.1.1–2, 9.

the Tannaim of the Second generation (along with Gamaliel II) and was a disciple of Johanan ben Zakkai. He was probably a boy or a young man during the Jewish War.[22] It is clear from his description, that the temple guards were by no means a police or security force, but only a ritual guard. Indeed, there is no indication that they were armed. It is interesting that Jerome translates *strategos tou hierou* as *magistratus templi,* not with a military term. The way in which the New Testament completely misconstrues the Temple Guard is a strong suggestion that its authors were far from eyewitnesses and indeed were poorly informed about the realities of first century Palestine.

THE "ROMAN" GARRISON BEFORE THE JEWISH WAR

In the recent Mel Gibson movie *The Passion of the Christ*, the Roman soldiers who crucify Jesus are portrayed as speaking Latin. While this seems self-evident to the uncritical reader, it may well be that there were no Latin-speaking soldiers in Judea before the Jewish War. It is clear that at least part of the Judean garrison was Samaritan. Josephus tells us that 3,000 Samaritans in Herod's army stayed loyal during the uprising of 4 BCE and since Josephus tells us that the garrison was made up of five cohorts infantry and an *ala* or wing of cavalry, it makes sense to see these as the same force. One of these Samaritan cohorts and the cavalry *ala* are attested in inscriptions.[23]

There is, however, the Italian cohort, mentioned in Acts of the Apostles as the unit of the first Gentile convert to Christianity, the centurion Cornelius, and the Augustan Cohort, to which the centurion Julius, who escorts Paul to Rome, belongs. In an influential article, Michael Speidel showed that it was possible that such units did exist.[24] The Augustan cohort is attested in an inscription of a centurion named Lucius Obulnius dating to the 80s CE.[25] It is part of Agrippa II's army, but the centurion mentioned in

22. Another Eliezar b. Jacob lived much later and was a disciple of R. Akiba.

23. For all the references to these units see Mor, "Roman Army in Eretz-Israel," 577–578. Some are collected in *DMIPERP* §153, §154, §213, §219, §§221–245; cf. §131, §132.

24. Michael P. Speidel, "The Roman Army in Judaea under the Procurators: The Italian and the Augustan Cohort in the Acts of the Apostles," *Ancient Society* 13–14 (1982–83): 233–40 = pages 26–34 in the present volume. Denis B. Saddington, *The Development of the Roman Auxiliary Forces from Caesar to Vespasian (49 B.C.–A.D. 79)* (Harare: University of Zimbabwe Press, 1982) and Mor, "Roman Army in Eretz-Israel" accept Speidel's conclusion.

25. *DMIPERP* §12+13; cf. §§14–18 for more on Lucius Obulnius and §§30–32 on

the inscription has a Latin name, Lucius Obulnius. While, as Speidel notes, it is certainly possible that a Roman unit could serve in the army of a client king, it is equally possible that this is a Herodian unit, with either a Roman officer or a Jewish (i.e. native) officer with a Latin name. As for the Italian cohort, Speidel claims that it is *cohors civium Romanorum*. Whereas most auxiliary units were made up of non-citizens, there were cohorts, raised in Italy, made up of citizens. Speidel actually identifies a *cohors II Italica c.R.* that was in Syria as early as 63 CE, though it moved to Austria before the Jewish War. As he argues, this unit could be the one called the *speire tes kaloumenes Italike* in Acts 10. The unit is not mentioned by Josephus nor is there epigraphical evidence for it at Caesarea or anywhere in Judea. The increasing evidence that the Acts do not represent an eyewitness account, but rather were compiled much later in a different place suggest that perhaps the unit did not exist.

The Romans had a custom of simply enrolling the troops of client kingdoms when they were absorbed into a province. It is likely that even under Herod they were armed, equipped and trained in the Roman manner, and probably had some Roman officers. So, becoming a Roman unit meant only getting a Roman title, something like *cohors Sebastenorum*. While commands would have been giving in Latin, and military correspondence carried out in that language, the soldiers themselves would have continued to speak Aramaic. Indeed, their religious practices would also not have changed—auxiliary soldiers generally continued to worship their traditional gods, and as the Samaritans called themselves the Children of Israel, worshipped the same God as the Jews, revered Moses and the other prophets and had their own version of the Torah they were Jews in the modern sense of the word. The idea of the Jewish Roman soldier may strike one as odd. We naturally assume that Roman military service was incompatible with the Jewish religion, but as we have seen, there does not seem to have been anything to prevent Jews from serving in foreign military forces in all Jewish units. Individual Jews serving among non-Jews was more problematic, but while we have little evidence for it, it may have been more common than we think.

Diomedes also this unit. Speidel, "Roman Army in Judaea," 238 = pages 31–32 in the present volume.

PRO-ROMAN JEWISH FORCES IN THE JEWISH WAR

During the revolt of 4 BCE, parts of the Jewish army had revolted, but other portions remained loyal. During the Jewish War of 66–73 CE, a similar phenomenon occurred: the Jewish security forces reacted in various ways. Some defected to the rebels and others stayed loyal to the Romans. In some cases, entire units went one way, but in others units split. Interesting enough, after some sixty years of direct Roman rule, the Jewish army seems to have been more loyal in 66 than it had been in 4 BCE, when most of the army defected to the rebels (Josephus, *J.W.* 2.52). What is striking, however, is that Josephus rarely refers to the Roman garrison, that is the Samaritan cohorts. There is little doubt, however, that the unnamed Roman garrisons, for example at Masada, Ashkelon and indeed in Jerusalem, were Samaritans, that is, Jews in the modern sense of the word. These forces also must have taken part in the war itself, although they are never named specifically.

When the uprising threatened, the Jewish King Agrippa II sent Philip, called a *strategos* along with a *hipparch* Darius and 2,000 cavalry, including Bathyrans, to Jerusalem (Josephus, *J.W.* 2.421). It is noteworthy that the Romans seem to have relied primarily on the forces of the local client king for security. While the Herodians sent 2,000 men, the Romans had only a single cohort (480 men) in the Holy City. The initial attempt to put down the rebellion failed. The rebels allowed the Jewish army to leave the city, while the Romans were massacred. As noted, however, it is quite possible, however, that this "Roman" force was in fact a cohort of Samaritans, and that it was anti-Samaritan, not anti-Roman feeling that led to its massacre. The unit's commander, who was certainly a Roman was humiliated, but spared.

In Thucydidean manner, Josephus lays out the forces that Cestius Gallus, the governor of Syria, brought to crush the rebellion.[26] The force was made up of 16,000–20,000 Roman legionary and auxiliary infantry, plus allied forces from Commagene and Emesa totaling 13,500. When he got to Ptolemais, he was joined by a "large number" of *epikouroi*. These may well be Syrian or Greek militia of some type, as 2,000 "Syrians" are ambushed and defeated later in the campaign. This is the force that famously failed to take Jerusalem, although Josephus insists it was ripe for the plucking, and was then mauled by the rebels at Beth Horon, losing perhaps 10%

26. *J.W.* 2.500–502, for the legal relationship of Syria and Judaea see Israel Shatzman, "The Integration of Judaea into the Roman Empire," *SCI* 18 (1999) 81–84.

casualties. The rebels defeated them, and Philip escaped. The Bathyrans moved to Gamala, where Philip rejoined them. They remained loyal to the Romans. When the Gamalans attacked them, they were moved back to Bathyra.

What concerns us, however, is what is normally seen as a side-show. Agrippa II had moved forces into the Galilee in mid-March, long before Cestius Gallus set out. He is clearly acting aggressively and decisively in the Roman interests. The Jewish royal army, under the command of Modius Aequus, besieged Gamala in the Golan (Josephus, *J.W.* 4.11, 4.83). They kept this strategic city blockaded for seven months, before being relieved by Roman forces. This no doubt represented the bulk of the Herodian forces, including the Babylonian archers.

Another royal Jewish force was sent under a "decurion" (*dekadarche*) named Aebutius to engage Josephus' forces at Simonias, west of Nazareth (Josephus, *J.W.* 4.36). There is no reason, by the way, to think of this Aebutius as necessarily a Roman—he may very well have been a Jew with a Latin name. Josephus gives the size of this force as 100 cavalry, 200 infantry and an unknown number of "allies" *symmachoi*, from Gaba. This town, of course, was the site of a Herodian military settlement, which is clearly still functioning. The 300 "regulars" certainly represent the unit stationed there, but who are these "allies"? Josephus may be referring to other Jews in the settlement, who did not owe military service, but who volunteered to fight for their king. It is impossible to be sure, but this might be a clue to a pro-Roman feeling among some Jews. Josephus might be expected to mention such loyalty to Rome, but it might have been embarrassing, considering that he was still in rebellion at the time and fighting these very same individuals. Indeed, the story is entire omitted from the *Jewish War*. In any case, Josephus' force of 2,000 was defeated at the cost of only three royal Jewish soldiers, so the latter were clearly an effective force (*Life* 114–118).

Josephus mentions a third pro-Roman Jewish force, the royal bodyguard, which also fought in Galilee under the command of its captain, Sulla (*Life* 399–406). This is a very unlikely cognomen for a Roman of this period, but makes perfect sense as a nickname or cognomen for a Jewish officer. Josephus does not mention the size of this force, but it was probably around 500 men. The reason for this hesitancy is that Sulla's small force beat 5,000 of Josephus' men. Agrippa II's role in the rebellion was important. He held onto western Galilee, and although most of Eastern Galilee remained in revolt, he neutralized the important base at Gamala.

In 67, Vespasian took over command, and had his army gather at Antioch. Tiberius Julius Alexander, a member of one of the most important Jewish families in Egypt, and indeed in the Empire, was one of his high officers. Vespasian's army numbered some 55,000 to 60,000 men and included allied forces of some 15,000 (Josephus, *J.W.* 3.69; cf. Suetonius *Vesp.* 4.5–6). Vespasian moved into the Galilee and took Jotapata, at which point Josephus surrendered. In addition, he took Mt. Gerizim, where 16,000 Samaritans, who had joined the rebellion, were massacred (Josephus, *J.W.* 3.307–315). In July or August of 67 CE, Vespasian moved into Eastern Galilee. Josephus says this was done as a "personal favor" to Agrippa II (Josephus, *J.W.* 3.443–452). While there is no doubt that the Romans considered Agrippa's territory part of their Empire, and thus would not allow the rebellion to continue there, this nevertheless indicates that they were sensitive to the nominal independence of Agrippa's territory and waited to be invited in. Vespasian quickly reduced Tiberias and Tarichaeae, then swept the Sea of Galilee of rebels, who had taken refuge in boats. The ease of the campaign is a clue to the relative size of the insurgents and the Jewish Royal army. Both probably numbered in the low to mid-thousands, say, 5,000–10,000. This would explain why the royal army was unable to suppress a revolt that the Romans easily swept aside.

It seems that both the Jewish Royal Army and the rebels had focused on Gamala, as there was a seven-month siege there. Vespasian took over the siege and captured it after a month (Josephus, *J.W.* 4.83). There is no reason to think that the Jewish Royal forces left (Josephus *J.W.* 4.81), and so they certainly participated in the fighting. Josephus does not mention any of their activity, which is suggestive. Simply because the activity of Jewish forces is not mentioned, for example, later at Jerusalem, does not mean they were absent. Josephus mentions an interesting scene, in which a centurion named Gallus, called a "Syrian," sneaks into a house inside the walls and can understand the Aramaic of the Jewish defenders (*J.W.* 4.37–38). He is probably an Aramaic-speaking member of the Roman regular army, but it is possible that he was part of the Herodian army. The only other reference to the part played by the Jewish royal forces is that the two survivors of the siege were relatives of Philip ben Jakimus, commander of the Herodian army.

Jewish royal forces are not mentioned in any of the operations leading up to the siege of Jerusalem, but this does not mean, of course, that they were not present. Josephus does mention the presence of both high-ranking

Jewish officers and Jewish royal forces at the siege of Jerusalem (*J.W.* 5.42–46). Tiberius Julius Alexander was present, and in fact may have been the de facto commander of the Roman forces. Although his Jewishness is often denigrated or ignored, he came from the most notable Jewish family in Egypt. Josephus notes that the client kings' armies, including the Jewish Royal Army, made up the vanguard of Titus' army as it advanced on Jerusalem.

We cannot say exactly how the Jewish contribution to the Roman war effort was. Assuming that the Herodian army had around 3,000 to 5,000 and this might well be an underestimate and noting that the size of the Roman deployment changed over time, from a low of about 35,000 to a high of some 70,000, we see that this Jewish contribution varied from some 5% to 10% of the total Roman force. This was certainly a significant factor. If we add in the Samaritan cohorts, some 3,000 men, and call them "Jewish" then the total might rise to as high as 20% at some points in the conflict. That these forces were present throughout the war is proven by the fact that Vespasian removed them only after the end of the conflict (Josephus, *A.J.* 19.363). In addition, Jewish leaders such as Agrippa II and Tiberius Julius Alexander provided important guidance and advice. The latter might well have been the strategic planner of the Roman campaign.

The Jewish War is generally characterized as a War of Liberation or Independence Struggle, one that is tragically lost by brave proto-nationalists against a "arbitrary and cruel" Roman imperial state.[27] It is perhaps better characterized as a civil war, in which one side, driven partly by class considerations, partly by religious fanaticism, attack not only foreigners but fellow Jews, and another of rulers and religious leaders trying to integrate their traditional culture into a modern world to save what they consider most important. This division was not only present in Palestine, but is seen in other Jewish communities as well, notably Egypt.[28] While the anti-Romans, whom we can generally although perhaps not entirely accurately call Zealots, are portrayed romantically, they were a cruel and ruthless bunch. Those who either initially or in the course of events support the Romans are conversely seen as traitors and collaborationists, but they whom we might well call Moderates, are much more sympathetic in many respects.

27. Shatzman, "Integration of Judaea," 84.

28. Christopher Jones, "Egypt and Judaea under Vespasian," *Historia* 46 (1997) 249–53.

It has become normal to see the Jewish War in terms of World War II, with the Romans as Nazis and the Zealots and Sicarii as plucky Resistance fighters. This puts those who fought on the Roman side in the role of Vichy. Words like "collaborator" are bandied about, as well as "traitor," and Josephus has even been called a "Quisling." There was, however, good reason for rational people to support the Romans. One is reminded of the scene in Monty Python's *Life of Brian*, in which the Jewish Zealots ask, "What have the Romans done for us?" The period between the collapse of Seleucid rule and the direct Roman takeover in 6 CE was one of endemic civil war and invasion. Even factoring in the two bloody uprisings, Roman rule over Palestine was one where internal security, freedom from invasion and general economic prosperity was the rule, not the exception. Indeed, although the participants had no way of knowing it, the destruction of the Temple, and the archaic temple economy dominated by a priestly aristocracy, along with capital made available through Roman occupation, made the period from the third to the seventh centuries the richest and most densely populated period in the region's history up to the 20th century.[29] This affluence extended also to the Jewish population. It is true that Jews were subject to a special tax after the first revolt, and banned from Jerusalem after the second, but the Jewish population in the country was well-to-do, and Judaism was practiced without any interference until Christianity became the empire's official religion. It has long been noted that if Jews in general had followed the lead of Eleazar ben Jair, and not of Johanan ben Zakkai, there would be no Judaism today. Why then, do we laud the former and condemn the latter? From a historical perspective, there is a strong argument that those who fought on the Roman side better represented the interests of the majority of the Jewish people.

29. Jonathan P. Roth, "The Army and the Economy in Judaea and Palaestina" in *The Roman Army and The Economy* (ed. Paul Erdkamp; Amsterdam: Gieben, 2002), 375–97.

6

Sons of Israel in Caesar's Service

Jewish Soldiers in the Roman Military

ANDREW J. SCHOENFELD

ABSTRACT

The participation of Roman Jewish soldiers in the armies of Imperial Rome often goes unrecognized. This is mainly a result of a lack of recognition on the part of scholars who wish to use Rabbinic sources as the benchmark for Jewish practice in the Imperial Age. It is also difficult to identify Jewish soldiers, many of whom had Greek and Latin names, unless they are specifically identified as Jews or are found in a Jewish context such as dedicatory inscriptions from a synagogue. Nonetheless, by using a variety of sources from the period it is possible to appreciate the depth and breadth of Jewish service in the Roman legions from the time of Caesar down to the early fifth century. There were Jews who served as simple foot soldiers, influential generals like Tiberius Julius Alexander, and Jewish military units such as the Regii Emeseni Iudaei. Regardless of their relationship to "orthodox" Jewish communities of the time, the service of Roman Jews in the Imperial armed forces must be recognized.

INTRODUCTION

In the year 69 CE the Roman province of Judea was consumed by a three-year rebellion that pitted Jewish zealots against the authority of the Emperor and the House of Herod. Not only was the revolt a destabilizing factor in the eastern regions of the Empire but it also posed a significant challenge to the new emperor, Vespasian. In order to quell the Jewish revolt in his eastern marches, Vespasian resolved to send an army under the command of his son, Titus, with explicit orders to crush the insurrection. Although the emperor's young son showed exceptional talent and tact for leadership, he lacked the military experience deemed necessary for a Roman general. Therefore, the emperor was forced to choose an able commander capable of assisting Titus in the Judean expedition. A great number of prestigious military men were available for the post, including Annius Vinicianus, son-in-law to the famed general, Corbulo. But Vespasian made the unlikely choice of an Alexandrian Jew named Tiberius Julius Alexander to spearhead the Roman army in its effort to thwart the Jewish uprising. The emperor's decision was to prove fortuitous, as not only did Tiberius Alexander coordinate a Roman victory in Judea but he also became Titus' trusted advisor and may have eventually reached the rank of Praetorian Prefect.[1]

Despite the outstanding military career of this Alexandrian Jew, his name and his legacy are largely unknown outside a small circle of specialists. Likewise, the participation of Jews in the Roman military is a topic that is underemphasized or frankly ignored by historians. Most often, scholars quote the exemptions from military service granted to Jews at Ephesus and Delos[2] or elaborate on the difficulties that Sabbath observance and dietary laws posed to Jewish men interested in serving under the imperial flag.[3] When the issue of Jewish service in the Roman Army is addressed, it is not without a certain degree of skepticism, and Roman Jews in imperial service are often cast in the light of "renegades" or apostates.

Thus, without any documentation of sources, Scharf states that Jews in the Roman army were descended from the bodyguard of the Emesene and Judean royal families who had intermarried and become pagans.[4]

1. M. Williams, *The Jews among the Greeks and Romans: A Diasporan Sourcebook* (Baltimore, 1998), 95.

2. Josephus, *A.J.* 14.223–230, 14.236–237.

3. E. M. Smallwood, *The Jews under Roman Rule* (2nd ed.; Leiden, 1981), 127.

4. R. Scharf, "Regii Emeseni Iudaei: Bemerkungen zu einen spatantiken Truppe,"

Smallwood states that "military service . . . was always bound to cause difficulties for the Jews of the Diaspora because of their dietary laws, which made their inclusion in gentile units impracticable, and their inability to carry out any duties on the Sabbath."[5] Appelbaum claims that Jews in the Roman army were "renegades,"[6] and Tiberius Julius Alexander is often recast as an apostate even when it is acknowledged that there is no evidence of this fact.[7]

The lack of recognition given to Jewish soldiers who served in the Roman military stems primarily from three main issues: the dearth of inscriptions and manuscripts specifically addressing Jews in the Roman military, the inability to recognize Jews with Greek or Latin names unless they are identified as such, and the tendency of many scholars to rely on rabbinic works in order to reconstitute "normal" Jewish practices in the Roman world.

As a larger corpus of Jewish inscriptions and artifacts from the ancient period has become available, it has become clear that the observance of Judaism in the Roman world was much more variegated than previously supposed. Authors like Lee Levine[8] and Seth Schwartz[9] have now challenged the assertions of prior historians, claiming that Jewish practice in the Imperial period encompassed a broad range of religious activity: from the "orthodoxy" of the rabbinic academies to the syncretism of Jews who had Latin names and employed pagan motifs in synagogal decoration. With these facts in mind, the prospect of active Jewish participation in the military becomes tangible, and upon careful examination of primary sources it is possible to demonstrate the profound extent to which Roman Jews operated in the Imperial Army.

Latomus 56 (1997) 343–59.

5. Smallwood, *Jews under Roman Rule*, 127.

6. S. Applebaum, "Jews and Service in the Roman Army," in *Roman Frontier Studies 1967* (ed. S. Applebaum; Tel-Aviv, 1971), 181–84.

7. C. Roth, ed., *Encyclopedia Judaica* (1st ed.; Jerusalem, 1971), 15.1135.

8. L. Levine, "Contextualizing Jewish Art: The Synagogues at Hammat-Tiberias and Sepphoris," in *Jewish Culture and Society Under the Christian Roman Empire* (ed. R. Kalmin and S. Schwartz; Leuven, 2003), 91–132.

9. S. Schwartz, *Imperialism and Jewish Society: 200 BCE to 640 CE* (Princeton, 2001).

1

By the time of Caesar, Jews could already reflect on an illustrious three-hundred-year history of armed service in Persia and the Hellenic East, not to mention the military exploits of the Hasmonean dynasty in the Jewish state proper. Throughout the Ptolemaic period, Jews served in every capacity in the Egyptian army. There were military colonies at Elephantine, border guards at Pelusium and reservists in the *Epigone*. Queen Cleopatra III's top military commanders were both Jews: Chelkias and Ananias, the sons of the legendary High Priest Onias of Heliopolis.[10]

This military tradition continued into the early imperial period; Josephus makes specific mention of Jewish military colonists instrumental in pacifying the region of Trachonitis. To this effect, 500 Jewish horsemen from Mesopotamia were settled at Batanaea under the leadership of a captain named Zamaris.[11] These settlers and their descendants continued in their role as a garrison into the second century and supported imperial forces during the Jewish revolt.[12] Careful examination of sources from the Julio-Claudian period reveals a smattering of Jewish soldiers laboring in the imperial army. In the year 19, Emperor Tiberius forcibly conscripted 4,000 Roman Jews for military service on the island of Sardinia,[13] but there is also evidence of Jews serving in a voluntary capacity. Matthaius, a Syrian Jew, served in *legio I Adiutrix* under Nero and received Roman citizenship in 68.[14] Prior to the implementation of the *Constitutio Antoniniana* in 211, military service was one of the few ways that Jews could achieve Roman citizenship. This was granted after 26 years of service in the auxiliary as recruitment into the legions was confined to those who were already citizens of the empire.

Although dedicatory, funereal, and laudatory inscriptions give us the names of many Jews in the imperial ranks, only in the instance of the abovementioned Tiberius Julius Alexander can something of a career be gleaned from the sources.

10. Josephus, *A.J.* 13.284–285.

11. Josephus, *A.J.* 17.23–25; cf. Benjamin Isaac, *The Limits of Empire: The Roman Army in the East* (1st ed.; Oxford, 1990), 329–30.

12. Isaac, *Limits of Empire*, 330.

13. Josephus, *A.J.* 18.84.

14. *CIL* 16.8 [[=*DMIPERP* §293]].

2

Tiberius Julius Alexander, the Egyptian Jew who was destined to become one of the most powerful personas in the Empire, was born in the year 16 CE in Alexandria.[15] His father, Alexander Lysimachus, was a member of the Egyptian gentry and customs chief on the Arabian frontier. Tiberius' uncle was none other than the famous philosopher, Philo. Like many rich assimilated Jews in the city of Alexandria, Tiberius' family had received Roman citizenship during the reign of Augustus and expected their children to assume important posts in the imperial administration. From a young age, Tiberius and his brother Marcus were groomed for a position in the Roman bureaucracy. Their father eschewed a standard Jewish education and, instead, had his children tutored in the classics.[16] Once the boys reached manhood, Alexander Lysimachus arranged for his sons to enter disparate fields in Roman imperial service. Marcus would become influential in the family's native city of Alexandria and eventually married Princess Berenice, the daughter of King Agrippa I.

Meanwhile, Tiberius began his illustrious career in the Roman army, where his leadership skills and family connections allowed him to secure the post of Governor of the Thebiad in 42 CE. Tiberius' success in this position prompted Emperor Claudius to appoint him Procurator of Judea four years later. At this time, the Province of Judea was a hotbed of revolution as Jewish zealots struggled to throw off the yoke of Roman hegemony. Many of his coreligionists considered Tiberius a turncoat for serving the Roman emperor, but the historian Josephus records that Tiberius' time as procurator was a period of peace in Judea.[17]

Tiberius Alexander left his station in Judea in 48, and by 63 he had risen to become one of the highest ranking officers in the eastern army, a member of Corbulo's general staff. Tiberius conducted himself with honor during Corbulo's Armenian campaign, and in the role of advisor to the fifth legion was instrumental in initiating negotiations with the Armenian King, Tiridates.[18]

His success in the Armenian war secured Corbulo's backing, and with that general's recommendation Nero appointed Tiberius governor of Egypt

15. J. Modrzejewski, *The Jews of Egypt: From Rameses II to Emperor Hadrian* (Princeton, 1995), 185.

16. Josephus, *A.J.* 20.100.

17. Josephus, *A.J.* 20.220.

18. Tacitus, *Ann.* 15.28.3.

in 66. Through the time of troubles that followed in the wake of Nero's murder, Tiberius would prove himself a loyal Roman administrator. When the general Vespasian challenged the usurper Vitellius for the imperial purple, Tiberius became an early supporter of the old commander, with whom he had served in the east. Tiberius' backing allowed Vespasian to triumph over Vitellius, and his acclamation of the new emperor in Alexandria became the official date of Vespasian's advent.[19] Tiberius Alexander's Jewish background, personal talents and profound loyalty made him the perfect choice as chief of staff during Titus' invasion of Judea.

As military advisor to Titus, Tiberius experienced the same success that he had enjoyed in Egypt and Armenia. The Jewish insurgency was put down in less than a year, and Titus was hailed a great victor, quickly becoming the darling of the empire. Although he was merciless in his efforts to put down the Jewish revolt against Rome, Tiberius Alexander seemed to maintain some of his religious sensibilities during the last days of the war. Josephus states that in the final moments of the siege of Jerusalem, both Tiberius and Titus desperately tried to avert the burning of the Temple.[20]

Tiberius Alexander returned to Rome with Titus and, according to an Egyptian papyrus, was eventually appointed to the post of Praetorian Prefect.[21] Although the interpretation of this source has been contested, if Tiberius Alexander indeed attained this position he was undoubtedly the most powerful Jew at the time and must be recognized as one of the predominant Jewish men in military history.

Tiberius reached the pinnacle of his career with the victory in Judea and his possible appointment as prefect. With the death of his friend and patron, Emperor Titus, Tiberius Alexander makes an abrupt exit from the annals of history. In the end, the fate of this illustrious Jew from Alexandria remains unknown. It is possible that, at the ripe old age of 65, the man merely retired from public life, but it has also been postulated that he met a violent end in the purges of Titus' successor, Emperor Domitian. There is, however, no firm proof of Tiberius Alexander's ultimate fate and, until some yet undiscovered evidence comes to light, we are unfortunately relegated to the realm of conjecture.

19. *CPJ* 418a [[=*DMIPERP* §365]]; Modrzejewski, *Jews of Egypt*, 187.

20. Josephus, *J.W.* 6.251–256.

21. *CPJ* 418b [[=*DMIPERP* §366]].

3

Tiberius Julius Alexander was, without question, the most successful Jew to serve in the ranks of the Roman Army, but Jewish participation in the Roman military did not begin or end with this great Alexandrian adventurer. Indeed, from available sources, it would appear that the pinnacle of Jewish participation in the Roman military would not be reached until two centuries after Alexander's death.[22] To the consternation of many rabbis of the period, Jewish men formed a cadre in the Imperial Army from the time of Emperor Caracalla down to the reign of the late Christian Emperors. There were even exclusively Jewish units, such as the Royal Emesene Jews.[23]

Many Diaspora Jews were fully enmeshed in Roman culture, used Greek or Latin names, and were active in the civic administrations of numerous cities around the Mediterranean.[24] In this respect they approximate modern Reform Jews, and it is not surprising that some men of the Jewish faith would look to establish careers in the Roman military.[25] Unfortunately, this high level of integration puts the scholar at a certain disadvantage when attempting to identify Roman Jewish soldiers in the historical record. Unless their religion is specifically identified, Jews with Greek or Latin names escape our notice, and it is probable that more Roman Jewish soldiers will be lost to posterity than can ever be identified.

Based on the evaluation of what archeological and historical material is available, most Jewish soldiers seemed to have originated from three

22. G. Gilbert, "Jews in Imperial Administration and its Significance for Dating the Jewish Donor Inscription from Aphrodisias," *JSJ* 35 (2004) 177. This statement also based on the fact that, considering the primary sources available, most inscriptions and material mentioning Roman Jewish soldiers have been dated to the third and fourth centuries. For further reading see: D. Noy, *Jewish Inscriptions of Western Europe*, vols. I and II (Cambridge, 1993); D. Noy, A. Panayatov, and H. Bloedhorn, *Inscriptiones Judaicae Orientis*, vols. I and III (Tübingen, 2004); Schwartz, *Imperialism and Jewish Society*.

23. Noy, *Jewish Inscriptions of Western Europe*, I, 8.

24. A number of primary sources attest to these facts. For further reading of inscriptions addressing the preponderance of Greek and Latin names among Jews in the Roman Empire see Noy, *Jewish Inscriptions of Western Europe*; Noy, Panayatov, and Bloedhorn, *Inscriptiones Judaicae Orientis*, I–III; H. Leon, *The Jews of Ancient Rome* (1st ed.; Philadelphia, 1960). A worthy introduction to Jews in the civic administrations of Imperial Roman cities can be found in *CPJ*; Williams, *Jews Among the Greeks and Romans*; Schwartz, *Imperialism and Jewish Society*; P. Trebilco, *Jewish Communities in Asia Minor* (Cambridge, 1990).

25. Williams, *Jews Among the Greeks and Romans*, 95.

distinct regions of the empire. In the later Imperial period, the Jewish community of Italy provided many recruits, but the Hellenic-Jewish populations of Syria and Asia Minor and the Jews of Egypt probably contributed the most to the Roman Jewish military effort. As mentioned above, the Egyptian Jewish community already had a rich military tradition before the advent of Imperial Rome.

Roman Jewish soldiers who are mentioned in inscriptions and artifacts from the first and second centuries are almost entirely of Egyptian or Syrian extraction. An inscription from Jaffa mentions an Egyptian Jew named Thanoum the Centurion,[26] and a military diploma from Dacia speaks of the foot soldier Barsimsus Calisthensus, a Jew serving in the *cohors I Vindelicorum*.[27] Other artifacts from modern day Romania attest to the fact that many Jews were stationed in this province during the first century.[28] There was also a significant Jewish military presence in neighboring Pannonia. Two-thirds of all Jewish inscriptions from Roman Pannonia are those of legionaries, primarily members of the Aurelia Antoniniana: *I Syria sagittaria* and *I Hemesenorum sagittaria*.[29]

The policies of Emperors Caracalla and Septimius Severus further encouraged Roman Jews to seek careers in the Roman military. Without question, the vast majority of sources addressing Roman Jewish soldiers are from the two centuries following Caracalla's decision to grant citizenship to all free individuals of the Empire. Thus, by the end of the third century, we find several Jews in high military positions, especially in Syria and Asia Minor.[30] A donor inscription from Aphrodisias concerns a Jew named Theodotos who held the high imperial rank of *palatinus*.[31] During this period a Jew from Sardis named Aurelius Basileides was raised to the rank

26. *CIJ* 920 [[=*DMIPERP* §71]].

27. G. Levenson, "The Little Tailor's Synagogue," in *The Jewish People's Almanac* (ed. D. C. Gross; 1st ed.; Garden City, 1981), 542 [[=*DMIPERP* §296]]. The military diploma, discovered near the remains of ancient Tibiscum, has been translated as: "Barsimsus, son of Calisthensus from Caesarea, foot soldier."

28. B. P. Hasdeu, *Istoria Tolerantei Religiose in Romania* (Bucharest, 1868), 76.

29. R. Patai, *The Jews of Hungary* (Detroit, 1996), 22–24.

30. Trebilco, *Jewish Communities of Asia Minor*, 191.

31. Gilbert, "Jews in Imperial Administration," 176 [[. . . Θεόδοτος Παλατῖν(ος) . . .]].

of procurator.[32] Another mosaic from the synagogue of Sardis records a high military functionary and *comes*, the Jew Paulus.[33]

In this period Roman Jewish soldiers achieved success in regions outside of Asia Minor as well. A funereal tablet from the Jewish necropolis at Beth-Shearim in Israel speaks of the palatine Julianus,[34] and a dedicatory lintel from the Sepphoris synagogue tells us of another *comes* named Gelasius.[35] Iosses Maximinus Pannonius was a non-commissioned officer with *legio V Macedonica* at Oescus[36] and a Jewish community member named Cosmius was stationed as the commanding officer of the military post at Spondil.[37] A Greek inscription from Larissa mentions the Jew Alexander who held the rank of *prostates*.[38]

This era also witnessed the continuation of the Jewish military tradition in Egypt. The names of several Jewish troopers can be found in papyri mentioning their service with the Oxyrhynchan garrison and Egyptian cavalry.[39] The *legio comitatensis* of the above-mentioned troop of Royal Emesene Jews (*Regii Emeseni Iudaei*) was stationed at Alexandria in 356 and participated in the attack on Bishop Athanasius in the Church of Theonas.[40] This same unit can be located in Concordia, Italy in 409[41] and

32. G. Hanfmann, *Sardis from Prehistoric to Roman Times* (Cambridge, 1983), fig. 272 [[Αὐρ(ήλιος) Βασιλείδης ἀπὸ ἐπιτρόπων]].

33. Trebilco, *Jewish Communities in Asia Minor*, 49, inscription 4.7 [[εὐχὴ Παύλου κόμητος]].

34. *CIJ* 1006 [[. . . Ἰουλιάνου Παλατίνου . . .]].

35. Noy and Bloedhorn, *Inscriptiones Judaicae Orientis*, III, 7 [[. . . Ὑελασίου σχο(λαστικοῦ) κώ(μητος) . . .]].

36. Noy, Panayatov, and Bloedhorn, *Inscriptiones Judaicae Orientis*, I, p. 32 [[Ioses Arcisina(g)o(gus) et principales filius Maximini Pannoni . . .]].

37. *CIJ* 677 [[Ἀλεξά(ν)δρου σχολαστικοῦ καὶ προστάτου]].

38. Noy, Panayotov, and Bloedhorn, *Inscriptiones Judaicae Orientis*, I, 117. Cf. A. Panayotov, "The Jews in the Balkan Provinces of the Roman Empire: The Evidence from the Territory of Bulgaria," in *Negotiating Diaspora: Jewish Studies in the Roman Empire* (ed. J. M. G. Barclay; London, 2004), 38–65.

39. Noy, Panayotov, and Bloedhorn, *Inscriptiones Judaicae Orientis*, I, 34. [[=*DMIPERP* §183: Θερμαῦθ(ος) δοῦλ(ος) Ἀνιν(ίου) κεντ(ουρίωνος) Ἰουδ(αικοῦ τελέσματος) . . .]]

40. *Patrologia Latina* 13.916; D. Woods, "A Note Concerning the *Regii Emeseni Iudaei*," *Latomus* 51 (1992) 404–7. "Proba non te, sed Iudaeos destinasse militem ad Alexandriam, Iudaeorum militem obsedisse fores Dei domus, Iudaeorum militum ducem esse Syrianum. Proba Iudaeos ingressos basilicam cum armis, atque certum numerum interfecisse."

41. Noy and Bloedhorn, *Inscriptiones Judaicae Orientis*, III, 69. This reference presents the inscription from the sarcophagus of Flavia Optata, the wife of a soldier from the

is mentioned in the *Notitia Dignitatum* under the command of the western *Magister Peditum Praesentalis.*[42] At this time the *Auxilia Palatina* of the troop was stationed at Strasbourg.[43]

The third and fourth centuries would see an increase in the number of Jewish soldiers recruited from the communities on the Italian peninsula. A funereal tablet from the Roman catacombs tells us of the Jew named Rufinus who campaigned in the ranks for 25 years before retiring to an allodial settlement near the place of his birth.[44] Other Roman Jews who survived careers in the military and were rewarded for their service included Reginus and his comrade in arms, Agrius Evangelus.[45]

There was also a substantial Jewish presence in the auxiliary, or *limitani*, units that the Romans used as frontier guards. The famous rabbi, Simeon ben Lakish, was a foot soldier in the *limitani* before he retired to more scholarly pursuits.[46] In North Africa an extensive portion of Roman frontier troops was recruited from the native Berber population, among them the Jewish *Jerawa* tribe.[47]

4

The ascent of Christianity as the official religion of the Roman Empire would eventually spell the end of Jewish service in the military. However, the position of Jews in the Roman Army was not immediately affected by the declaration of Christianity as the state religion because members of the armed forces were slow to adopt the new faith.[48] Throughout the fourth and early fifth centuries Jewish soldiers and exclusive Jewish units like the Royal Emesene Jews would continue to play a role in the defense of the empire.[49]

---

troop of Royal Emesene Jews.

42. *Notitia Dignitatum* 6.49.

43. Woods, "A Note Concerning the *Regii Emeseni Iudaei*," 405.

44. Leon, *Jews of Ancient Rome*, 274 [[. . . Ρουφῖνος . . . στρατευσάμενος ἀπὸ τάξεων . . . Note that Schoenfeld's comments on Rufinus are largely speculative]].

45. Noy, *Jewish Inscriptions of Western Europe*, II, 231 [[Greek transliteration of Latin: Ἀγριο Εὐανγε(λ)ο βενεμερεντι, Ρηγεινους κολ(λ)ηγα]].

46. R. J. Z. Werblowsky and G. Wigoder, eds. *The Encyclopedia of the Jewish Religion* (New York, 1965), 360.

47. M. Brett, *The Berbers* (Oxford, 1996), 54.

48. M. Simkins, *The Roman Army from Hadrian to Constantine* (London, 1979), 17.

49. Noy, *Jewish Inscriptions of Western Europe*, I, 8.

The letter of Severus of Minorca informs us of several Jews in high military positions in the early fifth century.[50] In 400, the Jew Lectorius was elevated to the rank of *praeses* of the Balaeric islands, and in 418 both Theodore and Caecilianus, Equestrian Jews of Minorca, held the military title of *defensor civitatis*.[51] The late Roman general, Arrian, employed Iturean archers, whose ancestors had been forcibly converted to Judaism by the Hasmoneans, in his conflict with the Alan tribes.[52]

However, as the Christian church solidified its power in the Roman hierarchy, imperial legislation became more vociferous in its attitude towards Jews, and discontent appears to have developed in Jewish members of the military. Like their more religious brethren, assimilated Jews began to view the Roman Empire as an adversary, and unrest spread amongst the Jewish ranks in the army. Many Jewish soldiers sided with enemies of the Christian government, deserting to the Persians or supporting usurpers like Maximinus and Eugenius.[53]

Both out of a desire to limit the role of Jews in public life and because of suspicions regarding their loyalty to the Christian state, Emperor Theodosius I enacted the first legislation barring Jews from serving as officers in the Roman army.[54] This was shortly followed by an edict of Emperor Theodosius II, issued in 410, that expelled all Jewish soldiers from the Eastern Roman military.[55] Eight years later, the same emperor would openly exclude Jews from the army in Italy, demanding that "[the Jewish soldier's] military belt shall be undone without any hesitation, and . . . they shall not derive any help or protection from their former merits."[56] In 425 Theodosius II re-issued the same edict for the province of Gaul and, in 439, made it the law for every province in the Roman Empire.[57] With few exceptions, the edicts of Theodosius II effectively put an end to Jewish service in the Roman army, and no large body of Jews would come to serve

50. *Epistula Severi* 6.19.6.

51. *Epistula Severi* 6.19.6; S. Katz, *The Jews in the Visigothic and Frankish Kingdoms of Spain and Gaul* (Cambridge, 1937), 120.

52. S. MacDowell, *Late Roman Infantryman: 236–565 AD* (London, 1994), 30.

53. A. Ferrill, *The Fall of the Roman Empire* (London, 1986), 97–98.

54. *Codex Theodosianus* 16.8.16.

55. Williams, *Jews among the Greeks and Romans*, 106.

56. A. Linder, *The Jews in Roman Imperial Legislation* (Detroit, 1987), 281.

57. Katz, *Jews in the Visigothic and Frankish Kingdoms*, 121.

in such military fashion until the rise of the Khazar state three hundred years after the fall of Rome.

5

For the most part, contemporary Jewish scholarship has chosen to de-emphasize or ignore the important contributions of the Roman Jewish community in general and Jewish soldiers in particular. This has occurred partly because of the high level of assimilation enjoyed by these Diasporan Jews, but also because the religious individuals who recorded Jewish history at the time viewed them as traitors. The Roman Empire was responsible for the destruction of the Jerusalem Temple, and religious scholars could not fathom why their coreligionists would want to participate in the instrument of Imperial oppression. Echoing the sentiments of these scholars and rabbis, modern Jewish historians have also tended to view Jewish participation in the Roman military with skepticism, often labeling Jewish soldiers apostates or questioning their attachment to the Jewish community.[58] When considering these statements, it is important to remember that Jewish religious practices across the Roman Empire were extremely variegated, and one cannot attempt to reconstruct a type of "normative" Judaism from the texts of rabbinic scholarship.[59] The Roman Jewish soldiers' attachment to their ancestral faith and involvement in the community is confirmed by the presence of their names in Jewish funereal inscriptions and dedicatory lintels of synagogues. The palatine Julianus was the brother of a rabbi named Paregorius,[60] and Iosses Pannonius,[61] the *principalis* of *Legio V Macedonia*, was a high synagogue official.

Based on these examples from primary sources contained in the historical record, it is evident that Roman Jews served in the military from the beginning of the Pax Romana down to the days of the early fifth century. The many sources, papyri, and tablets referenced in this article form a corpus of incontrovertible proof that Roman Jews were active in the armed forces of the Empire. That these Jewish soldiers actually thought of

58. Williams, *Jews Among the Greeks and Romans*, 95. Cf. Applebaum, "Jews and Service in the Roman Army"; Noy and Bloedhorn, *Insciptiones Judaicae Orientis*, III, 69; Noy, Panayotov, and Bloedhorn, *Inscriptiones Judaicae Orientis*, I, 34.

59. J. M. G. Barclay, *Jews in the Mediterranean Diaspora* (Edinburgh, 1996), 416.

60. *CIJ* 1006.

61. Noy, Panayotov, and Bloedhorn, *Inscriptiones Judaicae Orientis*, I, 34.

themselves as *Jews* is clear from the fact that they are mentioned as such in their inscriptions, were active as officials and members of synagogues, and were buried in Jewish cemeteries with religious symbols on their tombstones and sarcophagi. Whether these Jews were as scrupulous in their religious observance as the Rabbinic authors of the Talmud and Mishnah is a moot point. Authors who question the authenticity of these soldiers' religious conviction detract from our understanding of Jewish history in the Roman period and render an injustice to the memory of these Roman Jews, who felt strong enough in their faith to participate in their religious community, make dedications in their synagogues and use Jewish markers on their graves.

In summation, various sources from the works of Josephus to sarcophagi and the letters of Church fathers show the varied roles that Roman Jews played in the ranks of the Imperial Army. Roman Jewish soldiers, including influential personalities such as Tiberius Julius Alexander, must be given their place in Jewish history, regardless of their relationship to "orthodox" Jewish communities of the time. This recognition will not only fill a lacuna in the field of Roman military history but will also bring to light part of the brilliant compilation that was the Jewish community in the Imperial epoch.

7

'Romans Go Home'?

Rome and Other 'Outsiders' as Viewed from the Syro-Arabian Desert

Michael C. A. Macdonald

ABSTRACT

Whereas twenty years ago there was relatively little evidence for contact between the nomads in the deserts east of the Ḥawrān and their settled neighbours, there is now a great deal more, albeit fragmentary and often enigmatic. Almost all this evidence comes from the Safaitic graffiti carved by the nomads of southern Syria, north-eastern Jordan, and northern Saudi Arabia between the first century BC and the fourth century AD. These texts show that their authors had considerable contact with the settled areas, and probably that some served in units of the Nabataean and/or Roman armies drawn from their tribes. They also indicate that many were well informed of events in the settled areas, not merely on the desert's edge but in Palestine and even Antioch. These graffiti give the strong impression, not of 'insiders' and 'outsiders', but of constant symbiosis and communication—as well as occasional conflict—between the nomads and the settled populations of the local kingdoms and Roman provinces of this region.

Some twenty years ago, I remarked on the paucity of evidence for interaction between the settled populations of the Ḥawrān and the nomads to the east of it from the first century BC to the fourth century AD. I suggested that this was almost certainly not evidence for lack of contact between the two communities, since throughout the history of the region a constructive symbiosis between the nomadic and settled communities has been the norm. Instead, I thought it was a function of the difference between the two principle types of evidence which have come down to us: the monumental Greek and Latin inscriptions from the Ḥawrān and the Safaitic graffiti from the desert.[1] Now, two decades later, a great many more Safaitic inscriptions are available and a study of these in the light of texts already known seems to provide more evidence for contact than was previously thought.

*The Safaitic inscriptions are graffiti in an Ancient North Arabian dialect,[2] related to, but distinct from, Arabic, and carved in one of a family of alphabets which was unique to ancient Arabia. From their distribution and content it is clear that they were carved almost entirely by the nomads of the deserts of southern Syria, north-eastern Jordan, and northern Saudi Arabia who, for the only time in their history, had learnt to read and write. However, finding themselves with only rocks to write on, they used the skill mainly to pass the time while doing boring jobs such as guarding their flocks and herds while they pastured. This gave these writers ample time to carve their thoughts, hopes, fears, prayers, and—when taken together—these tens of thousands of graffiti present us with often vivid glimpses of

1. See M. C. A. Macdonald, 'Nomads and the Ḥawrān in the Late Hellenistic and Roman periods: A Reassessment of the Epigraphic Evidence', *Syria* 70 (1993) 303–413 at 352 (repr. with addenda and corrigenda in Macdonald, *Literacy and Identity in Pre-Islamic Arabia* [Variorum Collected Studies 906; Farnham, 2009], Ch. II); see also M. C. A. Macdonald, 'Literacy in an Oral Environment', in P. Bienkowski, C. B. Mee, and E. A. Slater (eds.), *Writing and Ancient Near Eastern Society. Papers in Honour of Alan R. Millard* (Library of Hebrew Bible/Old Testament Studies 426; New York, 2005), 49–118 at 74–84 (repr. with addenda and corrigenda in Macdonald, *Literacy and Identity*, Ch. I).

2. See M. C. A. Macdonald, 'Reflections on the Linguistic Map of Pre-Islamic Arabia', *Arabian Archaeology and Epigraphy* 11 (2000) 28–79 at 32–36 (repr. with addenda and corrigenda in Macdonald, *Literacy and Identity*, Ch. III).

the daily life of these nomads. It is unfortunate that there is no equivalent source for the settled rural or urban populations of the Roman provinces of Syria and Arabia at this time. Gravestones, signatures, official inscriptions, and so on, can provide a great deal of information but they do not give us the thoughts of 'the man or woman in the Boṣrā street' equivalent to this intensely personal information from the desert.

However, the personal nature of these inscriptions also brings problems. The Safaitic graffiti represent self-expression not communication and were carved for the pleasure of the authors with no thought for the needs of a reader. They can be written in any direction, and employ no vowels of any sort, or diphthongs, and no division between words. More serious for our purposes is the fact that an individual author obviously knew what he wanted to say and since he did not expect anyone to read his text, felt no need to clarify, add details, or explain allusions. Nevertheless, despite these problems, we must be grateful for these graffiti since they form our only source for the everyday 'point-of-view' of nomads in this region in the Roman, or indeed any, period.

As I have said, it is a mistake to think that these nomads lived in isolation from their settled neighbours. There are Safaitic texts in which the authors say they spent periods in Gilead,[3] in one of the Abilas,[4] in Palmyra,[5]

3. See KRS 15 . . . *w mṭy m gl'd l tdmr* . . . '. . . and he hastened from Gilead to Tadmur [Palmyra] . . .', and possibly *CIS* V 2473: . . .*w 'hmd 'bl f rdf m gl{'}d* . . . though the meaning of this is not clear. Note that in transliterations of Safaitic *{ }* marks letters the reading of which is doubtful, *[ ]* marks letters which are restored, and ---- indicates that one or more letters are damaged or otherwise unreadable. The ellipsis, . . . , has its normal meaning of text which has been omitted.

4. That is 1) Abila in the Lebanon, 18 Roman miles from Damascus on the way to Heliopolis, which was the capital of the 'Tetrarchy of Lysanias' (Josephus, *Antiquities of the Jews* 18.237) which Caligula gave to Agrippa I in AD 37; 2) Abila of the Decapolis; or 3) a toparchy (administrative division) of Peraea, south of the territory of Pella and west of those of Philadelphia and Gerasa, see Josephus, *Antiquities of the Jews* 4.176, with E. Schürer, *The History of the Jewish People in the Age of Jesus Christ (175 B.C.—A.D. 135)* 2 (rev. English ed. G. Vermes, F. Millar, and M. Black; Edinburgh, 1979), 6–7 (n. 11).

5. **Tdmr* is mentioned in ten Safaitic inscriptions, as a destination and a place the author is coming from, and in references to relations with its people. In one inscription (WH 1067) it is even used as a personal name. There are also a number of Safaitic inscriptions which have been found in the region around Palmyra, see D. Schlumberger, *La Palmyrène du Nord-Ouest. Villages et lieux de culte de l'époque impériale. Recherches archéologiques sur la mise en valeur d'une région du désert par les Palmyréniens. Suivi du recueil des inscriptions sémitiques de cette région de H. Ingholt et de J. Starcky avec une contribution de G. Ryckmans* (Bibliotheque archeologique et historique 49; Paris, 1951), nos 2quater, 21bis, 34ter, 54b, 60, 63bis, 63quater, 80, 81a–c, 82a–b.

and other places. We have brief Greek/Safaitic bilinguals,[6] and graffiti in Greek by members of tribes otherwise known only in Safaitic;[7] occasional Nabataean/Safaitic[8] and Palmyrene/Safaitic[9] bilinguals, as well as Safaitic inscriptions by people calling themselves 'so-and-so the Nabataean'.[10] *One even claims affiliation to the people of the town of Ṣalkhad in the Ḥawrān.[11] There were Roman forts and Safaitic graffiti at major watering places like Azraq,[12] or smaller ones like al-Namārah (which is frequently mentioned in Safaitic).[13] There, the Safaitic texts mingle with Latin and Greek graffiti carved by the soldiers, some of which mention the villages in the Ḥawrān from which the soldiers came.[14] There is also the famous Greek inscription from an area called Jathūm in the basalt desert of north-eastern Jordan which is a complaint by Abchoros the barber and Diomedes the lyre-player who, to their horror, had been dragged from the bright lights of the Ḥawrān to serve the commander of an infantry unit posted to this desolate wilderness.[15]

6. See e.g. in Macdonald, 'Literacy in an Oral Environment', 76–77 (Fig. 2), and M. C. A. Macdonald, M. Al Mu'azzin, and L. Nehme, 'Les inscriptions safaitiques de Syrie, cent quarante ans apres leur decouverte', *CRAI* (1996), 435–94 at 485–87.

7. See e.g. in Macdonald, 'Literacy in an Oral Environment', 76–77 (Fig. 3), and Macdonald, Al Mu'azzin, and Nehme, 'Inscriptions safaitiques de Syrie', 480–85.

8. *E.g. F. H. al-Khraysheh, 'Eine safaitisch-nabataische bilingue Inschrift aus Jordanien', in N. Nebes (ed.), *Arabia Felix. Beiträge zur Sprache und Kultur des vorislamischen Arabien. Festschrift Walter W. Müller zum 60. Geburtstag* (Wiesbaden, 1994), 109–14, and Macdonald, 'Nomads and the Ḥawrān', 348.

9. See Macdonald, 'Nomads and the Ḥawrān', 347.

10. E.g. Macdonald, Al Mu'azzin, and Nehme, 'Inscriptions safaitiques', 444–49.

11. See Macdonald, 'Literacy in an Oral Environment', 82–83.

12. On the castle at Azraq, see e.g. D. L. Kennedy and D. Riley, *Rome's Desert Frontier from the Air* (London, 1990), 181–83 and references there. For the inscriptions see *CIS* V 5200–5208.

13. *M. C. A. Macdonald, 'Transformation and Continuity at al-Namāra: Camps, Settlements, Forts, and Tombs', in K. Bartl and 'A. Moaz (eds), *Residences, Castles, Settlements. Transformation Processes from Late Antiquity to Early Islam in Bilad al-Sham* (Orient-Archaologie 24; Rahden, 2009), 317–32, and H. Zeinaddin, 'Die Inschrift en von al-Namāra', in the same volume, 333–37.

14. E.g. *IGLS* 2265–66, 2268–69.

15. *See L. Mowry, 'A Greek Inscription at Jathum in Transjordan', *BASOR* 132 (1953) 165–70, and for a discussion see Macdonald, 'Nomads and the Ḥawrān', 349–50 and references there. On στρατηγὸς ὀπλειτῶν, J. and L. Robert remark in 'Bulletin epigraphique', *REG* 68 (1955) 185–298 at 276 (no. 248) that 'la mention du στρατηγὸς ὀπλειτῶν est surprenante; nous y verrions non un titre reel, mais une denomination classicisante

I should define what I mean by the 'Ḥawrān' and other ancient geographical terms since they are sometimes used very loosely and this can cause confusion.[16] The term 'Ḥawrān' is used by modern writers in both a narrow and a broader sense.[17] The narrow sense is the one which corresponds to ancient Auranitis, that is the central part of Jabal Ḥawrān (modern Jabal al-ʿArab/Jabal ad-Drūz) and part of the plain to the west of it. 'Ḥawrān' in the wider modern sense is used of the whole of Jabal al-ʿArab and all of the plain to the west including Boṣrā and even as far south as Umm al-Jimāl. However, it is important to emphasize that in both defi nitions, the *ḥarrah* or basalt desert to the east of Jabal al-ʿArab/Jabal ad-Drūz is not part of the Ḥawrān. I shall be using the wider definition of Ḥawrān, that is Auranitis, plus the rest of Jabal al-ʿArab and the plain to the west of it.

There are a number of inscriptions which mention their authors' dealings with the Ḥawrān and which suggest that they sometimes pastured their animals there. For instance, one says that he drove his camels back to the desert on account of snow in the Ḥawrān,[18] and several say that they

(Athenes) emanant sans doute du citharede'. One might expect something like πέζαρχος. However, see F. Zayadine, 'L'espace urbain du grand Petra. Les routes et les stations caravanieres', *Annual of the Department of Antiquities of Jordan* 36 (1992) 217–39 at 221–22 for a sixth-century Greek inscription from the 'suburbs' of Petra which refers to a ΜΑΓΙΤΡΟΥ ΟΠΛΙΤΩ.

16. E.g. recently by T. Bruggemann, 'Ἐθνάρχος, Φύλαρχος and Στρατηγὸς νομάδων in Roman Arabia (1st–3rd Century). Central Power, Local Administration, and Nomadic Environment', in A.S. Lewin et al. (eds), *The Late Roman Army in the Near East from Diocletian to the Arab Conquest. Proceedings of a Colloquium Held at Potenza, Acerenza and Matera, Italy (May 2005)* (BAR International Series 1717; Oxford, 2007), 275–84: 'the indigenous tribes living in Djabal Ḥawrān in ancient times were nomadic' (p. 276); 'nomadic tribes, whose migration routes were totally on the territory of the empire' (p. 282); 'the north-east corner of the Djabal Ḥaurān . . . even in Roman times . . . remains the territory of nomadic (Safaitic) tribes' (p. 282); etc. On the inappropriateness of using the name of a script to label a people (in this case 'Safaitic'), see Macdonald, 'Nomads and the Ḥawrān', 306–10, and 'Some Reflections on Epigraphy and Ethnicity in the Roman Near East', *Mediterranean Archaeology* 11 (1998) 177–90 at 182–89 (repr. with addenda and corrigenda in Macdonald, *Literacy and Identity*, Ch. IV).

17. Macdonald 'Nomads and the Ḥawrān', 309 (n. 39).

18. *R.M.A. Harahsheh, *Nuqūš ṣafāʾiyyah min al-bādiyyah al-urduniyyah al-šamāliyyah al-šarqiyyah, dirāsah wa-taḥlīl* (Amman, 2010), 127–29 (no. 218): . . . *w ngs*[2] *h- ʾbl m ḥrn mn ṯlg b-rʾy ngm* '. . . and he drove the camels from the Ḥawrān on account of snow at the pools of Ngm'. Cf. SIJ 30: . . . *w tẓr h- ṯlg ʿl- {ḥ}{r}n* '. . . and he was waiting for snow [to fall] on the {Ḥawrān}'.

began their migration eastwards to the inner desert from there.[19] Since this migration begins with the first rains in October, this suggests that they had been spending the dry season, *qyẓ* (July to October), in the well-watered Ḥawrān. This reflects one aspect of the symbiosis between nomads and agriculturalists whereby the nomads bring their animals to the fields after the harvest to feed on the stubble and, in return, the animals manure the fields ready for sowing the next crop. This is in good years. But if there is a drought, the nomads are even more hard-pressed than the villagers and some will move out of the desert into the settled areas seeking water and grazing for their animals, and this inevitably results in conflict. One Safaitic inscription says that its author was ‘driven out of the Ḥawrān and so pastured his animals wherever he could’.[20]

An intriguing text is dated to ‘the year the people of the Ḥawrān complained to Caesar about Philippus’,[21] an event which I have suggested, may refer to complaints made to Vespasian against Philippus son of Iachimus son of Zamaris, whose family Herod the Great had settled in Batanaea with instructions to bring order to the Trachonitis, that is, the Lejā. Philippus was a close friend and general of Agrippa II and other complaints about him had been quietly ignored.[22] In passing, it should be emphasized that the Lejā was not (and is not) a grazing ground for nomads as is sometimes assumed. This is because it largely consists of solid, unbroken, lava, riddled with caves and with some areas of very rich soil used by agriculturalists. In antiquity, and until relatively recent times, it was famous as the lair of bandits and other miscreants and these should not be confused with nomads.[23]

19. *Harahsheh, *Nuqūš*, 112–15 (no. 197): . . . *w ’*s^2*rq m ḥrn b-’bl-h* s^2*‘r b-r’y y’m{r}* . . . ‘. . . and he migrated to the inner desert from the Ḥawrān with his camels [to] the herbage at the pools of Y’mr . . .’; *CIS* V 2021: . . . *w ’*s^2*rq m ḥrn* . . . ‘and he migrated towards the inner desert from the Ḥawrān; *CIS* V 3339: . . . *w ’*s^2*rq [w] bn m ḥrn (h-)rḥbt m{n} mḥ{l}* ‘. . . and he migrated towards the inner desert [and] went from the Ḥawrān to this *raḥaba* [an area where water collects in the rainy season and herbage grows] {because} of a dearth of {pasture}’.

20. WH 161: . . . *w ṭrd mn ḥrn f r‘y kll ’rḍ* ‘and he was driven (out) of (the) Ḥawrān and so he pastured in every region’.

21. KRS 1991 [[=*DMIPERP* §145]]: . . . *s¹nt qbl ’l ḥrn qṣr ‘l-fl f{ṣ}*.

22. M. C. A. Macdonald, ‘Herodian Echoes in the Syrian Desert’, in S. Bourke and J.-P. Descoeudres (eds), *Trade, Contact, and the Movement of Peoples in the Eastern Mediterranean. Studies in Honour of J. Basil Hennessy* (Mediterranean Archaeology Supplements 3; Sydney, 1995), 285–90 at 289.

23. B. Isaac, ‘Bandits in Judaea and Arabia’, *HSCP* 88 (1984) 171–203; and Macdonald,

*There are some 30 Safaitic inscriptions which mention either the author's relations with *rm* or which are dated to events involving the Romans.[24] In addition there are 19 texts dated to events involving the emperor, who is referred to simply as *qṣr* (Καῖσαρ). Once again, I should emphasize that since the authors knew what they meant and were not writing with a reader in mind, the events by which texts are dated can be purely local such as, 'the year Gmm son of S^{1}r died'[25] where Gmm son of S^{1}r was presumably either a 'local hero', a member of the writer's extended family, or a friend. Even more frustrating are dates such as 'the year of ʿbdt's death',[26] where we do not know whether *ʿbdt* is a local person or one of the three Nabataean kings of that name. In other cases, we are given details, but not of the sort that can help us identify the event, such as 'the year the people of Rome smote S^{2}mt son of ʾs^1 the Qʿs^{2}ite',[27] where we have no idea who this person was, or even 'the year of the struggle between Rome and the Nabataeans'[28] where we cannot tell whether this was some 'little local difficulty'—perhaps one of the raids by the Nabataeans into the newly formed province of Syria, mentioned by Strabo[29]—or an otherwise unattested struggle, for instance at the time of the Annexation of the Nabataean kingdom. There are other unhelpful dates such as 'the year the king died' and even 'the year Caesar

'Nomads and the Ḥawrān', 313–14: 'There is no suggestion in these texts [i.e. the passages in Josephus and Strabo dealing with the Trachonitis and the "edict of Agrippa" (*IGLS* 2329 [= *OGIS* 424], with AAES III 404 and PUAES IIIA 766)] either that these outlaws were nomadic—their "migrations" appear to have been triggered not by seasonal rainfall but by the approach of punitive expeditions—or that they were in any way related to the nomads who pastured in the deserts east of Jabal Ḥawrān and wrote the Safaitic inscriptions. The Trachonitis, or Lejā, is an area well outside that in which Safaitic texts are normally found. Indeed, only one such text [*CIS* V 1] has so far been discovered in the Lejā and I know of no evidence that the nomads from east of the Jabal made more than an occasional visit to it. From the other side, there is no indication in the Safaitic inscriptions that their authors led a life of brigandage'.

24. For my caveats about assuming that *rm*, *ʾl rm*, *hrm*, and *ʾl hrm* always mean the Romans see Macdonald, 'Nomads and the Ḥawrān', 328–29. There are however a sufficient number of texts where this would seem to be the most likely meaning to allow us to take the identification as a working hypothesis when there is no evidence to the contrary.

25. *CIS* V 4757: . . . *s^{1}nt myt gmm bn s^{1}r* . . . .

26. A. Naji, 'Kitābah ṣafawiyyah min ṣaḥrāʾ al-ruṭbah', *Sumer* 18 (1962) 165–70: . . . *s^{1}nt mʿt bdt* . . . .

27. *CIS* V 4439: . . . *s^{1}nt ṭrq ʾl rm s^{2}mt bn ʾs^1 h- qʿs^{2}y* . . . .

28. *CIS* V 4866: . . . *s^{1}nt ws^{1}q bn rm nbṭ*.

29. Strabo 16.4.21.

died'[30] without specifying which king or emperor, since the author knew which one he meant, and that was all that mattered.

However, there are some which are more enlightening. Thus, 'the year Syllaeus came from Rome'[31] would seem to refer to an event in the period between 9 BC when we know that the Nabataean minister, Syllaeus, was in Rome[32] and 6 BC when Josephus tells us Syllaeus returned to Rome at the same time as Herod's son Antipater.[33] *Unfortunately, no photograph, or even a tracing, of this inscription has been published, only a reading and discussion.

*One text is dated to 'the year Caesar's son died and he [the author] heard that Philippus had died, but scoffed'.[34] I have suggested that in this case 'Caesar's son' may refer to Germanicus, the adopted son of the Emperor Tiberius, who is mentioned in another Safaitic inscription.[35] After a tour in Syria which seems to have created a considerable public impression, he died suddenly at Epidaphne near Antioch in AD 19. The mourning and upheavals following his death would have ensured that the news spread quickly. The author is dismissive about the reports of Philippus' death, saying that he had *heard* that he had died, but scoffed. AD 19 would be in the middle of Philip the Tetrarch's long reign in the Ḥawrān, about which we know remarkably little, and it is possible that an unfounded rumour that he had died spread at this time.

30. SIJ 911 and WH 387: . . . *s^1nt myt h-mlk* [or *hmlk*], where it is not clear whether 'the king' or someone called *Hmlk* is meant (see Macdonald, 'Nomads and the Ḥawrān', p. 343). Cf. *s^1nt myt qṣr* in e.g. KRS 2375 and Safaitic inscriptions nos NBR 2 and 4 recorded by the Safaitic Epigraphic Survey Programme between Zalaf and Ruḥbah in southern Syria (publication in preparation).

31. S. Abbadi, 'Naqš ṣafawī ğsadīd yuʿarraḫu ilā ʾl-rubaʿ al-aḫīr min qarn al-awal qabl al-mīlad', *Abḥāṯ al-yarmūk. Silsilat al-ʿulūm al-insāniyyah wa-ʾl-iğtimaʿiyyah* 13 (1997), pp. 141–51: . . . *s^1nt ʾty s^1ly m- rm* . . . .

32. Josephus, *Antiquities of the Jews* 16.282–99, 16.335–53. Although Augustus condemned Syllaeus to death (*Antiquities of the Jews* 16.352: καὶ πέρας εἰς τοῦτο μετέστη Καῖσαρ ὡς τοῦ μὲν Συλλαίου καταγνῶναι θάνατον) in fact he was 'sent back (16.353: ὁ μὲν Συλλαίος ἀνεπέμπετο) to Nabataea to pay the penalty and what he owed his creditors, and then be punished accordingly'. However, it seems that he was not executed in Petra and had recovered his reputation sufficiently to feel that it was worth setting out for Rome again in 6 BC.

33. Josephus, *Jewish War* 1.573–574.

34. Safaitic inscriptions in preparation for publication by M. C. A. Macdonald, no. Ms 44: . . . *s^1nt myt bn qṣr w s^1mʿ ʾn myt fl fṣ f s^1ḫr* . . . .

35. *PUAES IVC 653: . . . *s^1nt lgy[n] grmnqṣ b- nqʾt* . . . 'the year the legion(s) of Germanicus were at Nq't'.

Another of the Herodian rulers of the Ḥawrān, Agrippa II, is also the only monarch to have a Safaitic inscription dated by one of his regnal years. During the Princeton University Archaeological Expeditions to Syria at the beginning of the twentieth century, one of the camp servants made a bad copy of a Safaitic inscription at a hill-top called al-ʿĪsāwī, in the Wādī Shām.[36] E. Littmann published his attempted reading of it and thought that it ended with the words 'year eighteen' which, understandably, he assumed referred to the era of Boṣrā, that is, AD 123/24. However, almost a century later, my friend and colleague H. Zeinaddin rediscovered the inscription and realized that the earlier copyist had treated the end of the inscription as a separate text, which he had copied particularly badly, and that in fact the date read 'year eighteen of King Agrippa', which would be AD 67/68.[37] This is therefore one of the most precisely dated Safaitic inscriptions we have so far.

We have other references to a King Agrippa, again almost certainly Agrippa II. One text is dated to the year King Agrippa died (that is, AD 92/93)[38] and another, from al-Namārah, is dated to 'the year King Agrippa laid siege to the city'.[39] This may refer to the part Agrippa II took in the Roman suppression of the First Jewish Revolt of AD 66–70. He was present with auxiliary troops at Cestius Gallus's disastrous attack on Jerusalem in AD 66[40] and at Vespasian and Titus's successful siege of Gamala, in both of which his only part seems to have been vain attempts to persuade the inhabitants to surrender, at least according to Josephus.[41] He may also have been present at the siege of Jotapata in June/July 67, and/or at the final

36. *This is PUAES IVC 1064 + 1065.

37. The stone was found on the Safaitic Epigraphic Survey Programme, directed by the author, which in three seasons between 1996 and 2002, made a systematic survey of the site of al-ʿĪsāwī recording 3423 Safaitic inscriptions. The complete inscription is as yet unpublished and has the field number H 763. Note that in contrast to the other Safaitic texts mentioning Agrippa, the name here is spelt *ʾgrfṣ* rather than *grfṣ*.

38. *. . . *s*^{1}*nt myt grfṣ h-mlk* . . . in inscription no. SESP.U 8 recorded by the Safaitic Epigraphic Survey Programme (in preparation for publication).

39. *. . . *s*^{1}*nt kbs*^{1} *h-mlk grfṣ h-{m}dnt* . . . . This text which has the field number HN 91 was recorded in 1996 by H. Zeinaddin in the course of the Namārah Rescue Survey, directed by the author. See Macdonald, 'Transformation and Continuity' for the survey in general, and Zeinaddin, 'Inschriften von al-Namāra', p. 335 for the inscription [[=*DMIPERP* §143]].

40. Josephus, *Jewish War* 2.523–526; Schürer, *History of the Jewish People* 1, 487–88.

41. Josephus, *Jewish War* 4.14–16.

capture of Jerusalem, though Josephus does not mention this.[42] *However, it seems possible that, from the point of view of his subjects back in the Ḥawrān,[43] and thence the nomads in the desert beyond, it was Agrippa who was leading the attack in some or all of these engagements.

There are some tantalizing other references to the Jews. One is dated simply to 'the year of the Jew',[44] and another possibly to 'the struggle of the Jew',[45] while a third states that the author 'was guarding (or was on the look out for) the queen of the Jews'.[46] While it is difficult to link any of these to identifiable events, it is possible that the third refers to Queen Berenice, the sister of Agrippa II.[47]

The date to 'the year [in which] Malichus king of Nabataea smote thirty centuries [?] of Roman soldiers'[48] could be an exaggerated reference to one of the skirmishes between the Nabataeans and the Romans in the years after the creation of the province of Syria in 63 BC. This took place during the reign of the Nabataean King Malichus I who was defeated in 55 BC by the first governor of Syria, Aulus Gabinius. On the other hand, Zeinaddin, who discovered this text, has placed it after the annexation of the Nabataean

42. Josephus, *Jewish War* 3.145–288, 3.316–39; Schürer, *History of the Jewish People* 1, 493.

43. In AD 53, the Emperor Claudius had granted Agrippa II the tetrarchy of Philip (Batanaea, Trachonitis, and Gaulanitis), the tetrarchy of Lysanias (Abila), as well as the territory of Varus in Lebanon.

44. *CIS* V 2732: . . . *s¹nt h- yhdy* . . . .

45. *CIS* V 3360: . . . *s¹[n]t (w)s¹q h-y{h}d{y}*.

46. *. . . *w ḫrṣ mlkt 'l yhd* . . . . The inscription was originally recorded by Littmann at al-ʿĪsāwī (= PUAES IVC 353) [[=*DMIPERP* §139]] but this particular passage was unclear on his copy and he was not able to make satisfactory sense of it. It was re-recorded, this time with photographs, by Madame M. Al Muʿazzin on the Safaitic Epigraphic Survey Programme, and the reading is now assured.

47. See Schürer, *History of the Jewish People* 1, 474–80.

48. . . . *s¹nt ṭrq mk mlk nbṭ ṯlṯn m't qtl 'l rm*, in a Safaitic inscription reported on by H. Zeinaddin in an unpublished paper entitled 'Al-'alāqāt al-ṣafā'iyyah al-nabaṭiyyah min ḫilāl al-kitābāt al-ṣafā'iyyah wa-ḏikr al-malik mālik al-ṯāliṯ malik al-anbāṭ' given at a conference in Petra 29–31 October 2002. The name of the Nabataean kings known to us as Malichus II and probably Malichus III, was spelt *Mnkw* in Nabataean. In Safaitic a post-vocalic /n/ is often assimilated and so *mnk > mk. Zeindaddin assumes that there is a *w* missing between *ṯlṯn* and *m't*, but if restored this would produce a peculiar form of the number 'one hundred and thirty'. On the translation of *m't* as 'centuries' see below. Here there is no mention of cavalry and one could assume that normal Roman centuries (i.e. infantry) were meant. Exaggeration of this sort is of course common in accounts of battles. I am most grateful to my friend and colleague Ahmad Al-Jallad for suggesting that I reconsider Zeinaddin's interpretation.

kingdom making it one of a number of possible references to the events surrounding the creation of *provincia Arabia*. In this case, the Malichus here would be the supposed successor of the Nabataean King Rabbel II, by the first year of whose reign a Nabataean inscription in Madā'in Ṣāliḥ is thought to be dated.[49] If one accepts the existence of this 'Malichus III', and that he may have resisted the annexation, one might attribute other Safaitic references to conflict between the Nabataeans and Romans to the same period, such as 'the year of the struggle between Rome and the Nabataeans',[50] or 'the year of the Nabataeans' rebellion against the Romans'.[51]

An event which is used to date several inscriptions, all by members of the same family, is *s¹nt ngy qṣr h- mdnt*,[52] the interpretation of which is not easy. In Arabic, the root *N-Ǧ-Y* can mean 'to be saved, to escape' and in the causative stem 'to rescue'. In many contexts in Safaitic this would seem to be what is required. So it would be possible to translate *s¹nt ngy qṣr h- mdnt* as 'the year Caesar saved the city', or even 'the province' since the word *mədīnâ* in Aramaic (from which it is borrowed into Arabic and possibly Safaitic) has a much wider implication than 'city', meaning 'any area of jurisdiction', such as a province.[53] This would then refer to an event which we cannot identify, possibly one of the Persian invasions or one of the Jewish Revolts? But it is difficult to imagine what Caesar 'saving' the province of Syria or of Arabia would have meant to a nomad east of the Ḥawrān, and we have no record of an emperor 'saving' a city in this region, or indeed 'escaping' from one.

However, there is another more daring interpretation, which I suggest extremely tentatively but which, if correct, seems to me to open up intriguing possibilities. In Minaic and Sabaic, the verb *ngw* appears to mean 'to announce, declare'[54] and it seems just possible that *ngy* in these particular

49. For a clear and helpful assessment of the arguments for and against this theory see L. Nehme, 'Quelques elements de reflexion sur Hegra et sa region a partir du IIe siècle apres J.-C.', in J. Schiettecatte and C. J. Robin (eds), *L'Arabie à la veille de l'Islam. Bilan clinique* (Orient et Mediterranee 3; Paris, 2009), 37–58 at 42–44.

50. *CIS* V 4866: . . . *s¹nt ws¹q bn rm nbṭ*.

51. WH 2815: . . . *s¹nt mrdt nbṭ 'l- 'l {r}m* . . . .

52. *WH 1698, 1725b, and Safaitic inscriptions recorded by A. Betts in north-eastern Jordan (publication in preparation), nos 3–9.

53. S. Fraenkel, *Die aramäischen Fremdwörter im Arabischen* (Leiden, 1886), 280–81.

54. *A. F. L. Beeston et al., *Sabaic Dictionary (English-French-Arabic)* (Louvain-la-Neuve, 1982), 93 s.v. *NGW*, in Ja 567 (a Sabaic inscription from Maḥram Bilqis, Mārib, Yemen, published in A. Jamme, *Sabaean Inscriptions from Maḥram Bilqîs (Mârib)*

Safaitic dating formulae could have a similar meaning. Thus *s¹nt ngy qṣr h- mdnt* might mean 'the year Caesar announced the province', that is, the declaration of *Arabia adquisita*, in AD 111.[55] It is likely that rumours that the Nabataean kingdom had been brought to an end would have been rife after the death of Rabbel II, with considerable confusion as to the exact political consequences. For many nomads this change would have been of more than academic interest since it would inevitably affect their relations with the settled areas. Firm news that Rome—which the nomads already knew from their dealings with the provincial authorities in Syria—had now officially taken over the Nabataean kingdom would therefore have been of keen interest to the nomads and could well have been used as an event by which to date their texts. I should repeat that this is no more than a tentative suggestion and I shall return shortly to other possible examples of *ngy* used in this sense.

Another text appears to be dated to 'the year Caesar sent reinforcements to the province and put the province in good order . . .', though this interpretation is not certain.[56] If correct, this could refer to Septimius Severus' placing of troops (including Gothic *gentiles*) in desert outposts in what is now north-eastern Jordan and southern Syria, together with his reorganization of the provinces of Syria and the northern parts of Arabia in the early years of the third century AD.[57] The writer's attitude is also interesting, since he seems not only well-informed of what was happening in the settled areas, but to approve of the emperor's actions. This should alert us not to assume that nomads were by definition hostile to good government in the provinces.

[Publications of the American Foundation for the Study of Man 3; Baltimore, 1962], 49–53), line 8, *CIS* IV 67, line 12 'give out, intimate, announce to *s.o.*'. Minaic, e.g. *RES* 3306A = G. Garbini, *Iscrizioni sudarabiche* 1. *Iscrizioni Minee* (Pubblicazioni del Seminario di Semitistica, Istituto Orientale di Napoli. Ricerche, 10; Naples, 1974), 83 (no. 293A) = as-Sawdā' (Minaic inscriptions from as-Sawdā', Yemen, in *Corpus of South Arabian Inscriptions*, available online at http://csai.humnet.unipi.it/csai/html/index.html), no. 36, line 6.

55. *Its first governor C. Claudius Severus, successor of A. Cornelius Palma Frontonianus, governor of Syria, who *Arabiam Petraeam domuit et in provinciae formam redegit* (Dio Cassius 68.14.5, see M. Sartre, *Trois études sur l'Arabie romaine et byzantine* [Collection Latomus 178; Brussels, 1982], 78), had probably been there since AD 107. See also G.W. Bowersock, *Roman Arabia* (Cambridge, MA, 1983), 83–84.

56. . . . *s¹nt 'md qyṣr h-mdnt w s¹wy h-mdnt* . . . in Macdonald, Al Mua'zzin, and Nehme, 'Inscriptions safaitiques de Syrie', 453–58 for the interpretation of the verbs.

57. Bowersock, *Roman Arabia*, 113–20.

To return to the verb *ngy*, there are a considerable number of texts with dating formulae of the form *s*^{1}*nt ngy* N *hdy*, and the like. Now the word *hdy* means 'leader' and it seems unlikely that *ngy* in these texts has its Arabic meaning of 'escape' or 'save', since this would produce 'the year N, a leader, escaped' or 'the year N saved a leader'. Since the same formula occurs with a number of different personal names this would require a great many leaders escaping or being saved.[58] Tentatively, therefore, I would suggest that *ngy* here may have the same sense as I have proposed above, namely 'announce, declare, appoint' and that the formulae would therefore mean 'the year so-and-so was declared [that is, appointed] commander'. This would then make more sense of the abbreviated version of this formula 'the year so-and-so was, or became, a leader'.

If we accept this interpretation as a working hypothesis, the question arises what were these people appointed leaders of. One might perhaps think of the temporary command of a raiding party or a group of nomads setting out for war. In these circumstances, the Bedouin accept a commander and agree to obey his orders, and the same could have been the practice in antiquity. But this is solely for the duration of the raid or battle and not for a predetermined length of time, such as a year, indeed there might be several different leaders in one year, depending on the number of raids or battles. It is also possible that the leadership of a trading caravan was implied. Here the outward and return journeys—at least to South Arabia for frankincense, if that was the destination—could be expected to take approximately a year and it is therefore possible that the appointment of a particular person as caravan leader could be used for dating. But we have no evidence at all that the nomads who carved these graffiti were involved in the caravan trade and, given that they describe many of their other activities, it would be strange if they were entirely silent about this.

In Palmyrene, the word *hdy* is found in the phrase *hdy nṭryn* meaning 'commander of guards'[59] and I would therefore suggest that it is just possible that these men were commanders of units of the Roman, or indeed the Nabataean, armies drawn from the nomads. The date would then refer to

58. There are however inscriptions in which the verb *ngy* clearly does have the meaning 'escape' as in . . . *w ngy mḥrn mks*^{1}*ʿ* . . . 'and he escaped from the Ḥawrān wounded'. This would suggest that there were perhaps originally two roots, N-G-W 'to announce' and N-G-Y 'to escape' which fell together as *ngy* in Safaitic. I am most grateful to my friend and colleague A. Al Jallad for this suggestion.

59. R. Du Mesnil du Buisson, *Inventaire des inscriptions palmyréniennes de Doura-Europos (32 avant J.-C. à 256 après J.-C.)* (rev. ed.; Paris, 1939), 20–22 (no. 39, line 3).

the year of their appointment, without the implication that they would have command for only a year. We know virtually nothing about the structure of the Nabataean army and frustratingly little about the units which the Roman army levied from the inhabitants of the eastern provinces in the first two or three centuries AD. So this can remain no more than a suggestion.

In my article of twenty years ago, 'Nomads and the Ḥawrān', I argued that titles such as στρατηγὸς νομάδων in the Greek inscriptions from Jabal al-ʿArab referred to Roman officers charged with liaison with the nomads, and that the phrases παρεμβολὴ νομάδων and ἔθνος νομάδων were Roman administrative terms for military units raised from the nomads. I have also argued elsewhere that the terms Θαμουδηνῶν ἔθνος / *šrkt tmwdw* in the Ruwāfah inscription refer to a *natio*, or indigenous auxiliary unit in the Roman army, as described by Pseudo-Hyginus, though, unfortunately, he gives us no clue as to the structure and command of these units.[60] As Speidel puts it:

> . . . the ethnic units, whether qualified by one of the terms discussed [that is, *numeri*, *vexillationes*, *milites*, *equites*, and so on], or just by their ethnic name [as with the *nationes* listed by Pseudo-Hyginus],[61] might differ far more from each other than has been assumed up to now . . . .[62] . . . Each unit must be judged on its own in such matters as origin, recruitment, composition, strength, organization, command, pay, conditions of service, permanence, status, tactical function, etc. . . . While some groups of them, such as the regular *nationes*, certainly shared some common characteristics, other units, even of the same tribes, may have followed quite different patterns and played vastly different roles . . . .[63]

60. Macdonald, 'Nomads and the Ḥawrān', 368–77, and 'On Saracens, the Rawwāfah Inscription and the Roman Army, in idem, *Literacy and Identity*, 10–11 (English trans. with addenda and corrigenda of 'Quelques reflexions sur les Saracenes, l'inscription de Rawwāfa et l'armee romaine', in H. Lozachmeur [ed.], *Présence arabe dans le Croissant fertile avant l'Hégire* [Paris, 1995], 93–101).

61. These are *Palmyreni, Gaesati, Daci, Brittones, Cantabri* (Pseudo-Hyginus 29), to which one might add, if I am correct, the Θαμουδηνῶν ἔθνος / *šrkt tmwdw* of the Ruwāfah inscription.

62. M. P. Speidel, 'The Rise of Ethnic Units in the Roman Imperial Army', in *ANRW* 2.3 (1975), 202–31 at 207 (repr. in idem, *Roman Army Studies* 1 [Mavors Roman Army Researches 1; Amsterdam, 1984], 117–48).

63. Speidel, 'Rise of Ethnic Units', 208.

Now, the word for such a unit in Safaitic appears to be *ms¹rt* which is related to, and may be a loan from, Aramaic *mašrītā'*.[64] In Syriac, the latter has exactly the dual meaning of Greek παρεμβολή, that is, 'a camp', or 'a military unit', and is used to translate it in both meanings in the Syriac Bible.[65] The word *ms¹rt* occurs in a number of Safaitic inscriptions most notably in one whose author describes himself as *'qrb bn 'bgr bms¹rt 'l 'mrt frs¹* that is ''qrb son of 'bgr a horseman in the military unit of the 'mrt lineage'.[66] It may be significant that 'qrb bn 'bgr dates his text to 'the year Ġwṯ bn Rḍwt was appointed'—if my interpretation of *ngy* is correct—and though he does not specify what Ġwṯ was appointed to, one could speculate that it was to the command of the unit in which the author was serving. The structure of this text can be compared with that of the Palmyrene inscription set up by a Nabataean some twenty-six years after the Roman annexation of the Nabataean kingdom.[67] He describes himself as *nbṭy' rwḥy' dy hw' frš [b-] ḥyrt' w b-mšryt' dy 'n'* 'the Nabataean, of the tribe of Rwḥw, who is a cavalryman in Ḥrt' and in the regiment of 'n'.[68]

64. *A much less likely alternative explanation would be that *ms¹rt* is a loan from Sabaic *mns³rt* 'vanguard' which occurs in e.g. 'Abadān 1, lines 13, 19; Mafray-al-Mi'sāl (Sabaic inscriptions, in *Corpus of South Arabian Inscriptions*, available online at http://csai.humnet.unipi.it/csai/html/index.html), no. 5, line 11. One would then have to assume that the /n/ was assimilated, as happens sporadically in Safaitic. However, given the proximity of the Nabataeans to those who wrote the Safaitic inscriptions, a loan from Aramaic seems far more likely.

65. Thus, in the sense 'camp', in e.g. Numbers 12:14: Hebrew *maḥaneh*, Greek παρεμβολή, Syriac *mašrītā*. In the sense of a host, military unit, see, for instance among numerous examples, 1 Maccabees 7:42: Greek παρεμβολή, Syriac *mašrītā*.

66. Safaitic inscriptions in preparation for publication by M. C. A. Macdonald, no. Ms 64: *l 'qrb bn 'bgr b- ms¹rt 'l 'mrt frs¹ s¹nt ngy ġwṯ bn rḍwt* 'By 'qrb son of 'bgr, a horseman in the military unit of the 'l 'mrt, in the year Ġwṯ son of Rḍwt was appointed'. On the involvement of nomads in Roman cavalry units, see below.

67. *CIS* II 3973.

68. If we take *'n'* as personal name, rather than a place name equivalent to 'Ānah on the Euphrates, we avoid the linguistic problems noted by E. Littmann, *Publications of an American Archaeological Expedition to Syria in 1899–1900* 4. *Semitic Inscriptions* (New York, 1904), pp. 71–72 who points out that all ancient spellings of this place name (Syriac, later Hebrew, Greek, and Latin) end in *-t* not -'. It also avoids the problem of the author being posted in two different places, *ḥyrt'* (al-Ḥīrah?) and 'Ānah. Thus, I would suggest translating '. . . 'bydw son of 'nmw [son of] Š'dlt, the Nabataean of the lineage of Rwḥw, a cavalryman [in] Ḥyrt' and in the regiment of 'n'. . .'. A personal name spelt *'n* is common in Safaitic, and, since no vowels are shown in Safaitic orthography, this could represent e.g. *'Anā (among other vocalizations) which would be spelt *'n'* in Palmyrene. There are also two references in Safaitic to a lineage group spelt *'n* (PUAES IVC 160 =

Other texts describe their authors’ service in such units, for example ‘he was on guard at the rear of the unit’ or ‘he was on guard for the unit’, and in three cases ‘the year Mty was appointed commander’.[69] Occasionally we get more detail as in ‘the year ’bgr travelled with the unit (*ms^{1}rt*) and was put in command of a cavalry detachment to control the Ruḥba’ (an area of rich pasture not far from the Roman military post at the wells of al-Namārah).[70] It seems likely that the word *ms^{1}rt* is a loan from Aramaic, even specifically from Nabataean where the title *rb mšryt’* (commander of the unit or camp) is found in a Nabataean inscription at al-Jawf, in northern Saudi Arabia,[71] though the fact that there is a verb *s^{1}rt* in Safaitic (see below) means that this is not certain.[72]

Another inscription,[73] whose author was also able to write his name and those of his father and grandfather in Greek on an adjacent stone,[74] says that he built a structure for someone called Hn’ and tracked a horseman of a region called the Ms^{1}ty in the year (members of) the ’l Ḍf (one of the two largest lineage groups mentioned in these texts) were cut to pieces.

LP 160, KRS 949).

69. WH 599: . . . *w nẓr b‘d h- ms^{1}rt* . . . ‘. . . and he was on guard at the rear of the unit . . .’; WH 619a: . . . *{w} nẓr b‘d h- ms^{1}rt s^{1}nt ngy mty hdy* ‘. . . and he was on guard at the rear of the unit, the year Mty was appointed commander’; WH 610: . . . *w nẓr l- ms^{1}rt s^{1}nt ngy mty hdy* ‘. . . and he was on guard for a unit, the year Mty was appointed commander’; WH 1027: . . . *w nẓr l- h- ms^{1}rt s^{1}nt ngy mty h[d]y* ‘. . . and he was on guard for the unit, the year Mty was appointed {commander}’.

70. *CIS* V 2553: . . . *s^{1}nt ---- {’}bgr b- ms^{1}r{t} w ‘mm s^{2}ḥn b- rḥbt* . . . ‘. . . the year ’bgr [. . .] troops (?) in the unit and was put in command of a cavalry detachment to control the Ruḥbah . . .’ For *‘mm* cf. Arabic *‘ummima* ‘he was made a chief or lord over others’ (Lane 2148c); *s^{2}ḥn* cf. Arabic *šiḥan* (plural of *šiḥnah*) ‘a cavalry detachment keeping guard or controlling a town or country’.

71. M. R. Savignac and J. Starcky, ‘Une inscription nabateenne provenant du Djof’, *Revue biblique* 64 (1957) 196–217.

72. In theory, *ms^{1}rt* could be a noun derived from such a verb. If we knew how the word was vocalized we might be able to tell if *ms^{1}rt* has an Aramaic or an Arabian form, but since Safaitic orthography omits vowels of all sorts it is not possible to choose between these possibilities.

73. WH 1849: *l whblh ẓn’l bn whblh bn mlk w bny l- hn’ h- s^{1}trt w qṣṣ frs^1 h- ms^{1}ty s^{1}nt bḥr ’l ḍff h lt s^{1}lm w ‘wd b- h- ms^{1}rt m’t frs^1* ‘By Whblh son of Zn’l son of Whblh son of Mlk: and he built a shelter for Hn’ and he tracked a horseman of H-Ms^{1}ty, the year [members of] the ’l Ḍf were cut to pieces. So, O Lt [grant] security and the return to the unit of a hundred horsemen’.

74. WH 1860 = Greek 2: ΟΥΑΒΑΛΛΑΣ ΤΑΝΝΗΛΟΥ ΤΟΥ ΥΟΥΑΒΑΛΛΟΥ.

He prays to the goddess Lt for security and for the return to the unit of a hundred horsemen (*m't frs¹*).[75] I shall return to this latter expression below.

First of all I would like to turn to an interesting term which occurs in a number of these texts. This is the verb *s¹rt*. It is always found in the 3rd person masculine singular of the suffix conjugation, so we can be sure that the *t* is part of the root. From the contexts in which it occurs in Safaitic, it would seem to mean 'to perform military service, to serve in a military unit'. However, there is no verb from such a root in Arabic and, tentatively, I would suggest two possible derivations. Firstly, it might be a loan word from the Greek verb στρατεύω 'to serve in the army'.[76] Semitic languages simplify initial consonant clusters in loan words and so the *strat-* at the beginning of the word is likely to have become **s¹arat*, just as Latin *strata* was adopted into Arabic (via Aramaic) as *ṣirāṭ*.[77] One problem with this is that, since Latin was the language of the Roman army, one would expect a loan from that language rather than from Greek for such a basic military term. Moreover, σ is more often represented by *ṣ* than *s¹* in Safaitic transcriptions. A second possibility is that it is cognate with the Hebrew root *Š-R-T*, the etymology of which is disputed, but which produces the common pi'el verb *šērēt* meaning to 'serve' in both secular and religious contexts, though, as far as I can find, not in a military sense. However, this is not to say that a cognate of this verb in Safaitic could not have had such a sense.

*There are several texts in which the author says that he *s¹rt*, which I would suggest means 'he served in a military unit',[78] with his father, or

75. Note that in Arabic the verb *'āda* can be used with the preposition *fī* in the sense of 'return to' (Lane 2188c) and since *b* is generally used instead of *fī* in Ancient North Arabian *'wd b- h- ms¹rt* would seem to mean 'a return to the unit'.

76. LSJ s.v. στρατεύω.

77. Greek σ can be represented by either *s¹* or *ṣ* in Safaitic, e.g. *tts¹* (< *Titus*) and *'qlds¹* (probably < *Claudius*) as against *grmnqṣ* (< *Germanicus*) and *(')grfṣ* (< *Agrippas*).

78. The texts in which this word occurs are *CIS* V 65: . . . *w s¹rt m' 'ḥrb* . . . which I would translate as '. . . and he served with 'ḥrb . . .'; *CIS* V 320: . . . *w s¹rt m' 'b -h b- m't frs¹* 'and he served with his father in a hundred horsemen [see below]; *CIS* V 321: . . . *w s¹rt m' 'ḥrb* '. . . and he served with 'ḥrb'; *CIS* V 781: . . .*w s¹rt s¹nt n{g}y qdm bn 'mm hdy* 'and he served the year Qdm son of 'mm was appointed commander'; *CIS* V 2041: . . .*w s¹rt* 'and he served'; *CIS* V 2076: *{w} s¹rt 'l- (ḥ)dd 'bgr b- 'lf rgl w m't f [r]s¹* . . . '. . . and he served on the borders of 'bgr [perhaps the territory of Edessa?] with a thousand foot soldiers and a hundred horse . . .'; *CIS* V 4276: . . .*s¹nt s¹rt h'ṣ* . . . '. . . the year H'ṣ served . . .'; KRS 1024: . . .*w s¹rt '{l-} ḫr hdy* . . . '. . . and he served under Ḫr's command' [literally, 'he served upon Ḫr being the commander'], cf. Arabic *'alayhi amrun* 'command lies upon him, he is in command', Lane 2145a]; Safaitic inscription recorded by the Safaitic Epigraphic Survey Programme at Rijm Qa'qūl in southern Syria (publication in

another family member, or with a friend, and one dates his text to 'the year Mlk served in the "great army" [*h- arḍ/irḍ*]'.[79] Another text seems to say that its author 'served on the borders of 'bgr [perhaps the territory of Edessa, where Abgar seems to have been the throne name of successive kings?] with a thousand foot soldiers and a hundred horse'.[80]

This brings me to several texts which contain the expression *m't frs*^{1} 'a hundred horsemen' or simply *m't* 'hundred'.[81] Numbers are rare in the Safaitic inscriptions and we have no texts which mention say twenty camels or ten donkeys, or even 150 horses, only this expression 'a hundred horsemen'. It is tempting to think that this refers to a mounted military unit of some sort, though in the Roman army, of course, the *centuria* was an infantry not a cavalry unit. However, among the auxiliary units of the imperial Roman army was the *cohors equitata* which consisted of six centuries of infantry and four *turmae* of cavalry, each of the latter comprising approximately 30 horsemen. Thus, for instance, according to Josephus the *cohortes equitatae* in Vespasian's army in AD 60 each had 600 infantry and 120 cavalry,[82] and while the figure for the infantry is thought in fact to have been considerably lower, that for the cavalry seems to be generally accepted.[83] In the following century, Pseudo-Hyginus still has the ideal total of cavalry in a

preparation), no. RQ.A 10: . . .*s*^{1}*rt 'l- mlk h- s*^{1}*lṭn* . . . perhaps '. . . he served while Mlk was in power. . .' (?) or '. . . he served on government property . . .' (?); PUAES IVC 326 (from a photograph taken by the Safaitic Epigraphic Survey Programme, see n. 37 above): . . .*s*^{1}*nt s*^{1}*rt mlk b- h 'rḍ* . . . '. . . the year Mlk served in the great army . . .', on *arḍ/irḍ* see Lane 2007a, 2008a; WH 1141: . . .*w s*^{1}*rt* . . . '. . . and he served . . .'.

79. See the previous note.

80. See n. 78 above.

81. *CIS* V 320: . . . *w s*^{1}*rt m' 'b -h b- m't frs*^{1} '. . . and he served with his father in the hundred horsemen'; *CIS* V 2076: . . . *{w} s*^{1}*rt 'l- (ḥ)dd 'bgr b 'lf rgl w m't f[r]s*^{1} . . . '. . . {and} he served on the borders of 'bgr with a thousand infantry and a hundred {cavalry} . . .'; RQ.A 10 (see n. 78 above): . . . *w s*^{1}*rt 'l- mlk h- s*^{1}*lṭn s*^{1}*nt* . . . *w b- m'ty frs*^{1} 'perhaps '. . . he served while Mlk was in power. . .' (?) or '. . . he served on government property . . . and two hundred horsemen'; WH 1849: . . . *w qṣṣ frs*^{1} *h- ms*^{1}*ty* . . . *f h lt s*^{1}*lm w 'wd b- h- ms*^{1}*rt m't frs*^{1} '. . . and he tracked a horseman of the Ms^{1}ty . . . and so O Lt [grant] security and the return to the unit of the hundred horsemen' (see n. 73 above); KRS 1468: . . . *w qṣṣ b- m't frs*^{1} *b'd 'l ḍf* . . . 'and he tracked, in a hundred horsemen, following [members of] the 'l Ḍf . . .'; an unpublished text from Jabal Says, southern Syria: . . . *w bh' b m't* 'and he moved camp with a hundred [horsemen?]'.

82. Josephus, *Jewish War* 3.67.

83. P. Holder, *The* auxilia *from Augustus to Trajan* (BAR International Series 70; Oxford, 1980), 7.

cohors equitata quingenaria as 120.[84] It is possible that these writers of Safaitic inscriptions had served in *cohortes equitatae* and referred to them by the rough total of horsemen in the unit, as *m’t frs*^{1} (‘a hundred horsemen’) occasionally abbreviated to *m’t* (‘hundred’). But this can be no more than a suggestion.

As well as horsemen, there are also references to the author’s *rgl* which, in the contexts, must surely mean ‘foot soldiers’, ‘infantry’,[85] perhaps suggesting that the author was some form of commander.[86] In one text *rgl* is contrasted with *frs*^{1}.[87] From the civilian side, we have an indignant graffito by a victim of military brutality. A certain Ḫlṣ was apparently minding his own business pasturing the camels when ‘the army’ (presumably a military unit) beat him up and scattered his camels which at the time of writing he was still trying to retrieve.[88]

We also have quite a number of graffiti which say that their authors were running away from the Romans or Roman territory.[89] Unfortunately,

84. Pseudo-Hyginus, *De munitionibus castrorum* 27. In the same passage he says that the *cohors equitata miliaria* has 240 horsemen and ten centuries of infantry (ideally 760 men).

85. Cf. Arabic *rāǧil* ‘a foot soldier’ (as opposed to *fāris*^{1} ‘a cavalryman’), Sabaic *’rgl* ‘unmounted troops’ (A. F. L. Beeston, *Warfare in Ancient South Arabia [2nd.–3rd. Centuries A.D.]* [Qahtan: Studies in Old South Arabian Epigraphy 3; London, 1976], 12), Hebrew *raglī* ‘a foot soldier’ (e.g. in 1 Samuel 4:10, 15:4, 2 Kings 13:7, etc.), and Syriac *ragālā* and *reglāyā* ‘foot-soldier’, and in the plural ‘infantry’ (as opposed to *farāšā* ‘cavalry’; e.g. Judith 2:5; 1 Maccabees 6:30, etc.). In all cases, these words also mean men on foot in a non-military context. Note also that the Greek inscription from Jathum (see n. 15 above), lines 8–10 mentions that a στρατηγὸς ὁπλειτῶν ‘a captain of infantry’ was stationed there.

86. PUAES IVC 597 = LP 597: *l* N *w ḫrṣ ‘l rgl -h w ḥḍr* ‘By N and he watched over/guarded his infantry men and camped at a place of permanent water’; KRS 1903: *l* N *w ḫrṣ ‘l- rgl -h* . . . ‘By N and he watched over/guarded his infantry men . . .’.

87. *CIS* V 2076: . . . *{w} s*^{1}*rt ‘l- (ḥ)dd ’bgr b ’lf rgl w m’t f[r]s*^{1} . . . ‘{and} he served on the borders of ’bgr with a thousand infantry and a hundred cavalry . . .’.

88. This, at least, is one interpretation of *CIS* V 2556: . . . *w ḥll h- dr f ws*^{1}*q[-h] h- ‘rḍ r‘y h- ’gml w ḫrṣ h- ’b<n>l* . . . ‘. . . and he camped here and then the army hurt [him] while he was pasturing the camels and he was on the look out for the camels’. On *ws*^{1}*q h- ‘rd*: I suggest that the *-h* object pronoun was assimilated to the *h-* article. This is a common feature in Safaitic, cf. *w l h rgm* for *w l-h h- rgm, ‘and the cairn is his’ in WH 3420, V. A. Clark, *A Study of New Safaitic Inscriptions from Jordan* (PhD thesis, University of Melbourne, 1979), nos. 412, 1046, etc.

89. **CIS* V 1713: . . . *w ḥl h- dr nfr m- h- rm w ḫl ḥwlt* . . . ‘. . . and he camped here escaping from the Romans and the horsemen of the ḥwlt’; Safaitic inscriptions recorded at Jabal Ṣaqa‘, north-eastern Jordan, by G. M. H. King and M. C. A. Macdonald (publication in preparation), no. MKJS 1: . . . *w s*^{2}*ty ‘nzt nfr mn ’- rm* ‘. . . and he spent the winter

they are not more specific and so we cannot tell whether they were deserters from Roman army units, or rebels or criminals fleeing punishment. Others say that they rebelled against Rome, or possibly mutinied.[90] One dates his rebellion to 'the year the Persians came to Boṣrā' and another to 'the year the Romans and the Persians fought at Boṣrā'.[91] Unfortunately, we do not know which of the Persian invasions this refers to, possibly that of AD 256, as Knauf has argued.[92] Perhaps linked to this is another date 'the year the legion departed Boṣrā'[93] and 'the year Caesar departed [or fled] to Boṣrā', but I cannot trace either of these events in the historical record.

To conclude, in this paper I hope I have been able to show that, in the last century BC and the first four centuries AD, the concept of 'inside' and 'outside' does not really apply to relations between the nomads to the east and south of the Ḥawrān and their settled neighbours. It is important not to deal in stereotypes: the incurably aggressive nomad and the peaceful sedentary who meet only when the former periodically raids or attacks the latter, are the *topoi* of classical and some modern writers, but do not reflect reality. The two ways of life are not only inextricably connected by mutual needs and advantages but there is no clear dividing line between them. Most tribes have both nomadic and settled sections and many nomads spend parts of their lives in the settled regions and in cities.

This is the picture we receive from the inscriptions. Nomads who spent time in Gilead, Palmyra, and Abila, nomads who served in the Roman army and sedentaries from the Ḥawrān who served in remote outposts in

---

at 'nzt whilst fleeing from the Romans' (for the use of ʾ- instead of *h*- for the definite article see Macdonald, 'Reflections on the Linguistic Map', 51–52 ; and A. Al-Jallad, *An Outline of the Grammar of the Safaitic Inscriptions* [Studies in Semitic Languages and Linguistics 80; Leiden, Brill 2015], 16–17); *CIS* V 3721, 3776, 3787; PUAES IVC 94; SIJ 352: . . . *w nfr mn- rm* '. . . and he escaped from Roman territory . . .'

90. Clark, *Study of New Safaitic Inscriptions*, no. 424: . . . *mrd ʿl- ʾ l rm* . . . '. . . he rebelled against the Romans. . .'; F. H. Khraysheh, 'New Safaitic Inscriptions from Jordan', *Syria* 72 (1995) 401–14 at 410–13 (no. 6): . . . *w mrd ʿl- ʾl rm ---- qyẓ ʿlf {t}yt* s^1*nt brḥ qṣr lbṣry* . . . '. . . and he rebelled against the Romans ---- he spent the dry season using dry fodder . . . [?] the year Caesar fled [?] to Boṣrā'; SIJ 78: . . . *w mrd ʾl- rm* s^1*nt ʾty h- mḏy bṣry* . . . '. . . and he rebelled against Roman [rule] the year the Persians came to Boṣrā . . .'

91. SIJ 78, see the previous note; *CIS* V 4448: . . . s^1*nt ḥrb h- mḏy ʾl rm b- bṣr.* . . '. . . the year the Persians fought the Romans at Boṣrā. . .'

92. E. A. Knauf, 'Als die Meder nach Bosra Kamen', *ZDMG* 134 (1984) 219–25.

93. H. Zeinaddin, 'Safaitische Inschriften aus dem ğabal al-ʾArab', *Damaszener Mitteilungen* 12 (2000) 265–89 at 282–83 (no. 15): . . . *{*s^1*}nt brḥ lgyn bṣry* . . . [*brḥ* 'to depart from' takes a direct object, see Lane 181a]; and Khraysheh, 'New Safaitic Inscriptions', 410–13 (no. 6), on which see n. 90 above.

the desert such as Jathūm and al-Namārah. Roman officials whose job was to act as intermediaries between the nomadic tribes and the government—at least if one accepts my interpretation of the ethnarchs and *strategoi* of the nomads—and an often surprising amount of information in the desert about important events not only in the Ḥawrān but as far away as Antioch, Palestine, and even Rome. We should not forget that Safaitic graffiti have even been found scratched into the plaster of a wall in Pompeii![94]

As mentioned at the beginning of this paper, from thousands of individual statements one can only build up an impression, but that impression is not one of 'inside and out' but of a social continuum: from the desert across the rich agricultural land of the Ḥawrān to the cities, and to the administrations and armies of the local kingdoms and the imperium. Of course, this continuum included different concepts of authority, nomads generally do not take kindly to being ordered about, unless they have agreed of their own free-will to accept someone's orders for a particular period and purpose, as in a military unit. Of course, too, there were good times and bad, conflicts and collaboration, occasional small military expeditions against particular tribes by the authorities and attacks on targets in the settled areas for specific purposes by small bands from individual tribes, and both types are recorded in the Safaitic inscriptions. These conflicts should not be confused with banditry which was mostly based in the Lejā, and had a quite different purpose and origin. The conflicts I refer to were part of living within the social continuum of the desert and the sown and the symbiosis of nomad and sedentary. At this period at least, which is the only one for which we have information from the nomads, there does not seem to have been a continuous and general 'nomadic menace', nor a definable border which—for the people on the ground—would have created a feeling of 'inside and out'.

94. J. Calzini Gysens, 'Safaitic Graffiti from Pompeii', *Proceedings of the Seminar for Arabian Studies* 20 (1990) 1–7.

ADDENDA (2019)

This article was written before the publication in March 2017 of the *Online Corpus of the Inscriptions of Ancient North Arabia* (OCIANA: http://krc2.orient.ox.ac.uk/ociana/). This contains all the Ancient North Arabian inscriptions (including Safaitic) except the so-called 'Thamudic' which will be added in the next phase. It is being constantly updated. Readings, translations, metadata, and images of all the Safaitic inscriptions mentioned here can be found on OCIANA. All references to OCIANA were consulted on 1 October 2018. Addenda are indicated in the main text by an asterisk (*).

"The Safaitic Inscriptions are graffiti . . ." —For a grammar and dictionary of Safaitic, and a convincing argument that the language of the Safaitic inscriptions is a form of Old Arabic, see now A. Al-Jallad, *An Outline of the Grammar of the Safaitic Inscriptions* (Studies in Semitic Languages and Linguistics 80; Leiden, 2015) and A. Al-Jallad and K. Jaworska, *A Dictionary of the Safaitic Inscriptions* (Leiden, 2019).

"One even claims affiliation to the people of the town of Ṣalkhad in the Ḥawrān." —There are now two inscriptions by authors claiming to be of 'the people of Ṣalkhad' (KRS 2813 and Damascus Museum 26750), and another (NEH 9) by someone who says that 'he lives in Ṣalkhad but spent the season of the later rains [here in the desert]'.

Footnote 5—There are now fourteen Safaitic inscriptions in which Tadmur (Palmyra) is mentioned including one on a stone tripod platter in the Damascus Museum (reg no. 32750) in which the author claims to be 'of the people of Tadmur'.

Footnote 8—See also H. Hayajneh, 'Ancient North Arabian-Nabataean bilingual inscriptions from southern Jordan', *Proceedings of the Seminar for Arabian Studies* 39 (2009) 203–22, which deals with Nabataean-Hismaic bilingual graffiti. Hismaic is the name of an Ancient North Arabian script and language mainly found in the Ḥismā sand deserts of southern Jordan and north-west Arabia (see the home page of the OCIANA website).

Footnote 13—Just under 1000 Safaitic inscriptions have been recorded at al-Namārah and its environs (enter "al-Namarah" in the "site" field of OCIANA to see them.

Footnote 15—The author of the inscription made several mistakes including omitting the sigma from ΜΑΓΙ[Σ]ΤΡΟΥ.

"There are some 30 Safaitic inscriptions which mention either the Author's relations with *rm* or which are dated to events involving the Romans. In addition, there are 19 texts dated to events involving the emperor, who is referred to simply as *qṣr* (Kαῖσαρ)." —There are now 45 references to *rm*, and 23 to *qṣr* see OCIANA.

"Unfortunately, no photograph, or even a tracing, of this inscription has been published, only a reading and discussion." —A photograph can now be seen in OCIANA under AbNSJ 1.

"One text is dated to 'the year Caesar's son died and he [the author] heard that Philippus had died, but scoffed.'" —There are 2 Safaitic inscriptions which are dated to the 'arrival of Caesar's son' (ZNam 1 and 3, see OCIANA). If this refers to Germanicus' arrival, it suggests that the visit was widely publicized.

Footnote 18—The phrase *b-rʾy ngm* has now been reinterpreted as "during the acronical rising of Virgo" in A.M. Al-Jallad, "An Ancient Arabian Zodiac. The Constellations in the Safaitic Inscriptions. Part II", *Arabian Archaeology and Epigraphy* 27 (2016) 84–106 at 85, 101.

Footnote 19—*b-rʾy yʾmr* has now been reinterpreted as 'during the rising of Capricorn', see Al-Jallad, 'An Ancient Arabian Zodiac', 92, 104 (HaNSB 197).

Footnote 30—on then-forthcoming publication, see now OCIANA.

Footnote 31—See also S. Abbadi, "A new Safaitic inscription dated to 12–9 BC," *Studies in the History and Archaeology of Jordan* VII, (Amman, 2001), 481–84; and OCIANA under AbNSJ 1.

Footnote 34—on then-forthcoming publication, see now OCIANA.
"We have other references to a King Agrippa, again almost certainly Agrippa II." —There are now five Safaitic texts dated to 'the year Agrippa died'. These are HSNA 1, 2, 6, 7, SESP.U 8, see OCIANA.

Footnote 37—on then-forthcoming publication, see now OCIANA.

Footnote 38—on then-forthcoming publication, see now OCIANA.

Footnote 39—on then-forthcoming publication, see now OCIANA.
"However, it seems possible that, from the point of view of his subjects back in the Ḥawrān, and thence the nomads in the desert beyond, it was Agrippa who was leading the attack in some or all of these engagements." - There is also a curious reference to 'the year of king Agrippa son of Herod' (*s¹nt mlk grfṣ bn hrdṣ*) in HSNS 5 (see OCIANA). Agrippa I was of course

the son of Aristobulus IV and so a *grandson* of Herod the Great, while his son, Agrippa II, was the great grandson son of Herod. Either the author of this inscription was (understandably) confused about the Herodian family-tree, or he was using *bn* ('son of') loosely to mean 'of the family of', i.e. 'the Herodian'.

"While it is difficult to link any of these to identifiable events, it is possible that the third refers to Queen Berenice, the sister of Agrippa II." See OCIANA under LP 353. —There are also some other remarkable dating phrases mentioning Jews. Thus SIJ 688 and ASWS 186 (see OCIANA) are dated respectively to 'the year of the expulsion of the people of the Jews' (*s^{1}nt nzz ʾl yhd*) and 'the year of the expulsion of Jews' (*s^{1}nt nzt yhd*) which it is tempting to suggest refer to the expulsion of Jews from Jerusalem after the Roman defeat of the Second Jewish Revolt in AD 135. AbHYN 1 [[=*DMIPERP* §134]] is dated to 'the year the Nabataeans plundered the Jews' or vice versa (*s^{1}nt ḥrb nbṭ yhd*) which could refer to any of the conflicts between the Maccabees or Herodians and the Nabataeans. Again we have references to the 'year of the war of the Jewish people' (*s^{1}nt ḥrb ʾl yhd* Al-Namārah.M 68; *s^{1}ntḥ rb yhd* BS 2003) and a fragmentary text referring to the 'affliction of the Jewish people' (C 1270.1).

Most surprising of all, perhaps, are two Safaitic inscriptions by the same author dated to 'the year ʾbkr the Jew was crucified' or 'the year ʾbkr crucified the Jew' (AbJ 1 and BES 18.1).

Footnote 52—on then-forthcoming publication, see now Betts 3–9 in OCIANA.

Footnote 54—See now the numerous Minaic references in the *Digital Archive for the Study of Pre-Islamic Arabian Inscriptions* (DASI: http://dasi.humnet.unipi.it/)

Footnote 55—For a recent discussion of the annexation see P. Cimadomo, 'The Controversial Annexation of the Nabataean kingdom', *Levant* 50 (2018) 258–66.

Footnote 56—This inscription is SESP.S 1 in OCIANA.

Footnote 64—For this now see DASI mentioned above.

Footnote 66—on then-forthcoming publication, see now Ms 64 in OCIANA. "There are several texts in which the author says that he *s^{1}rt*, which I would suggest means 'he served in military unit', with his father, or another family member, or with a friend, and one dates his text to 'the year Mlk served in the “great army” [*h- arḍ/irḍ*].” —A fascinating group of one Greek and four Safaitic inscriptions was found recently on one rock on the border of the basalt and limestone deserts in north-eastern Jordan. It will appear in A. Jallad, Z. Al-Salameen, Y. Shdeifat and R. Harahsheh ‘Gaius the Roman and the Kawnites: Inscriptional Evidence for Roman Auxiliary Units Raised from the Nomads of the Ḥarrah’ (forthcoming). The Greek inscription reads Ταενος Χεσεμανου Εσραθ that is ‘Zʿn son of Kḥs^{1}mn is serving [or: I am serving] (in a military unit)’. Clearly, this nomad knew Greek letters and how to transliterate his name and patronym into Greek, but did not know the Greek for ‘to serve in a military unit’ and so used the Safaitic word **ys^{1}rt* ‘he serves’ or possibly **ʾas^{1}rat* ‘I serve’. He also wrote his name in Safaitic on the same rock, as did someone who calls himself ‘Gaius the Roman’ (*gyṣ ḏ ʾl rm* literally Gaius of the lineage group of Rome’) who says ‘he is here from his posting at ʿrl or wrl’. Another inscription, possibly by a brother of Ẓʿn, on the same rock is dated to ‘the year Ẓnn son of Kḥs^{1}mn was appointed [leader]’. It would seem that the Roman name ‘Gaius’ may have been adopted by one of the nomads serving in the Roman army, possibly like the names *tts^1* (Titus) and *ʾqlds^1* (Claudius) in other Safaitic graffiti (see OCIANA for examples). This is because it is unlikely that a Roman used to the customs of Roman society would refer to himself simply by his *praenomen* rather than his family *nomen* (I am grateful to Josef Bloomfield for this insight). The rest of the inscription is in perfect Safaitic and again suggests that this was a nomad rather than a Roman.

Footnote 78—On all then-forthcoming publications, see now OCIANA.

Footnote 88—On assimilation of this type see M. C. A. Macdonald, ‘Clues to How a Nabataean May Have Spoken, from a Hismaic Inscription’ in G. J. Brooke, A. H. W. Curtis, M. Al-Hamad and G. R. Smith, eds., *Near Eastern and Arabian Essays: Studies in Honour of John F. Healey* (Journal of Semitic Studies Supplement 41; Oxford, 2018), 231–39.

Footnote 89—on then-forthcoming publication, see now OCIANA.

Further Reading: Annotated Bibliography

The present book provides only a very small sampling of important works that may be of interest to New Testament scholars. The present annotated bibliography may help direct interested readers to further reading on topics of interest. Works centred upon the various Jewish Wars or biblical texts are omitted from this list, as these are often already in the "domain" of biblical scholarship and usually more likely to be known to New Testament scholars. The list is geared toward the English language, though a few publications in other languages are included. As with most of the book, it adopts a post-Luttwak and post-Revised-Schürer purview (i.e., 1976 and later).

Applebaum, Shimon. 1989. *Judaea in Hellenistic and Roman Times: Historical and Archaeological Essays*. Studies in Judaism in Late Antiquity 40. Leiden: Brill Academic.

Two chapters are especially relevant to the present study. "The Troopers of Zamaris" (47–65) discusses a colony of Jewish Babylonian cavalry in the Batanaean colony of Bathyra. These soldiers ultimately comprised nearly half of Agrippa II's army, if Josephus is to be believed. "The Beginnings of the *Limes Palaestinae*" (132–42) concerns the issue of a border defense in Judaea/Syria Palaestina and the date of its formation—Applebaum co-authored some publications with Gichon, so his work on the *limes* tends to be of the variety that Shatzman criticizes in the chapter present in this volume.

Braund, David. 1984. *Rome and the Friendly King: The Character of Client Kingship*. London: Croom Helm.

This book remains essential reading on client kingship in the Roman era. One chapter, "The King of the Frontier" (91–104), discusses the military component of client kingship extensively, including numerous examples of the Herodian dynasty in Palestine. The entire book is worthy of study.

Cotton, Hannah M. 2006. "The Impact of the Roman Army in the Province of Judaea/Syria Palaestina." In *The Impact of the Roman Army (200 BC—AD 476): Economic, Social, Political, Religious, and Cultural Aspects*, edited by Lukas De Blois and Elio Lo Cascio, 393–407. Impact of Empire 6. Leiden: Brill.

Hannah Cotton has published extensively on various papyri and epigraphs concerning the military in early Roman Palestine, though these works are not the most accessible. "The Impact of the Roman Army," however, is a good entry point for her important work. This chapter skillfully synthesizes such work (along with archaeological insights) for how these often difficult-to-interpret data might inform the study of soldier-civilian relations in Roman Judaea.

Dąbrowa, Edward. 1993. *Legio X Fretensis: A Prosopographical Study of Its Officers (I–III c. A.D.)*. Historia Einzelschriften 66. Stuttgart: Steiner.

Legio X Fretensis was the primary military garrison in Judaea following the Jewish War and this book remains the definitive study of the legion, despite the subsequent discovery of numerous inscriptions erected by the legion or its soldiers. Because of this, readers would be advised to look into more recent publications before drawing firm conclusions from Dąbrowa's discussions that are built around individual inscriptions.

Devijver, H. 1989. "Equestrian Officers in the East." In *The Eastern Frontier of the Roman Empire*, edited by David H. French and Chris S. Lightfoot, 1.77–111. British Archaeological Reports International Series 533. Oxford: BAR.

Devijver has devoted much of his work to the study of equestrian officers and the Roman East, with this particular publication probably being the most relevant for scholars of the New Testament.

Eck, Werner. 2014. "The Armed Forces and the Infrastructure of Cities during the Roman Imperial Period—The Example of Judaea/Syria Palaestina." In *Cura Aquarum in Israel II: Water in Antiquity*, edited by Christoph Ohlig and Tsvika Tsuk, 207–14. Schriften der deutschen wasserhistorischen Gesellschaft 21. Siegburg: Deutsche Wasserhistorische Gesellschaft and Israel Nature and Parks Authority.

Eck, Werner. 2016. "Soldaten und Veteranen des römischen Heeres in Iudaea/Syria Palaestina und ihre inschriftlichen Zeugnisse." In "*Let the Wise Listen and Add to Their Learning" (Prov 1:5): Festschrift for Günter Stemberger on the Occasion of His 75th Birthday*, edited by Constanza Cordoni and Gerhard Langer, 127–40. Studia Judaica 90. Berlin: de Gruyter.

One of the most prolific scholars alive, Werner Eck has published over 700 peer-reviewed articles, dozens of which are important studies on the military in Roman Palestine (not to mention being co-editor on the important *Corpus Inscriptionum Iudaeae/Palestinae* book series—along with Hannah Cotton and Benjamin Isaac, among others). That being said, most of his publications are among of the most inaccessible writings on the topic of the military in Roman Palestine: these tend to be the *editio princeps* of new military diplomas or other inscriptions, situating the discovery within histories of administration and troop movement that might strike many biblical scholars as antiquarian minutiae. The two articles listed here are among his most accessible on the topic and provide a clear framework for interpreting inscriptions that might otherwise be of confusing relevance for New Testament scholars.

Fuhrmann, Christopher J. 2012. *Policing the Roman Empire: Soldiers, Administration, and Public Order*. Oxford: Oxford University Press.

Since most of the Empire lacked any sort of localized policing force, this set of duties often fell upon soldiers garrisoned in the area. The book is full of insights and even begins with a discussion of Acts 21 and the question of policing in that context.

Gichon, Mordechai. 2002. "45 Years of Research on the *limes Palaestinae*: The Findings and Their Assessment in the Light of the Criticisms Raised (C1st–C4th)." In *Limes XVIII: Proceedings of the XVIIIth International Congress of Roman Frontier Studies*, edited by Philip Freeman, Julian Bennett, Zbigniew T. Fiema and Birgitta Hoffmann, 1.185–206. British Archaeological Reports International Series 1084. Oxford: BAR.

Mordechai Gichon was the central target of the article by Israel Shatzman in the present volume and this chapter presents his strongest and ultimately final defense of a robust *limes Palaestinae*. I leave to the reader whether Gichon or Shatzman is ultimately more convincing.

González Salinero, Raúl. 2003. "El servicio militar de los judíos en el ejército romano." *Aquila Legionis* 4:45–91.

This is perhaps the single most important article ever published on Jews in the Roman army. If the reader found the chapters by Roth and Schoenfeld in the present volume compelling, they should immediately seek out this article, which is considerably longer and very detailed. No English translation is presently available, though González is presently preparing a monograph on the topic in the English language; its anticipated publication date is yet unknown.

Gracey, M. H. 1986. "The Armies of Judean Client Kings." In *Defence of the Roman and Byzantine East*, edited by David L. Kennedy and Philip Freeman, 1.311–23. British Archaeological Reports International Series 297. Oxford: BAR.

Gracey's work focuses primarily on the army of Agrippa II, whose soldiers seem particularly prolific in erecting inscriptions. Whereas the Speidel article in the present volume is centred upon the possibility of Acts' reliability, Gracey's scope is considerably wider and may be useful for those interested in the social historical significance of the military under the Herodian client kings.

Haynes, Ian. 2013. *Blood of the Provinces: The Roman Auxilia and the Making of Provincial Society from Augustus to the Severans*. Oxford: Oxford University Press.

The most recent full-length study of the *auxilia*, who comprised the entirety of the Judaean garrison 6–66 CE and a sizable portion of it following the Jewish War. Haynes' study is remarkably thorough and touches on numerous topics that will interest biblical scholars, including religion among auxiliaries, daily life for soldiers, and recruitment practices.

Holder, Paul A. 1980. *Studies in the Auxilia of the Roman Army from Augustus to Trajan*. British Archaeological Reports International Series 70. Oxford: BAR.

Before the arrival of Haynes' important volume, Holder published what was long the standard work on the *auxilia*. Though much of it has been improved upon by Haynes, this book remains useful today.

Isaac, Benjamin. 1991. "The Roman Army in Judaea: Police Duties and Taxation." In *Roman Frontier Studies 1989: Proceedings of the XVth International Congress of Roman Frontier Studies*, edited by Valerie A. Maxfield and Michael J. Dobson, 458–61. Exeter: University of Exeter Press.

Isaac, Benjamin. 1992. *The Limits of Empire: The Roman Army in the East*. 2nd ed. Oxford: Clarendon.

As noted in the introduction, Benjamin Isaac's work is framed in direct contrast with the "modernist" depiction of Roman Grand Strategy articulated by Edward Luttwak. Isaac's monumental work is controversial and not always the most accessible for those not already initiated to the character of the "Grand Strategy" debate. It nevertheless has an immensely useful chapter on Judaea/Syria Palaestina (104–18) and several insightful chapters on soldier–civilian interactions. Because *Limits of Empire* can be difficult as an entry point, readers may prefer to start with his concise and focused study "The Roman Army in Judaea," which has a helpful overview of primary sources and paints a vivid portrait of soldier-civilian interactions in the region.

Kennedy, David L. 2004. *The Roman Army in Jordan*. 2nd ed. London: Council for British Research in the Levant.

This book will be of particular interest to scholars interested in the Decapolis, Batanaea, or Nabataean Arabia, which includes a social-historical discussion and a gazetteer for the sites where there is evidence of military occupation.

Luttwak, Edward N. 1976. *The Grand Strategy of the Roman Empire from the First Century A.D. to the Third*. 1st ed. Baltimore: Johns Hopkins University Press.

A controversial book, it nevertheless warrants reading by those interested in the military of early Roman Palestine. The first chapter (1–50) is most relevant for biblical scholars, as it discusses the Julio-Claudian period. I would not recommend the second edition (2016) in part because there are few substantial improvements, despite being a 40th anniversary edition, and the fact that this work is best read for understanding the history of scholarship rather than gleaning new insights to Roman military planning.

Macdonald, Michael C. A. 1995. "Herodian Echoes in the Syrian Desert." In *Trade, Contact, and the Movement of Peoples in the Eastern Mediterranean: Studies in Honour of J. Basil Hennessy*, edited by Stephen Bourke and Jean-Paul Descœudres, 285–90. Mediterranean Archaeology Supplement 3. Sydney: MeditArch.

Like Macdonald's chapter in the present volume, this chapter addresses the under-discussed matter of Safaitic inscriptions. The essay in the present volume briefly discusses Herodian client kings, instead preferring the relationship between the Safaitic-speaking nomads and the Romans. The essay noted here has a very extensive discussion of the numerous inscriptions about the Herodian client kings among these inscriptions. As one might guess, many inscriptions have subsequently been discovered—Macdonald's chapter in the present volume is a partial updating to his "Herodian Echoes," albeit with a diminished focus on the Herodian dynasty.

Millar, Fergus. 1993. *The Roman Near East: 37 BC—AD 337*. Carl Newell Jackson Lectures. Cambridge: Harvard University Press.

Millar's book on the Roman East may be the best starting point for those with little other experience on the topic. Including a helpful overview of the political history of the region, Millar has a chapter devoted to Judaea/Syria Palaestina (337–86) and an appendix concerning documents from the Bar Kokhba War (545–52).

Paltiel, Eliezer. 1991. *Vassals and Rebels in the Roman Empire: Julio-Claudian Policies in Judaea and the Kingdoms of the East*. Collection Latomus 212. Brussels: Latomus.

Whereas Braund's volume on client kingship is a largely synthetic work seeking to describe as accurately as possible the phenomenon of client kingship, Paltiel's work is one of thorough political history. Paltiel's neglected monograph presents a compelling portrait of the many client kingdoms and their precarious position within the Roman Empire—differing policies of a given emperor might lead to annexation and the end of one or another client dynasty.

Pollard, Nigel. 2000. *Soldiers, Cities, and Civilians in Roman Syria*. Ann Arbor: University of Michigan Press.

This work is beneficially read alongside Richard Alston's *Soldier and Society in Roman Egypt* (1995). Alston's book benefits from the incalculable number of papyri surviving from Roman Egypt (and thus gives a degree of specificity and detail impossible for any other Roman province), Pollard's work examines soldier-civilian interactions in a broadly "Syrian" manner that includes Judaea, Batanaea, the Decapolis, etc. Both of Alston's and Pollard's volumes will be of special interest to social historians of the New Testament.

Rocca, Samuel. 2008. *Herod's Judaea: A Mediterranean State in the Classical World*. Texts and Studies in Ancient Judaism 122. Tübingen: Mohr/Siebeck.

Samuel Rocca's work on the military of Herod the Great in this book has been subsequently published in a few smaller (and more accessible) volumes: *The Forts of Judaea* (2008) and *The Army of Herod the Great* (2009). This book is probably the most useful for biblical scholars, as it has a large chapter on Herod's army and fortifications (133–96; cf. 88–89). This book updates Shatzman's very important book on the armies of the Hasmonaeans and Herod the Great.

Roth, Jonathan P. 2002. "The Army and the Economy in Judaea and Palaestina." In *The Roman Army and The Economy*, edited by Paul Erdkamp, 375–97. Amsterdam: Gieben.

In this article, Roth explores how the destruction of the Jerusalem Temple led to an economic and political vacuum that was filled in large part by the post-War military garrison.

Saddington, D. B. 1986. "The Administration and the Army in Judaea in the Early Roman Period (from Pompey to Vespasian, 63 B.C. to A.D. 79)." In *Pillars of Smoke and Fire: The Holy Land in History and Thought*, edited by Moshe Sharon, 33–40. Publications of the Eric Samson Chair in Jewish Civilisation 1. Leiden: Brill.

Saddington, D. B. 2009. "Client Kings' Armies under Augustus: The Case of Herod." In *Herod and Augustus*, edited by David M. Jacobson and Nikos Kokkinos, 303–23. IJS Studies in Judaica 6. Leiden: Brill.

Unlike many historians of the Roman military, Denis B. Saddington occasionally spoke directly to biblical scholars, notably in a brief article in the *Journal of Biblical Literature* ("The Centurion in Matthew 8:5–13"; 2006) and an entry in *Aufstieg und Niedergang der römischen Welt* ("Roman Military and Administrative Personnel in the New Testament"; 1996). Though this is commendable, there are times when Saddington showed unfamiliarity with the methods and assumptions of biblical scholarship in these two articles (suggesting, e.g., that the Gospel of Peter and the Acts of Pilate may contain the actual names of the soldiers who crucified Jesus). This should not be taken as an indicator that Saddington's work is too flawed to be useful; his discussion of the social-historical significance of the military and its institutions remains excellent, he merely falters when diving too deep into biblical waters. Thus, Saddington's two articles above are deeply insightful and provide helpful overviews from a military historical perspective and can be read with considerable profit.

Sartre, Maurice. 2005. *The Middle East under Rome*. Translated by Catherine Porter and Elizabeth Rawlings. Cambridge: Belnap.

Maurice Sartre's magnum opus extends beyond the realm of New Testament Palestine, though it overlaps in considerable ways. Sartre's command of the literary and epigraphic evidence of the Roman Near and Middle East will benefit all readers.

Schürer, Emil. 1973. *The History of the Jewish People in the Age of Jesus Christ (175 B.C.—A.D. 135)*. Translated and revised by Geza Vermes, Fergus Millar, and Matthew Black. Revised and updated English edition. Vol. 1. Edinburgh: T. & T. Clark.

The first volume of the revised Schürer is commonly cited in discussions of the military in Roman Judaea, especially 360–68. The book has been updated from its earlier 1891 English translation, though the argument is substantially the same on this point, albeit incorporating more recent discoveries. Schürer's contention that the military units in Judaea 6–66 CE were the *cohortes et ala Sebastenorum* remains important and his arguments remain standard.

Shatzman, Israel. 1991. *The Armies of the Hasmonaeans and Herod: From Hellenistic to Roman Frameworks*. Texte und Studien zum Antiken Judentum 25. Tübingen: Mohr/Siebeck.

Nearly half of the book is devoted to the military of Herod the Great (129–276). It is both detailed and insightful, providing the basis for Rocca's similarly strong study listed above. Shatzman here is less interested in the *Limesgeschichte* debate seen in his chapter in the present volume and instead how the Herodian army can be seen as a cultural institution at the nexus of the Hellenistic and Roman cultures.

Stiebel, Guy D. 2015. "Military Dress as an Ideological Marker in Roman Palestine." In *Dress and Ideology: Fashioning Identity from Antiquity to the Present*, edited by Shoshana-Rose Marzel and Guy D. Stiebel, 153–67. London: Bloomsbury.

Guy Stiebel's publications are commonly in the form of excavation reports, but this synthetic work will be of interest to those studying Roman ideology in Judaea and Syria Palaestina.

Wheeler, Everett. 2007. "The Army and the *Limes* in the East." In *A Companion to the Roman Army*, edited by Paul Erdkamp, 235–66. Blackwell Companions to the Ancient World. London: Blackwell.

Luttwak's thesis concerning a clear grand strategy among the Romans has not fared well under criticism, though Wheeler presents a modest case for such a grand strategy in the Roman East; it is among the best arguments for such a system in recent years.

Zeichmann, Christopher B. 2018. *The Roman Army and the New Testament*. Lanham, MD: Lexington/Fortress Academic.

Zeichmann, Christopher B. 2018. "Military Forces in Judaea 6–130 CE: The *status quaestionis* and Relevance for New Testament Studies." *Currents in Biblical Research* 17:86–120.

Zeichmann, Christopher B. forthcoming. *Military Sites in Early Roman Palestine (37 BCE—130 CE): Documents, Maps, and Gazetteer*.

The present writer has published a handful of studies aimed at making study of the Roman military more accessible for New Testament scholars. *The Roman Army and the New Testament* has an extended discussion of military demographics and soldier-civilian interactions in both pre-War and post-War Palestine. "Military Forces in Judaea" is an attempt to provide an updated account of the military units in the province of Judaea. Finally, *Military Sites* is an extended study about the locations of military presence in early Roman Palestine in three distinct periods: the Herodian period (37 BCE—6 CE, the pre-War period 6–66 CE), and the post-War period (70–130 CE), detailing the evidence—whether archaeological, literary, or epigraphic, at each site. It is also designed to be accessible to New Testament scholars and includes the text and translation of all relevant military texts in *DMIPERP*.

Index of Ancient Sources

BIBLE

Numbers

12:14 122 n. 65

1 Samuel

4:10 126 n. 85
15:4 126 n. 85

2 Kings

13:7 126 n. 85

Judith

2:5 126 n. 85

1 Maccabees

6:30 126 n. 85
7:42 122 n. 65

Mark

5:1–20 xi

Acts of the Apostles

1:23 86 n. 17
4:1 87
5:17–42 87
10:1 19, 20–22, 26–30, 89
18:7 86 n. 17
21:33 5
23:22 22 n. 133
23:23 19 n. 111
25:13 33
27:1 15
27:2 23–24, 31–34, 88–89
28:16 24–25

Philippians

1:13 24 n. 142

Colossians

4:11 86 n. 17

RABBINIC LITERATURE

Babylonian Talmud Shabbat

121a 78 n. 42

Genesis Rabbah

76:8 74 n. 22

Jerusalem Talmud Dedarim

4.9.38d 78 n. 42

Jerusalem Talmud Eruvin

5.22b 70 n. 7

Jerusalem Talmud Shabbat
16.7.15d 78 n. 42
16.15d 69 n. 6

Jerusalem Talmud Yoma
8.5.45b 78 n. 42

Megilat Ta'anit
6 63 n. 108

Mishnah Qiddushin
10:1.1–2 87–88
10:1.9 87–88

Tosefta Demai
1:11–14 74 n. 23
1:12–13 74 n. 21

Tosefta Shabbat
3:9 78 n. 42
13 (14):9 69 n. 6

GRAECO-ROMAN LITERATURE

Appian
Civil Wars
2.49 8 n. 29
2.71 8 n. 29
5.3 11 n. 65
5.87 8 n. 34

Syrian Wars
50 70 n. 11

Arrian
Discourses of Epictetus
13 20 n. 118

Aulus Hirtius (pseudo-Julius Caesar)
Alexandrian War
69.1 11 n. 64

Cicero
Letters to Atticus
5.18.2 7 n. 24
5.20.3 8 n. 28
14.9.3 8 n. 32

Letters to Family
15.1.5 7 n. 24
15.14.2 8 n. 28

Codex Theodosianus
7.4.30 39–40 n. 10
16.8.16 105 n. 54
16.8.29 39–40 n. 10

Dio Cassius
39.56.3 7 n. 26
40.31–32 4 n. 9
47.26–27 8 n. 32
55.31–32 21 n. 123
60.17 22 n. 132
67.22.4 13 n. 91
69.12.2 73 n. 18

Epistula Severi
6.19.6 105 n. 50, 105 n. 51

Historia Augusti
Life of Marcus
21 21 n. 122

(Pseudo-)Hyginus
De Munitionibus Castrorum
16 5 n. 16, 5 n. 18
27 5 n. 12, 126 n. 84
29 121 n. 61

Jerome
Letters
126.2 45 n. 27

Index of Ancient Sources

Josephus

Antiquities of the Jews

4.176 110 n. 4
12.147–153 81 n. 5
13.284–285 98 n. 10
13.375–378 93 n. 9
14.99–100 7 n. 25
14.119–122 8 n. 28
14.127–136 8 n. 30
14.137–139 8 n. 31
14.203 71 n. 15
14.223–230 96 n. 2
14.236–237 96 n. 2
14.271–272 8 n. 33
14.295 9 n. 40
14.361 47 n. 39
14.449 8 n. 35, 9 n. 38
14.468–469 8 n. 34
15.72 9 n. 41
15.293 83 n. 9
15.294 84 n. 10
16.198–199 83 n. 8
16.271 84 n. 11
16.271–299 64 n. 111
16.282–299 115 n. 32
16.292 84
16.295 84 n. 11
16.332 87
16.335–353 115 n. 32
16.352 115 n. 32
16.353 115 n. 32
17.3 83
17.23–25 98 n. 11
17.24 83
17.31 86 n. 16
17.266 83 n. 9, 87
17.286 10 n. 45, 10 n. 76
18.59 19 n. 108
18.84 98 n. 13
18.147 84 n. 12
18.237 110 n. 4
19.176 28 n. 5
19.356–357 18 n. 104
19.364–366 18 n. 104
19.365 14, 19 n. 105
19.365–366 23 n. 136
20.7 65 n. 122
20.100 99 n. 16
20.122 14, 19 n. 106, 23 n. 137
20.176 18 n. 104
20.220 99 n. 17

Jewish War

1.175–177 7 n. 26
1.180 8 n. 28
1.187–192 8 n. 30
1.202–203 8 n. 31
1.225 8 n. 33
1.301 9 n. 43, 85
1.324 8 n. 35
1.345–346 8 n. 34
1.397 83 n. 8
1.403 83 n. 9
1.535 87
1.573–574 115 n. 33
1.672 9 n. 44, 83 n. 8, 85
1.673 86
2.9 85 n. 15
2.13 85, 86
2.18 86
2.36 84 n. 10
2.40 10 n. 45, 12 n. 76, 18 n. 101
2.52 9 n. 42, 18 n. 102, 23 n. 135, 85, 87, 90
2.53 27 n. 3
2.55 83, 86
2.58 23 n. 135, 85
2.64 86
2.66 17 n. 95
2.66–67 10 n. 45
2.67 12 n. 76, 19 n. 109
2.74 87
2.174 19 n. 108
2.186 17 n. 96
2.224–226 19 n. 110
2.236 19 n. 106
2.523–526 116 n. 40
2.260–263 19
2.263 14

Josephus, *Jewish War* (continued)
2.266–270 19 n. 109
2.268 18 n. 103, 28 n. 5
2.296 20 n. 113
2.318 20 n. 113
2.332 20 n. 113
2.421 86, 90
2.460 20 n. 115
2.484 20 n. 112
2.499–500 10 n. 53, 12 n. 68
2.500 12 n. 82, 13 n. 92, 17 n. 97
2.500–502 90 n. 26
2.507 20 n. 117
2.540–555 12
3.12 15, 20 n. 116
3.31–34 62 n. 100
3.65–66 23 n. 137
3.66 17 n. 98, 19 n. 106
3.66–67 5 n. 14
3.68 47 n. 40, 62 n. 99
3.69 92
3.110–111 10 n. 54
3.120 2 n. 2
3.145–288 117 n. 42
3.233–234 10 n. 54
3.307–315 62 n. 98, 92
3.309 62 n. 100
3.316–339 117 n. 42
3.324–325 13 n. 86
3.409–412 10 n. 54
3.428–431 62 n. 101
3.443–452 92
4.11 91
4.14–16 116 n. 41
4.36 91
4.37 80
4.37–38 92
4.81 92
4.83 91, 92
4.120 62 n. 101
4.130 62 n. 101
4.402–404 58 n. 86
4.444 62 n. 98
4.444–449 62 n. 98
4.445 62 n. 102
4.446–448 61 n. 97
4.510 84
4.551 63 n. 103, 63 n. 104
5.39–41 12 n. 83
5.42 17 n. 99, 62 n. 99
5.42–46 10 n. 55, 93
5.50 63 n. 104
5.67–68 13 n. 85
5.290 62 n. 99
5.460–465 47 n. 40
5.467 13 n. 85, 13 n. 87
6.68–80 13 n. 85
6.237 13 n. 85
7.5–17 10 n. 56
7.18 11 n. 62, 12 n. 81, 13 n. 84
7.75–88 47 n. 40
7.89–95 47 n. 40
7.117 13 n. 88
7.163 63 n. 108
7.219–228 12 n. 71, 47 n. 40
7.252 63 n. 108
7.407 63 n. 106
7.443–446 47 n. 40
Life
61 86
114 86
114–118 91
180–181 86
394 62 n. 100
399–406 91
422 10 n. 56

Julius Caesar
Civil War
3.88.2 11 n. 57

Gallic War
8.4.3 11 n. 63
8.54 11 n. 57

Pseudo-Julius Caesar (cf. Aulus Hirtius)
Spanish War
30.7 11 n. 57

Livy
21.43.16 80
22.57.11 21 n. 122
23.35.6 21 n. 122

Lucian
Alexander
44 42 n. 18

Macrobius
Saturnalia
1.11.33 4 n. 10, 22 n. 124

Notitia Dignitatum
6.49 104 n. 42
22 40 n. 10
27 43 n. 20
33.33 15
34.18–20 45 n. 29
34.22 45 n. 29
34.26 45 n. 29
34.40 45 n. 29
34.45 45 n. 29

Pliny the Elder
Natural History
5.15 58 n. 86
33.45 3 n. 4

Pliny the Younger
Epistles
7.31 14
Epistles to Trajan
57 24 n. 142

Plutarch
Antony
3 7 n. 26
37.3 8 n. 36
42 11 n. 58
50.1 9 n. 37
51.1 9 n. 37
Crassus
20 7 n. 27

Ptolemy
Geography
4.5.14 42 n. 18
5.14.18 46 n. 33
5.15.3 46 n. 35
5.15.5 46 n. 34, 46 n. 36, 46 n. 37, 47 n. 38
5.15.7 47 n. 39
5.16.4 48 n. 37
5.17.3 43 n. 22

Rufinus
Ecclesiastical History
2.6 43

Socrates
Ecclesiastical History
4.36 43 n. 23

Sozomenos
Ecclesiastical History
6.38 43 n. 23

Strabo
16.4.21 114 n. 29
17.1.12 10 n. 46, 12 n. 76
17.1.30 10 n. 46, 12 n. 76

Suetonius
Augustus
25 4 n. 9, 21 n. 123
48 33 n. 18

Vespasian
4 12
4.5–6 92
6 11 n.60

Tacitus
Annals
1.17 3 n. 4
2.57 10 n. 51
2.85 22 n. 126

Tacitus, *Annals* (continued)
4.5 10 n. 47, 12 n. 77
12.23 30 n. 11
13.7 33 n. 18
13.35 13 n. 89
13.40 10 n. 52
15.6 12 n. 79
15.6–17 13 n. 90
15.26 11 n. 67, 12 n. 80, 13 n. 91
15.28.3 99 n. 18

Histories
1.76 30 n. 11
2.74 11 n. 60
2.83 12 n. 69, 20 n. 119
2.85 11 n. 60
3.24 4 n. 6
4.3 11 n. 61
4.39 12 n. 70
5.1 17 n. 99

Theodoret
Ecclesiastical History
4.20 43 n. 23

INSCRIPTIONS AND PAPYRI

AE (*L'Année* épigraphique)
1888.66 16
1895.78 14
1897.44 16
1899.177 14
1911.161 14
1920.78 12 n. 73
1922.109 14
1923.28 24 n. 143
1925.121 32 n. 14, 35; cf. *DMIPERP* 12+13
1927.44 13, 14–16, 22 n. 130, 22 n. 131; cf. *DMIPERP* 225
1948.150 28 n. 4; cf. *DMIPERP* 131
1948.151 28 n. 4; cf. *DMIPERP* 132
1966.493 32 n. 16, 33 n. 17; cf. *DMIPERP* 23
1967.525 32 n. 16; cf. *DMIPERP* 148
1974.226 30 n. 12
1985.828 35

BGU (*Aegyptische Urkunden aus den Königlichen Staatlichen Museen zu Berlin, Griechische Urkunden*)
696 5 n. 13

CIG (*Corpus inscriptionum graecarum*)
2.3497 14

CIJ (*Corpus inscriptionum judaicarum*)
677 103 n. 37
775 81 n. 5
920 102 n. 26; cf. *DMIPERP* 71
1006 103 n. 34, 106 n. 60

CIL (*Corpus inscriptionum latinarum*)
2.1970 16
2.4201 14
2.4251 14
3.504 12 n. 78
3.507 12 n. 78
3.509 12 n. 78
3.6001 15
3.6687 32 n. 16; cf. *DMIPERP* 201
3.6707 14
3.6814 12 n. 73
3.6815 12 n. 73

3.6816 12 n. 73
3.6628 87 n. 18
3.6741 11 n. 59
3.6742 11 n. 59
3.6742a 11 n. 59
3.8261 16
3.8262 16
3.13483a 29 n. 9; cf. *DMIPERP* 147
3.14165.13 11 n. 66; cf. *DMIPERP* 387
5.3936 38 n. 8
5.4191 10 n. 49
5.4987 10 n. 49
6.3339 33 n. 19
6.3508 23 n. 140
6.3528 21
6.3614 33 n. 19
6.31856 16
8.2394 15
8.2395 15
8.7079 13 n. 84; cf. *DMIPERP* 187
8.9358 6 n. 20
8.9359 6 n. 20
8.17904 15
8.21044 6 n. 20
10.3887 10 n. 49
10.6100 16
10.6426 14
11.1058 12 n. 75
11.6117 21
11.6721.28 12 n. 74
11.6721.29 12 n. 74, 12 n. 75
11.6721.30 12 n. 74
14.171 20 n. 118
14.5351 33 n. 16
16.8 98; cf. *DMIPERP* 293
16.22 16
16.31 14
16.33 16; cf. *DMIPERP* 202
16.35 15, 16, 30 n. 12; cf. *DMIPERP* 225
16.45 14
16.87 17, 33 n. 16; cf. *DMIPERP* 211
16.94 15
16.106 16
16.107 6; cf. *DMIPERP* 296
16.117 15
16.128 16
16.159 30 n. 10; cf. *DMIPERP* 295
16.171 14
16.183 15

CPJ (*Corpus papyrorum judaicorum*)
418a 100 n. 19; cf. *DMIPERP* 365
418b 100 n. 21; cf. *DMIPERP* 366

DMIPERP (Database of Military Inscriptions and Papyri of Early Roman Palestine)

3 87
12 32, 35–36, 88 n. 25
13 32, 35–36, 88 n. 25
14 35
15 35
16 35
17 35
18 35
23 32 n. 16, 33 n. 17
30 23 n. 139, 32 n. 14, 88 n. 25
31 88 n. 25
32 88 n. 25
43 59 n. 87
71 102 n. 26
131 28 n. 4, 88 n. 23
132 28 n. 4, 88 n. 23
139 117 n. 46
143 116 n. 39
145 113 n. 21
147 20–21, 29 n. 9
148 32 n. 16
150 11 n. 56
153 88 n. 23

DMIPERP (continued)
154 88 n. 23
183 103 n. 39
187 13 n. 84
188 13
189 72 n. 17
201 22 n. 129, 23 n. 138, 32 n. 16
202 16–17
211 17, 33 n. 16
213 88 n. 23
219 88 n. 23
221 88 n. 23
222 88 n. 23
223 88 n. 23
224 33 n. 16, 88 n. 23
225 13, 22 n. 130, 22 n. 131, 30 n. 12, 88 n. 23
226 88 n. 23
227 88 n. 23
228 88 n. 23
229 88 n. 23
230 88 n. 23
231 88 n. 23
232 28 n. 4, 30 n. 12, 33 n. 16, 88 n. 23
233 28 n. 4, 88 n. 23
234 28 n. 4, 88 n. 23
235 28 n. 4, 88 n. 23
236 28 n. 4, 88 n. 23
237 28 n. 4, 88 n. 23
238 28 n. 4, 88 n. 23
239 28 n. 4, 88 n. 23
240 28 n. 4, 88 n. 23
241 28 n. 4, 88 n. 23
242 28 n. 4, 88 n. 23
243 28 n. 4, 88 n. 23
244 28 n. 4, 88 n. 23
245 28 n. 4, 88 n. 23
259 13, 22 n. 131
293 98 n. 14
295 30 n. 10
296 6, 102 n. 27
365 100 n. 19
366 100 n. 21
387 11 n. 66

IGLS (*Inscriptions grecques et latines de la Syrie*; volume number indicates "new" series)
1906 42 n. 15, 42 n. 17, 42 n.18
1906a 42 n. 16
2033 42 n. 17, 42 n. 18
2112 32 n. 14; cf. *DMIPERP* 30
2265 111 n. 14
2266 111 n. 14
2268 111 n. 14
2269 111 n. 14
2329 114 n. 23
16.197 35; cf. *DMIPERP* 12+13

IGRR (*Inscriptiones Graeci ad res Romanas pertinentes*)
1.824 14
3.1136 15, 23 n. 139, 32 n. 14; cf. *DMIPERP* 30

ILS (*Inscriptiones Latinae Selectae*)
1999 15
2683 15, 22 n. 129, 23 n. 138, 32 n. 16; cf. *DMIPERP* 201
2724 13, 14–16; cf. *DMIPERP* 188
2733 16
9057 13, 14–16, 22 n. 131; cf. *DMIPERP* 259
9108 11 n. 67
9168 15, 20, 29 n. 9; cf. *DMIPERP* 147
9488 33 n. 16

OCIANA (*Online Corpus of the Inscriptions of Ancient North Arabia*)

All Safaitic inscriptions can be found on *OCIANA*, though no *OCIANA* numbers are given in this volume

OGIS (*Orientis graeci inscriptiones selectae*)

421 23 n. 139, 32 n. 14; cf. *DMIPERP* 30
424 114 n. 23
425 32 n. 16; cf. *DMIPERP* 23

P.Mich.

7.444 87 n. 18

P.Ryl.

2.189 72 n. 17; cf. *DMIPERP* 189

RMD (*Roman Military Diplomas*)

1.3 30 n. 12, 33 n. 16; cf. *DMIPERP* 232
1.69 33 n. 16; cf. *DMIPERP* 224

RMR (*Roman Military Records on Papyrus*)

63 31 n. 13
68 75 n. 29
69 75 n. 29
70 75 n. 29
77 75 n. 29
83 75 n. 29

SEG (*Supplementum Epigraphicum Graecum*)

7.1100 32 n. 15; cf. *DMIPERP* 14
9.346 42 n. 15
9.414 42 n. 15
33.1306 35
35.1321 35
35.1322 35

www.ingramcontent.com/pod-product-compliance
Lightning Source LLC
Chambersburg PA
CBHW071459150426
43191CB00008B/1393
* 9 7 8 1 5 3 2 6 5 6 3 8 5 *